I Call to the Eye of the Mind:

A Memoir by Sara Hyland

Edited by Maureen Murphy

D1615661

Attic Press
Dublin

DEDICATION

Do mhuintir Diolún
a thug Gaeilge do
bheirt againne: Sara
agus mé féin

CONTENTS

List of Illustrations   6

Editor's Note   7

Introduction   11

1893 - 1897   Household Life   19
1898 - 1903   The Yeatses arrive in Dundrum   31
1903 - 1908   Lolly and Lily Yeats   47
1907 - 1909   Sara goes to Dun Emer   61
1909 - 1913   W B Yeats   71
1913 - 1918   Jack Yeats entertains
                  the Cuala Girls   85
1916 - 1922   The Easter Rising   99
1923 - 1928   Cois Fhairrge   121
1928 - 1933   Tailteann Games and Medals   141
1933 - 1938   Lily's Retirement   157
1938 - 1943   Sara Becomes a Teacher   167
1943 - 1972   Epilogue   173

Chapter Notes   176

Works Cited   195

Manuscript Sources   196

Index   197

LIST OF ILLUSTRATIONS

Sara's silver Tailteann medal   10
The Hyland's Cottage in Dundrum.   18
Larry Hyland and Sara's twin, Jimmy   27
Advertisement for the Dun Emer Guild from
            a local church magazine, 1915   43
Portrait of Lily Yeats by John B Yeats
            (National Gallery of Ireland)   46
The Yeatses house in Dundrum   58
Outside the Cuala Industries   60
Lily Yeats and her girls in the
            embroidery room at the Cuala Industries   70
Sara and two friends from the
            Cuala embroidery room   73
Lolly Yeats and her girls in the Cuala printing
            room (Trinity College, Dublin)   98
Jimmy Hyland, Sara's twin, as a young man   120
Cois Farraige, Irish College   128
Letter informing Sara that she had won the
            Tailteann medal   140
Sara's first prize silver Tailteann medal   150
Detail of a cushion embriodered by Sara
            and designed by Jack B Yeats   166
Sara at work, in later life   172

EDITOR'S NOTE

This book began with a call from Elizabeth Butler Cullingford inviting me to the 1989 Yeats Summer School in Sligo. Liz said that she planned to have women and the arts as one focus of the School, so I proposed a talk on the Yeats sisters: Susan Mary (Lily) and Elizabeth Corbet (Lolly). When I mentioned the subject of my paper to my friend, Eilís McDowell, she told me that her Dundrum neighbours, the Dixons, had a memoir written by their grand-aunt Sara Hyland, who had worked for Lily Yeats. Eilís's introduction to the Dixons was the first of many debts in what has become a shared project. Her knowledge of matters archival and architectural, her intimate knowledge of twentieth-century Irish history and her willingness to ramble around south County Dublin searching for Sara sites has made this book both a reality and a great pleasure.

The Dixon family's permission to use Sara's Memoir for my talk about the Yeats sisters led to my suggestion that the Memoir be edited for publication. Sara's niece Josie Hyland Dixon, and her husband Ken had taken an early interest in Sara's Memoir and Ken arranged to have the manuscript typed and duplicated. Sara's grand-niece, Diane Dixon, who lives in the Hyland cottage, has been a valuable help in reconstructing

Hyland family details, in researching Dundrum lore and in sharing samples of Sara's work with me. Among Sara's other relatives and neighbours, I thank her niece, Joseph's daughter, May Hyland O'Brien and Sara's past pupil, Marie Mason.

Róisín Coyle and Elizabeth Solterer recalled their experience as little girls in Lolly Yeats's painting class and how she would rush in full of talk, break bits of flowering branches for each girl and urge her to begin boldly with a big splash of paint. Their impression, still vivid after seventy years, was that she was a gifted teacher. Elizabeth's lively memories of literary Dublin provided me with glimpses of many people Sara mentioned in her Memoir. For details about Sara's Army Flag project, I thank Maurice Cogan and the late Séamus Mac Neill.

Among Yeatsians, my greatest debt is to William M Murphy whose *Prodigal Father* introduced his readers to Lily, the heroine of the Yeats family. His generosity in sharing his early draft of *Family Secrets*, the work of his thirty years spent studying the Yeats family, has been an indispensable source for documenting Sara's work life. Hilary Pyle made helpful points about Jack Yeats's relationship with his sisters and with the Cuala Industries. That great encourager, Ann Saddlemeyer, who is working on the life of George Yeats, another remarkable and till-Ann-unsung Yeats woman, has dispensed advice and good cheer in equal measure. When Anne Yeats visited the Summer School in 1989 for the opening of her exhibition of paintings, I was grateful for the opportunity to hear her affectionate and amusing recollection of her aunts.

Perhaps the most delightful surprise in Sara's Memoir was to discover that both Sara and I went to the same house in Teach Mór, Indreabháin. While my *bean a' tighe*, Jude Diolún Uí Fhatharta was one of the children farmed out to her grandparents, she remembers Sara among the early group of students who came to that best of all houses for learning Irish. Máirtín O'Flarthartaigh was able to identify many of the people and places Sara associated with some of the happiest days of her life. In this project, as in so many things, I have been blessed with the friendship and hospitality of Anraí and Donla O'Braonáin.

I thank my Irish Studies colleagues whose advice and friendship is only ever a call away: Francis and Janet Carroll, Adele Dalsimer, Jim Doan, Tom and Jane Hachey, Emmet Larkin, Robert Lowery, Larry McCafferty, Margaret Mac-Curtain, Lucy McDiarmid, Janet Nolan, Jim McKillop, Norma and Robert Rhodes, Mary Helen Thuente, Catherine Shannon, Maryann Valiulis and Alan Ward. Closer to home I am grateful to my family for their stalwart support and to my friend Jean Connolly, who prepared the manuscript, Karen Spencer, my WordPerfect guru and Diana Ben-Merre, my most attentive reader. Finally, I would like to thank the Dundrum Library, the National Library of Ireland, the New York Public Library and the Library of Yale University.

I have let Sara speak for herself and kept my editing to matters of clarity and to tidying. I've resisted the urge to shape chapters leaving it to Sara to pick up the threads of her story as she told it. My notes are meant to provide resources for those who would like to know more about people and events in the Memoir. Readers will notice that details like dates are often at odds with Sara's account. What is important in oral tradition is significance not accuracy, for it is our impressions of events and our memories of the past that shape our lives and the lore that we pass to others.

Sara's silver Tailteann medal
(reverse side page 150)

INTRODUCTION

Sara Hyland was born into Victorian Ireland and came of age with Irish Independence. The year of her birth Gladstone's Second Home Rule Bill was defeated in the House of Lords; the year she died the Republic of Ireland prepared to join the European Community. Her mother brought her to see Queen Victoria; her brother drove for Michael Collins. She saw the advent of automobiles and aeroplanes, Sinn Fein and votes for women, Abbey Players and Gaelic Leaguers. As one of Lily Yeats's assistants, she met those who shaped the literature and culture of modern Ireland. Sara's story is remarkable not only for its glimpse of the Irish Literary Revival from the vantage point of the embroidery workroom of the Cuala Industries but for its portrait of a south County Dublin family living in the village of Dundrum from the turn of the century to the 1940s.

Her father James Hyland was a jarvey who worked from the Dundrum station on the old Harcourt Street line; her mother, Annie Kiernan Hyland, did hand-laundry at home. Parents, seven children, a cousin reared in the house, and an occasional boarder thronged into one of the dozen gabled, brick and granite three-room Pembroke Cottages built in the laneways off the village main street. A happy family, doors open to neighbours and to village life, early schooling and full-time

11

employment for fourteen-year-old school leavers helped ease the density at number 10 Pembroke Cottages, so one feels none of the misery of crowded urban living that contemporary Dublin city dwellers report. It was only years later when Sara returned from a month in the West of Ireland that she felt the cottage claustrophobic.

In Sara's childhood, life was village centred. She wandered into local shops, visited farms and forges and played, on winter afternoons, in the cozy waiting room of the railway station. Like her brothers, Sara found part-time work to add to the household income. The Hyland boys delivered papers and Sara did odd-jobs before getting a place running errands and helping on Saturday evenings in Browne's, a drapery and hardware shop on the site of the present Deveney's in Dundrum.

Summers the children played in the open fields surrounding the village. There was a yearly excursion to their grandfather Kiernan in Lusk with the excitement of a train - or even better - a jaunting car journey and the renunion with cousins. For Sara there were other outings with the 'Bun Lady', a regular customer of her father who found the lively little girl good company.

The years were marked by the seasons, by the liturgical calendar and by the landmarks of Irish life: first communions, weddings, wakes and funerals. Excursion-goers on their way to the Scalp or to Enniskerry enlivened Sunday morning in summer, and the children learned that a hearty cheer was often rewarded. Occasionally, the local gentry treated the village children to a party or to an outing.

Hyland family life was enriched by Sara's mother's artistic sensibilities. She loved paintings and decorated her home with reproductions - changed each year - cut from copies of *Pear's Annual*. Even her meals appeared with touches of extra colour: vegetables, herbs and flowers. Annie Hyland taught her children poems and told them folktales and legends some of which she believed herself like the one of the changeling that appeared in the house where she worked before she married. It was from her mother that Sara heard Aesop's Fables and Shakespeare.

Above all, the Hyland household was a musical one with a special passion for the opera. Again it was Annie Hyland's lore and love of opera that inspired her children. They saved for excursions to the Gaiety where they sat in the gods to hear the travelling companies: Carl Rossa, Moody Manners, Joseph O'Mara, Harrison Frewen and the Quinlan Opera Compnay. According to Sara, during opera season Dublin was a lyrical city where newsboys whistled arias, the heirs, perhaps, of those gallery boys whom Mr Browne, sitting around the Misses Morkan's table in James Joyce's 'The Dead', recalled unyoking the horses and pulling the carriage of a visiting prima donna through the streets of Dublin.

Along with her early appreciation of the arts, Sara showed an interest in politics - first the politics of nationalism and later party politics. She records the rising sense of nationalism in the Ireland of her childhood, nationalism that could lead to some tension with the local Unionists. Chief Baron Palles's annual Christmas party for the village children was cancelled over the matter of a small Union Jack placed at the top of the tree. Parents objected; the Palleses persisted and so the parties were discontinued. Similarly, Catholic children were refused admission to programmes at the Protestant school because Catholics were known to refuse to stand at the singing of 'God Save the King'.

Sara loved a local election, remembering a General Election when the Dublin South Nationalist candidate defeated the Unionist MP. The Liberal Party was returned and with them the possibilty of Home Rule. Recalling the singing of 'A Nation Once Again' at that time, Sara credited the Gaelic League and Arthur Griffith's Sinn Fein philosophy with fostering self-confidence and national resolve.

Sara's image of England as a great black hag with bird-like claws spread over Ireland recalls another image of Ireland enchanted: Douglas Hyde's crow in his essay 'The Return of the Fenians'.

> *What is this darkness on the sky? What is this*
> *blackness on the sun? What is this mist overhead,*
> *robbing us of daylight, choking us with its weight?*
> *- looking at the dark cloud getting wider and larger,*
> *look at it putting out two wings like a great crow*
> *from one side to the other.*

The centre of Sara's life, and the focus of her Memoir, was her work for the Cuala Industries in the embroidery room of Lily Yeats. Susan Mary 'Lily' Yeats and Elizabeth Corbet 'Lolly' Yeats returned to Ireland from London in 1902 to share a joint business venture with Evelyn Gleeson who had leased a house called Runnymede on the Sandyford Road just outside the village of Dundrum. They renamed the house Dun Emer, an allusion to a scene in the Book of Leinster version of the 'Táin' which describes Emer teaching embroidery to her foster sisters outside of Forgall's fort. The Industries were divided into three sections: Evelyn Gleeson directed the carpentry and tapestry production; Lily headed the embroidery department and Lolly managed the Dun Emer Press.

While the Dun Emer founders did not consider themselves feminists along the lines of the Irish suffragettes of Hanna Sheehy Skeffington, they created employment for the village girls and the Dun Emer Press employed the first women printers in Ireland. The Dun Emer prospectus of 1903 suggests that the plan was for some of the girls to become teachers and to spread the scheme throughout Ireland, but many stayed their working lives with the Yeats sisters. Sara did, in fact, become a teacher, but it was only after Lily Yeats retired.

Sara went to Dun Emer in April, 1907, at the age of fourteen. By the time she arrived the Dun Emer arrangement was proving to be unworkable, so the partnership dissolved and the Yeats sisters formed their own Cuala Industries and leased a four-room cottage on the Churchtown Road. The fifteen years the Industries spent there, Sara's fifteenth through her thirtieth year, were happy ones although letters written by the Yeatses reveal their personal worries and their business anxieties. Undercapitalized at the best of times, during World War I, Cuala suffered first from a decrease in sales and then from wartime shortages. With the Troubles, there were further disruptions to their business that lasted from 1916 till the end of the Civil War in 1923.

Sara's own recollections of 1916 and the Troubles are insights into what the times meant to ordinary people living in south County Dublin. Her mother was caught in Glasnevin on Easter Monday; there were alarming reports from the city and panic when the food supplies began to run out. Sara's brother drove for Michael Collins and Collins's devoted aide was a frequent visitor to the Hyland household; yet, it appears the Yeats sisters were not aware of these connections though they would have been sympathetic to the nationalist cause.

During the Civil War, Republicans fired on the village Exchange; the roads were barricaded, and for a week Dundrum was cut off from Dublin. Lily Yeats reported that Cuala was raided by the Free State Army, but Sara mentions nothing about it. She was there, but perhaps she thought to have mentioned the raid would have implied a criticism of the Treatyite position she shared with the Yeats sisters.

While history may have intruded into the peace of Cuala, the picture of life in the Industries from 1908 to 1923, according to Sara, was one of contentment. She found her work

satisfying and took great pride in what she produced; there
were interesting visitors to the cottage and the Yeats sisters
arranged parties and outings for their girls whom they treated
as their extended family. For example, the Cuala girls were
invited to the sisters' cousin Ruth Pollexfen's wedding and
dressed for the occasion in white dresses and blue flowered
straw hats.

While the girls admired both the sisters, it was Lily who
had their hearts. As she was the heroine of William Murphy's
biography of John B Yeats, *Prodigal Father* (1978), Lily Yeats
is the heroine of Sara's Memoir. Sara praises her fairness, her
kindness and her active interest in the lives of all her girls.
When Sara and her pal May Courtney began to spend their free
afternoons in Dublin, Lily advised them what to see - particular
paintings in the National Gallery, certain Georgian houses and
later, with the permission of the girls' parents, plays at the
Abbey with passes provided. In the twenties, when Sara won
scholarships to study Irish at the summer colleges in Cois
Farraige Gaeltacht, Lily worked out an arrangement so that
Sara could have the extra time off to attend.

The nature of work in the embroidery room certainly
contributed to the intimacy between Lily and her girls.
Photographs of the time as well as Sara's Memoir portray the
girls sewing in a circle around Lily, an image of Victorian
mothers and daughters with their eyes lowered and heads bent
over their work. It was a natural setting for the exchange of
confidences. Sara recalled:

> She loved talking and imparting knowledge to us.
> There was scarcely any traffic on the road which
> was about forty feet from the cottage and with no
> other work being done in the room, it was easy for
> us to hear all she said.

The Cuala Press room, on the other hand, operated differently.
The girls and Lolly worked alone at their typesetting and
colouring. While there was repetition, the precision and
concentration required offered less opportunity for social
interaction.

After Sara left the Industries to become a teacher of
embroidery in the Technical School in Dundrum, Lily was her
inspiration. Sara modelled her own teaching on Lily's and Lily
supported her efforts with encouragement and with permission
to teach the girls her Cuala designs. Sara's Memoir closes with
her last visits to talk about teaching and to reminisce with Lily

15

who lived on, an invalid in Gurteen Dheas after Lolly's death. As she believed the interest in her life was her association with the Yeats sisters, Sara's story ends with Lily.

Encouraged by Monk Gibbon, a Yeats cousin who wrote his own memoir of his poet cousin, *The Masterpiece and the Man: Yeats as I Knew Him* (1959), and whose father was rector of St Nahi's Church in Dundrum, Sara wrote her Memoir in order to be a kind of Boswell below the stairs to the remarkable sisters and, loyal Cuala girl, she does not tell the family tales. While we know from William Murphy's work on the Yeats family and from the Yeats's letters that there was stress at the Industries and at home between Lily and Lolly and between Lolly and most everyone, Sara charitably characterized Lolly as highly-strung and nervous, stopping short of describing her irritable mannerisms that tried the patience of others - incessant talking and fidgeting. While Sara herself gave notice in 1934, she loyally does not mention the matter in her Memoir.

Sara chose the first line from W B Yeats's 'At The Hawk's Well' - 'I call to the eye of the mind' - for the title of her Memoir. Of course a line from Yeats gave her story a certain *cachet* but she was, no doubt, also taken with the idea of the mind as the imagination, the act of creative retelling. Yeats called up an image of desolation: barren and weed-choked, while Sara brings to her eye of the mind a life brimming with family, friends, meaningful work and interests. She emerges from her story as an energetic, confident woman - perhaps a bit bossy - writing from the self-sufficiency of middle age, a woman with strong opinions about politics - nationalist, Free Stater, Fine Gaeler and a with passion for the Irish language and culture.

Perhaps Sara's most endearing quality is her sense of adventure. It is especially striking because autobiographies and memoirs of her contemporaries are not marked by such spirit. It may be, as Carolyn Heilbrun observes in *Writing a Woman's Life*, that most middle-class women's lives precluded the quest theme that is so central to most men's biographies. Lives of Irish middle-class daughters of Sara's era were generally prescribed by marriage and family; however, a girl from the cottages not only worked until marriage but she often continued in domestic service or worked at home as Sara's mother did. Sara's work life, from her earliest odd-jobs, was marked by a sense of accomplishment and independence.

Some of those same qualities are apparent in the way she embraced the cultural life of Dublin. She had the advantage of her Cuala connection, but it was personality as well as opportunity. Spunky and resourceful, she knew her Shakespeare but read 'Love's Thorny Path' in the hayloft over Browne's shop; she went to the Abbey but saw *Sins of the Rich* at the Queen's on the sly. While she represented herself as a woman with her feet firmly on the ground, she was game for a ride, in 1927, in an open plane.

She was an eager traveller alert to the nuances of a new place. Not surprisingly, she especially noted what people wore. Her recollections of her Connemara summers draw on careful observation of people and folkways. Her description of traditionally-dressed women on the road to Mass reminds one of James Herbert Craig's painting 'Going to Mass' and of Máirtín O Direáin's elegiac poem 'Cuimhne Cinn'.

Her prose is descriptive rather than evocative. Indeed at times she is self-consciously literary, aware, perhaps, of her subjects' literary associations. When she speaks with her own voice, a voice that links language with her own life, she can be lyrical as when she describes the mountains around Dublin as an Elizabethan collar on a dull dress.

We can only speculate about what Sara left out of her account. We know she was careful about the Yeats sisters, but she was also selective about the rest of her story. She tells us about some disappointments, but we have no real sense of her feelings except for her profound sense of loss in the early thirties after her mother's death and after Lily's retirement from Cuala.

Sara's story remains for us a unique account of village life in Dundrum, an account that has already contributed substantially to local histories. As we become more interested in women's lives and women's work, Sara's Memoir becomes more important for its story of employees rather than employers - even employers as admirable as the Yeats sisters. Finally it is a story of a woman who lived in interesting times in modern Ireland, a woman who has left us her own patchwork of those times embroidered with its people and events.

Maureen Murphy
1995

The Hyland's Cottage in Dundrum

CHAPTER ONE

(1893-1897)

Sara's family - Household life - Village school - Dundrum and countryside - Local characters - Village musicians - Beggars - Moneylenders - Coinage - Meals - Mother's stories - Cures - Prayers - Manor Mill Laundry - Fleas - Queen Victoria's visit - The Gaelic League - St Patrick's Day.

I was born in the village of Dundrum, County Dublin at 6.00 on Sunday morning, March 12, 1893 - one of a pair.[1] My twin brother Jimmy and I did not resemble each other in appearance or in character; he was flaxen-haired and very quiet while I was dark-haired and lively. We had two older brothers, Joseph and Bartholomew or 'Batty', and we were to have three younger ones: Larry, Patrick and Willie. My parents were hardworking people with a great love for children. We had a very happy life. Houses were small[2] and families were large when we were young. Less than seven children was scarcely considered to be a family, and there was one family in the Dundrum area with twenty-one children.

Our house[3] had a large room that served as living room and kitchen, two small bedrooms that opened off of it and a smaller room that could be used as a bedroom. We had a good-sized

19

backyard and outbuildings. The living room, or kitchen as we called it, was very bright with two big windows that faced each other and there was an open fireplace where my mother did all the cooking for the family.

My mother was passionately fond of pictures. We had so many that it would take a long while to look at them all. The large ones were changed each Christmas. My mother watched eagerly for *Pears Annual* and the other periodicals that gave free coloured pictures and she selected from them choosing those which fit into the frames we had. She often had to forego a picture she liked because it did not fit the frame intended for it. We children had our favourites and often objected when they were exchanged for new pictures.

The pictures also had a practical use. Before going to bed, my father hung his collar and tie from their corners and he hung his hat on the antlers of a deer. Small plaster ornaments fitted between the pictures so that there was not even enough room for a postage stamp to slip between them. In later years, I was to see the same condition in the Yeats's house in Churchtown but there was nothing hanging from their picture corners - nor was that permitted in our house during the daytime.

To keep our house tidy we lived as if we were on board a ship. We did not have wardrobes for our clothing. Two large presses in the kitchen held our Sunday clothes and other articles. My mother brushed, folded and put away our Sunday clothes immediately after breakfast on Monday mornings. My father's clothes were placed first on the shelf and then the boys' clothes according to their ages so that anything that was needed during the week could be found without difficulty.

We did not have many clothes. Our overcoats and other everyday clothes hung on the back of the bedroom door: high pegs for the older boys, lower ones for the younger. We also had long wooden boxes with lids that opened halfway across the top and were, therefore, easily pulled from under the bed and clothes or bed linen dropped into them and stored away.

Beds were not the same as those we have today and you should have heard the rattle of the iron slats when a bed was being dismantled for cleaning or repairing. Cheap beds had plain railings at the head and at the foot while more expensive beds had brass knobs and flowers where the rails met. The iron sides had eight or ten lozenge-shaped knobs on each side that could be turned by a pincer or by strong fingers. Lightweight slats about three inches wide fit on the knobs and were laced crosswise. Knobs were tightened to keep the slats in place. Finally, a heavy bar that made the bed quite rigid was slipped into place. A tightly-packed paillasse or straw mattress lay over the slats; then, a horsehair, hair and fibre or even a feather tick, which many people liked, covered the paillasse. The rest of the bedding was just as it is today.

In winter we did not have hot water jugs or rubber bottles to put in our beds to warm them. Well-to-do people had warming pans with long handles. Maids filled them with hot coals, covered them and moved them about slowly between the bed sheets. Poor people made do with a heated brick wrapped in brown paper or in another covering. Once we had a slight accident with a hot brick and the burn holes in the bedclothes reminded us to be careful.

My mother did a great deal to help with household expenses. She knitted and mended men's socks and she hand-washed garments that the gentry considered too fragile to send to the local laundry. When the high quality of her work became known, she often had to refuse work. We loved to help her and she taught us 'to work is noble, to beg is to be ashamed'.

My earliest and most vivid recollection is going to school[4] at the age of three with Jimmy and my older brothers. Most children in the parish who lived near the school started at an early age because Dundrum was a very small community and all pupils, even very small ones, were welcome. It was a great help to mothers of young families. The girls' school,[5] a large, open room fifty feet by twenty feet, accommodated eighty-six little girls. Five low steps at the gable end of the room led to the gallery which accommodated the youngest pupils who were under the care of a monitress or an older pupil who was, in turn, supervised by a teacher or head mistress.

On my first day at school I climbed to the top seat of the gallery to have a look over the side down on a class of older pupils. They were very amused but my teacher quickly put an end to the distraction. I was made to sit in the centre of the lowest seat of the gallery, right in front of her, and I expected she saw to it that I remained there.

The boys had a similar building adjoining the girls' school;

however, they had no gallery for babies. Both schools were located behind the Catholic church, about one hundred yards from the Main Street. The church was built in 1877 and I believe the schools were built at the same time. The playground sloped down to the Slang river. It was a heartache for the teachers, but we children loved walking barefoot in the river bed which was a slow-moving stream in the summer but a fast-moving torrent in the winter or after a heavy summer rain. The river, as it flowed toward the city, ran parallel with Main Street and parallel with the main road. When it reached Milltown, it joined the Dodder and then meandered through Ballsbridge to the sea.

We passed a blacksmith's forge on our way to school and often stayed to watch a horse having his shoes put on. It was lovely to see the sparks flying from the red-hot iron and to hear the music of the hammer striking the anvil. The blacksmith, a very big man in a leather apron, puffed a lot when he worked the bellows to keep the fire alight.

Main Street appeared to be divided by a bend in the middle, so you could never see more than half of it at once. It was neither very picturesque nor very tidy. There was always an empty house or shop with broken windows or palings. The railroad station[6] at the north end of Main Street was the hub of village life. It was a large building with comfortable waiting rooms and a well-stocked bookstall run by Eason's. The stationmaster lived in a large house nearby and there were accommodations for another official as well. The two ticket collectors, the signal box attendant and the two young porters were busy every day of the week. Trains arrived from Dublin's Harcourt Street Station and left Dundrum to continue to Rathfarnham and Bray. A large poster announced that this was the station for passengers going to St Columba's College.

My father was one of the five or six jarveys who met the train from Harcourt Street with a horse cab and car. They were very busy. They knew everyone and everyone knew them. I often went along to the station to ask my father for a ha'penny to buy sweets. I always hoped that I would get a whole penny, for a penny bought a good deal in my young days. Our favourite sweet was a farthing lucky orange, a large, orange-coloured ball of hard sugar that left our mouths orange and sticky. That it almost always held a farthing appealed to our gambling instinct. Another of our favourites was Peggy's Leg.

While Dundrum was untidy, the green fields and hills surrounding the village made it a beautiful place to live. To the south, we could see the Wicklow hills, or the Dublin mountains as we called them, encircling the village like a beautiful Elizabethan collar on a dull dress. Leaving Dundrum by any of its five roads took us right into the countryside to fields where cattle grazed and where wild flowers grew in profusion.

Early in the spring cattle were put out to graze during the day and, until all signs of frost were gone, they were taken back to their stalls each evening. The cows, mostly Ayreshire, were of a lovely red colour with large creamy patches. There were calves as well and maybe a pony or donkey or two. It was a beautiful sight to see them slowly cropping the rich green grass studded with buttercups, daisies, cowslips, and purple and white clover that made it look like an exquisite carpet. Hawthorn, blackberry, wild rose, foxglove, cow parsley, ponytail and every sort of wild flower grew in masses along the hedges which were broken here and there by bushes and lilac, hawthorn and laburnum trees.

Leaving the village from the station on the Upper Churchtown Road, we passed a quaint little huckster's shop that we entered by going down a couple of steps. It was dark inside because the floor of the shop was much lower than the road. The ledge of the small front window was just level with the road outside. The small back window of the shop was stocked with candles, soap and other merchandise. During Lent we could see dried fish called ling hanging outside. At other seasons, heavy nailed boots hung in their place.

Past the shop there was a wheelwright, a blacksmith, the ruins of the old National School and finally the old churchyard of St Nahi[7] where I spent many hours with my pals reading and puzzling at the lengthy inscriptions on the old tombs that dated from the seventeenth century.

Further on, there was an unusual gateway leading to a big house called Woodlawn. It looked like the entrance to a monastery and it had two enormous horse-chestnut trees, one on each side, which almost covered the gate and gave great shelter from a sudden shower of rain.

Dundrum was surrounded by a number of big houses[8] with acres of land that were owned by the mainly Protestant gentry.

They had servants: three or four maids, a gardener and a coachman. The wealthier ones also had a butler and a footman. The carriages were a lovely sight. One lady drove an unusual black buggy with bright yellow wheels and a pair of high-stepping horses. She dressed in a smart black riding suit to match her buggy. The footman, who sat on a high seat at the back but in sight of the driver, recalled 'Diana of the Chase'[9] or some Roman chariot.

In 1879, Father Brady,[10] one of our priests, was killed in the grounds of one of the big houses in Roebuck Park, while travelling by horseback at night to make a sick call. Roebuck Park had two entrance gates, one in Roebuck and one in Dundrum near the railway station, as well as the gates off the avenue. On this dark night, one of the avenue gates was left closed and the unfortunate priest was killed.

Like most country villages, Dundrum had its share of amusing characters who lived here or who came begging or on errands from the surrounding hills. My favourite was Jack who belonged to a well-to-do family who could afford to keep him nicely dressed and very clean. He had beautiful white hands. While he never spoke much to people, he could be very talkative to imaginary things.

He liked a drink, and though I never saw him drunk, he broke so many glasses in the local pub that he was not served unless he had a vessel with him. He was very fastidious so a jam jar or a tommy can would not do. One day he asked to borrow a milk jug from my mother. My mother never refused anyone who asked her for anything and as he had walked into the house and over to the dresser, she had to let him have a very pretty jug that happened to be empty. Fearing she would not see the jug again, she sent me after him. I probably followed him into the pub that was near our house, but what I recollect was sitting on the doorstep of a cottage on Main Street while Jack held the jug aloft and quoted poetry that I did not understand. Perhaps he was quoting from Omar Khayyám[11] and when he smashed so many public house glasses, he was only trying to 'turn down an empty glass!'

We had music of some description every day. Bonk-a-Bonk was a street musician who came to Dundrum every week. He was a tall, thin man who wore a funny, little, round hat and a long coat that was once black but which had, over the years, become several shades of green and brown. In winter his single concession to the season was a wide belt on his old coat. Crooked spectacles rested on the tip of his red nose which always had a drop ready to fall. He wore mittens and played a tiny concertina close to his ear. He sang only 'Annie Laurie' in a little, squeaky voice.

Another street musician was the German Band, a man with musical instruments on every part of his body: spurs on his heels with round bells on them, cymbals on his kneestraps, different bells on his elbows, coins hanging from epaulettes on his shoulders, more jangles from his cap, a small drum on a belt around his waist, a mouth organ clamped in his teeth and an accordion in his hands. I don't remember where he kept his drumstick but he did rally with it. We watched him, fascinated by his contortions and his ability to sound every instrument. He often sent us flying when he took a quick swing right around. He took off his cap and spurs when he finished his piece and that gave him a little freedom to walk to his next stop.

We had a barrel-organ grinder who had a good organ with nice tunes. He had a very nice little monkey who collected ha'pennies in his cap which he removed from his head on command. We felt he knew us individually and we loved to give him sweets or nuts and to see him scratch his forehead before replacing his cap. There was also Johnny-the-Whistle who got marvelous music out of a tin whistle. We had frequent visits, as well, from the military band going on a route march to Ticknock.

Among the beggars who came regularly to Dundrum was a very cross, plain-looking individual named Susan Crowe. Her short, grey hair seemed to grow out of the straw hat that she wore winter and summer. She came from the poorhouse or Union, as we called it, in Loughlinstown[12] near Shankill. My mother had great sympathy for her and she used the example of Susan to teach us not to be rude to anyone, no matter about his or her appearance. My mother also used Susan to warn us about what we might be like someday if we did not take care of ourselves.

There were many salesmen who called at our doors with ornaments, pictures, lengths of material and other goods. Our doors were never closed except in bad weather during the winter and if someone came while we were having a meal, he or she got a share of it.

Moneylenders came offering loans at a high profit to themselves. My mother would say about them, 'It would be a bad day for anyone to get into their clutches'. There were plenty of amusing stories of the women who did borrow from them and who would hide when they saw the collector coming. They would send their children to the door to say, 'My mother is out'. One young child was reported to have said to one of them nicknamed 'Click Click': 'Click Click, me mother is in the press.'

Coinage[13] during my childhood consisted of gold, silver and copper coins and bank cheques. A gold sovereign was valued at twenty shillings; the gold half-sovereign was ten shillings. Both were very beautiful coins engraved with St George slaying a dragon. Gold coins were withdrawn during World War I and replaced by the ten shilling and one pound notes. The silver five shilling piece, also engraved with St George, was a large, heavy coin. The four-shilling and two-shilling pieces carried a different design. The shilling, sixpence and threepenny bit had yet another design. The less common four-penny piece was a mixture of silver and copper. Pennies, ha'pennies and farthings were made of copper.

Wages were low but our requirements were few, and food was reasonably cheap. We ate all kinds of meat including rabbit, but we seldom ate fish. A cheap, American bacon called 'the lad,' had a firm - almost hard - fat and was full of juice. It cost between four and sixpence a pound and boiled with cabbage, it made a memorable meal. Another meal fit for a king was boiled pig's cheek, hot, with white cabbage and new potatoes. A generous butcher would sell a pluck[14] - the heart, liver and lungs of a sheep - for fourpence or he might just give it for free. We never paid for a sheep's head, but though my mother was a great cook, I did not care for the soup she made from it. She was fond of cooking with herbs and flowers: marigold flowers appeared with boiled beef and carrots. She achieved colour and effect with another favourite dinner - a dish of boiled mutton with carrots, white turnip, orange jellies and parsley sauce.

Roasting meat was a problem in an open fire. The meat hung in the fire from a staple or bar in the chimney breast. Long lengths of coarse grey wool were wrapped around the staple and a large hook in the meat was attached to the staple. A dish placed below the meat caught the drippings. We twisted the wool turning the meat by tipping it with a long-handled spoon in one direction until the string was spun tightly. Then, we let the meat unwind. We had to turn it slowly and carefully so the meat would cook properly. We had to look out for cinders falling into the grease pan, because they left a bitter taste.

It was a long job so we children took turns twisting the wool. We generally sat or knelt on one of the chairs placed around the fire to block the cold and draughts. As we twisted, we read our school books or posed riddles to one another to be solved. We had hundreds of them. While we tended the meat, my mother prepared the vegetables and finished other chores. Their experience cooking meat turned my brothers into first-class cooks.

Larry Hyland and Sara's twin, Jimmy

About this time I got a new baby brother[15] and I clearly recall seeing my mother nursing him. She had a beautiful, soft and very full breast which must have been a perfect haven for babies. My new brother must have been a couple of months old before I noticed him, but on this day when he was being fed, I stood watching him all curled up sucking as fast as he could. He moved his toes up and down as if to say, 'Good chaps, you are doing fine. Keep it up'. The baby suddenly gave a big push his hand but when he tried a conversation with the teat he got a smack on the bottom to remind him he had a job to do.

My mother had a small, sweet voice and generally crooned while nursing her babies. One of the many songs she sang had the queer words, 'till cherries grow on an apple tree'.[16] Another song about a stolen child with its last lines, 'Why destroy a mother's blessing - wherefore steal my baby boy?'[17] always brought tears to her eyes and a catch in her voice. She was a wonderful person full of all sorts of lore which she passed on to us. She recited long poems she had learned at school and she told us ghost stories that she heard or experienced.

She told us about a changeling she saw in 1872,[18] when she worked in the household of her father's relatives. She did not tell us whether the child was a member of that household, but she did describe the way the poor baby declined and its almost inhuman appearance at the end. She also told us a ghost story about Daw's Bridge, the bridge she crossed in a pony and trap on her journey home. She also told us that she heard the muffled thud, the thud of the body snatchers' car[19] as it passed her house on the way to the graveyard to steal the corpse of a recently buried person. The thud was produced by the ropes or other stuff wound around the wheel rims in an attempt to quiet them.

We were not brought to the doctor for minor complaints; our parents or neighbours cured such ailments. They treated a sore throat by filling a woolen stocking with warm salt and tying the stocking tightly around the neck when going to bed. Freshly boiled potatoes peeled and cut into small lumps did just as well. Sliced raw onion between two pieces of muslin made an excellent poultice for bronchitis while strong, cold tea eased sore eyes. A bottle placed in cold water, brought to the boil, emptied and applied directly to a boil would draw it painlessly and quickly unless there was water left in the bottle. In that case there would not be a vacuum and the victim would be scalded. If we suffered from lumbago, my mother would iron out the stiffness by putting a small folded blanket on the back and applying a very hot iron backwards and forwards till the patient felt relief. It seldom failed.

Some of the cures were delicious: a mixture of flax seed, liquorice, honey, lemon and brown sugar; a thin gruel with a knot of butter and a little whiskey and an egg flip were some of the things prescribed for a cold or a wheeze in the chest. We were dosed with electuary[20] in spring as well as senna tea. Sage kept our teeth white. Older people had their little comforts. One was mulled porter: porter in a jug with brown sugar and a stick of cinnamon which was warmed on the hob beside the fire.

Houses were poorly lit in our childhood. We had just one paraffin oil lamp that hung high on the wall out of our reach. The lamps were considered fairly dangerous, but when they were kept clean with a tidy, well-trimmed wick and a good reflector at the back, my mother said they were brilliant compared with lamps of her youth which were open containers with homemade wicks floating in oil.

It was usual for us to say the Rosary[21] every night before bed. My mother and father knelt at the big table and we children knelt at chairs or boxes. Sometimes we fell asleep and we got a scolding; the scoldings were worse if we mumbled or if we did not pay attention.

Thunderstorms were another occasion for storming heaven with our prayers. At the first clap of thunder we ran home and gathered round my mother who told us that God was angry with the world. If it was a big storm, she said God was very angry. We covered the mirrors[22] with cloths so they would not attract lightning, and the front door and back door were left open for the lightning to pass through the house. My mother kept us well out of its path. My oldest brother Joseph hid under his bed, but I felt much safer near my mother. When the storm passed, there was a smell of earth and a coolness in the air.

The laundry in Dundrum[23] gave good employment to girls and women, and local boys and men worked on the delivery vans. Its opening in 1887 must have been a great blessing to the impoverished people of this area in those difficult days. Histories of County Dublin record the great poverty that existed in the Dundrum area earlier in the nineteenth century.

Fleas are not nearly so troublesome as they were in our childhood. There were beastly things called creepers that were skin-coloured and slow moving. They were devils for giving a nip and leaving a red spot on the skin. We always were on the alert for them and it was hard work keeping free of them. Mothers particularly searched for them. If we came home shrugging or scratching, we'd be asked whom we were sitting beside at school and we'd be warned not to sit beside that person the next day.

One day in 1898 or 1899, my mother pushed the pram with her babies to the entrance gate of Mount Anville Convent to see Queen Victoria[24] arrive at the Convent to renew her friendship with one of the nuns. My mother was hoping to meet some of her friends who lived near the Convent and with whom she lived during the first year of her married life. They had a great gossip and she had a chance to show off her children to her old friends.

The Queen arrived with a great flurry of prancing horses and soldiers on horseback with beautiful uniforms. We children enjoyed the splendid sight, but that enjoyment was not shared by the majority of grown-up Irish men and women who hated those royal visits and considered them to be a great impertinence. When we grew up and learned more about the history of our country, we helped to break the chains that bound us.

In July, 1893, a movement to restore the Irish language[25] started in Dublin. It grew slowly at first, but as time went on, enthusiasm grew for it. Our local schoolmaster and his wife, also a teacher, took great interest in Irish and they taught the children as much as possible - Irish prayers and Irish songs; however, they had to be very careful not to offend the ministers on the Board of Education. I remember one St Patrick's Day seeing Joseph and other boys standing outside the church with tin mugs collecting for the Gaelic League saying, *Tabhair dom pingin ar son na Gaeilge.*[26] The brass buttons in their jackets showed they had the authority to collect the money. The pennies they got made a great noise as they dropped into the mugs, and the boys made a great show of pretending not to be able to hold up the mugs because of the weight of them.

St Patrick's Day was not only a church holiday but a great day for all sorts of activities connected with Irish culture. The Dun Emer Guild[27] took part in the Industrial Exhibition parade in Dublin city. They sent a horse-drawn dray with a carpet loom erected on it and one or two workers demonstrating how carpets were made. The dray was beautifully decorated with evergreens and large hanks of brightly-coloured wool used in carpet-making.

CHAPTER TWO

(1898-1903)

Summer excursionists - Weddings - Fashions - Christmas treats - The Zoo - A local asylum - Train accident - Dundrum Station - Songs and stories - The 'Bun Lady' - Outings to Lusk - First communion - 'Red Nellie' - Lent - The Yeatses arrive in Dundrum - Dun Emer - Odd jobs - The 1902 fire.

There was very little traffic in the village; however, on Sunday mornings in summer, excursion parties came through Dundrum on their way to the Scalp or to Enniskerry. They travelled in drags or wagonettes drawn by two horses. Drags were long, light vehicles rather high off the ground. Passengers faced one another on long benches that sat six people each. Passengers entered the drag by three steps and a very small door. The drags were not covered, so showery weather meant disaster.

The 'dickey,' or driver sat on a high seat behind the horses where he handled the team and the huge brakes that could be applied to the wheels when going downhill. There was room for a second person next to the brake handle, but the space was usually filled with straw hampers with food and drink for wayside picnics.

The excursionists were generally very merry. There were musical instruments in most drags so between the singsongs

31

and the laughter, it was great fun. Often they wore funny hats, or masks or long streamers - anything that would add to the fun-making. We watched eagerly for them and cheered their arrival and were frequently rewarded with fruit and sweets. We would wait for them on their return and they would get a great welcome from us, particularly if they had been generous on their way out.

The excursions started in May or early June and continued until September when the blackberry pickers arrived with their cans to walk the hills picking berries from the hedges that bordered the roads. Sometimes we joined them. Other times we had the excitement of the gathering of horses and hounds for a hunt. They gathered near the local public house to wait for their friends. They were free to walk their horses about, but the man in charge of the hounds had to stay put till it was time to move off. We also had the Harriers, young men in white singlets and shorts, who practised running and jumping in the fields at Meadow Brook. The soldiers from Portobello Barracks, accompanied by a band, also passed through the village on their march and we always walked a bit of the road with them, keeping in step with the music.

While every little happening was of interest to a child, a wedding was possibly the most exciting thing that could happen on Main Street. Lack of transportation limited the bridal party to six or eight people who arrived in two or three horse-drawn cabs or in a pony and trap. The ceremony, generally held in the afternoon, took only a few minutes. We children played at marrying one another at the end of the church. The great fun was to say, 'Till this day fornight' and 'With this ring I thee wed, and with this poker I'll break your head'.

The excitement came as the horse of the newlyweds' cab was whipped into action for the homeward journey. The groom and the best man leaned out of the windows and threw handfuls of small change called 'grush'.[1] We never knew from which window the money would come, so despite money falling all about, it was possible to finish up without a ha'penny.

Bride, groom, bridesmaid and best man travelled home in the same cab. Few people in those days went on a honeymoon trip, but there was generally a party to celebrate the wedding. Newlyweds were showered with rice to wish them plenty and the bridal pair usually followed custom in their dress: the bride in a pale grey dress with a white satin collar and the groom in a navy suit and tan boots.

Fashion in general was predictable and altered only slightly from year to year. Older women wore long, full skirts with brush braid sewn on the inside of the hem to protect them from the wear of rubbing against shoes or boots. The skirts were rather dull in colour except in summer when the dull browns and greys were replaced with pretty shades of mauve, pink, blue, green or buff. Better-off people wore skirts of a lovely material called tussore, a very fine, strong Chinese-type silk that could stand up to a lot of hard wear. Originally buff in colour, it later came in all pastel shades. We had a very nice, fine Irish material called dinsmore, which the more patriotic Irish women wore, and there were linens and muslins in pretty patterns.

Women wore blouses with short, shoulder capes which came to a little below the waist. Everyday blouses were plain, but there were ones with lots of trimming for Sundays and special occasions. I expect the blouses with their front openings were an absolute necessity for nursing mothers. Women wore bonnets, or toques or large, well-trimmed hats turned up on the left side. Shoes were not fashionable for either men or women as boots were considered to be better protection for the feet. Boots varied in length, cut and fastenings: some laced, some buttoned.

Children's dresses were not brightly coloured. Girls of all ages wore white pinafores that completely covered their frocks. Pinafores were often of very fine material and some were made with rows of lace and fine tucks. They were a Godsend to relations wishing to give a present to a young girl.

Our underwear was a problem in our young days. There were not ready-made children's garments so our mothers had to make them. Our school sewing classes also provided instruction. We graduated from patching to making an apron, and from there to a petticoat and finally to drawers or knickers as they are called today. Drawers were difficult because of the legs. We put bands at the knees so we could add lace (a farthing a yard at our local drapery shop) for summer and a coloured stitching on our winter flannelette ones. We loved to wear our drawers just long enough to show the lace or stitches beneath our dresses when we walked or ran. One of our schoolmates, called 'Long-drawers Mary', wore her drawers down to her ankles.

A Christmas treat was provided us by the first notable resident of the district, Lord Chief Baron Sir Christopher Palles,[2] the eminent lawyer and judge. Born in Dublin in 1831, he died in 1920 at Mount Anville House. He organized a Christmas tree party for us; the only requirement was that we be at least five years of age to attend. Sir Christopher's niece, Miss Bessie Palles, with the help of friends and some hired people, did all the work. They erected a Christmas tree about twenty feet high in the girls' school to which they fastened toys of every description. Toys similar to those on the tree were in a box on the floor. After we chose our toy on the tree, we were given the one in the box. Sometimes a child would refuse to take anything but the toy on the tree, so Miss Palles or one of her helpers climbed a step-ladder and took down the toy. Everything was done to make us happy. We had mugs of tea with buns or sweet cakes. In return we sang party songs taught to us for the occasion.

When we finished our tea, the tree was removed and we saw magic lantern pictures. In 1898, we must have seen a moving picture. It was a picture of a very mischievous-looking boy with a basket of fruit balanced on his head. While he whistled, out popped the little white head of a goose which seemed to peck at his nose before withdrawing back into the basket. We shrieked with delight and had to be shown the picture over and over again. I think we hoped to see the goose do something more.

Sir Christopher and Canon Matthews,[3] our Parish Priest, always arrived at the end of the party. Asked whether we enjoyed ourselves, we sang our party songs again. Our teachers thanked the Palleses on our behalf and with a loud cheer for our benefactors we were given a bag of sweets and put into our coats. Parents or neighbours took us home very tired and happy. The Christmas tree parties went on for years until parents objected to the Palles's custom of putting a small Union Jack on the top of the tree. Our hosts would not yield on this point so the party was discontinued.

One year, on the occasion of the coming of age of the young Earl of Pembroke, we were taken to the Zoological

Gardens on a fine day in early summer. We travelled in drags and all that I remember of the trip was that a sudden shower of rain soaked my pretty hat and that red colouring from the poppy flowers ran down my face on to my white dress. The sun came out and dried us, but I don't remember anything about the Zoo or about the return journey, and it was many years before I visited the Zoo again.

We Catholic children often envied our Protestant neighbours because their school had a large hall for concerts and other activities. We felt it was unfair to have such benefits in our country and that all Protestants should live in England. Didn't they wear Union Jacks and sing the English national anthem? When any of us tried to get in to one of their concerts, we were met with stiff resistance from the younger folk who knew we would get up from our seats so as not to be there for 'God Save the Queen'. They always sang it with great fervour, but it annoyed us to hear them.

Behind the shop at the crossroads of Sandyford and Upper Kilmacud, there was a private asylum,[4] a large house with twenty or more rooms. The main entrance of the house was hidden from Sandyford Road by trees and shrubs and from Upper Kilmacud Road by a row of two-storied houses. Further privacy was obtained by the solid wood door in the garden wall. A back gate at the end of the garden led into a field. Through a very small hole in the wicket gate, we children could observe an eccentric-looking middle-aged lady and some nurses. Another old lady seemed to get great satisfaction from tearing up things and we knew that great lengths of very cheap cotton were purchased frequently for her in the local drapery shop. Still another lady apparently liked to take her clothes off, and we got a great thrill one day to see a nurse pleading with her to come back into the house.

The lady in charge of the asylum was evidently very fond of clothes. A stout woman who favoured pretty colours, she wore extra-full skirts down to her toes. Satin bows and streamers flew around in all directions and she carried a parasol with more satin bows. She always wore a very large hat with fruit, flowers and frequently an artifical bird on top. She was one of the aristocracy; her doctor father had started the asylum for relatives of wealthy people. She was outspoken and her own class was a bit afraid of her because of the things she said. I'm sure they thought she was as odd as some of her patients. We certainly heard plenty of amusing stories about her.

My mother often took us along Upper Kilmacud Road for an outing to the church grounds where there were nice patches of grass and evergreens that bordered the path to the Protestant Taney Church. The grounds were kept beautifully by the sexton who lived in the gate lodge. We felt privileged to go in and sit on the grass with the babies. Our prams left outside the gate were safe enough because anyone passing would not interfere with them. Travelling to and from the church we passed over the railway bridge and were always thrilled to see a train going to Bray or returning toward the city.

In January, 1900, the brakes of the goods train[5] coming from Wexford failed. As it is downhill from Stillorgan to Harcourt Street Station, the train did not stop until it went through the wall and hung down into Hatch Street. Miraculously, the driver was only slightly injured. From then on we were always uneasy when the smoke of a train disappeared as it went under the bridge. It was a great relief to see it re-appear on the other side. We were close enough to see the engine driver and to shout to him. We were very happy when he waved to us in return.

We had one train that was so regular that house clocks were set by it. It was the 'nine luggage', a goods train that left Harcourt Street Station at nine o'clock on every night but Sunday. We could hear it away in the distance and were able to tell by the sound of it whether it had reached Milltown Station. It was so slow-moving that a person walking alongside the train would have to stop now and then for the train to catch up.

It made a gentle noise that seemed to ask for pity on account of the great load it carried. When coming into Dundrum Station, its rhythm seemed to say, 'I think I can. I think I can'. After a great shudder in the station and a few cheerful 'Chuff chuffs', its rhythm, as it left, quickened to a triumphant, 'I knew I could. I knew I could'. When the nine luggage passed our house, the windows would rattle. When the rattle was prolonged or heavy, someone always said, 'She must have a heavy load on tonight'. We always spoke of her with great affection.

We loved our Dundrum Station as well as the trains. The general waiting room was very big and always had a good fire burning during the winter. The smaller first-class waiting room also had a fire. On Sundays in winter we often went down to the waiting room after our dinner. We would bring our toys and books and meet some of our playmates there. It was almost like going to a friend's house. If there were strange children there, we were annoyed and glared at them until the train arrived in the station and took them off.

The waiting rooms were nicely furnished with a large table, a couple of chairs and built-in seating around two of the walls. We liked those seats best because we could place our dolls and toys on them. If we knelt down on the floor beside the seats, we were on a level with them. We played mothers or teachers and after one of us was in the hospital, the play was nurses and doctors.

The railway staff[6] enjoyed us and questioned us about our games. We knew how to keep ourselves in their good graces and were careful not to come out onto the platform when the train was coming into the station. The friendly station staff and a father who stood in the cab and car stand, and to whom we could fly for protection, made us feel very much at home.

Other friends were the policemen at the local RIC barracks on the Kilmacud Road. They kept pet rabbits that frolicked around in the rich green lawns in front of the living quarters and the courthouse. The rabbits burrowed into the earthen mounds near the house where the RIC men lounged in the warm weather. We never passed the barracks without calling in to see the rabbits with presents of dandelions, cabbage and lettuce leaves wilting in our little hot hands.

We were often rewarded with a pair of young rabbits to take home. This did not suit our parents, of course, who looked on rabbits as pests because of the trouble of housing and of cleaning up after them. We soon tired of them. They did not look the same in our backyards as they had in the wild at the barracks; however, we shed bitter tears when we were ordered to take them back and leave them where we got them. We were probably a bit ashamed at having failed in our ownership; yet, we knew that if we disobeyed our mother's instructions, she would go with us back to the barracks and make our task more humiliating.

I had another brother during those years[7] which made our family five boys and one girl. I was separated from the boys at this point and did not like it. If I tried to slip into their bedroom after they went to bed, I was pelted with anything they could get their hands on. They always seemed to know when I was coming and they were ready for me. I never thought it was fair that they had so much fun singing songs and laughing before going to sleep, and I did not understand why I could not join them.

The boys' songs were numerous and they varied with the seasons. My favourite was, 'One More River'. The older boys would start off merrily with, 'The animals came in two by two' while the younger boys waited impatiently to shout out the chorus, 'Only one more river to cross'. I waited eagerly in case they made a mistake to call out a correction thereby bringing their insults down on my head. When they stopped at animals 'ten by ten', I thought it was because our house number was ten. Other favourites were Moore's melodies, our school songs and parodies of war songs. Since the Boer War was just ended, we shouted, 'Hurrah for Billy Kruger'.[8]

About this time my mother started telling me Aesop's Fables. One she liked repeating to the family was 'The Lark in the Field of Corn.'[9] Although we did not understand it when we were young, the fable conjured up a pretty picture in our minds of baby larks telling their mother all that happened in her absence. In later years I often thought that I must have been brought up on fables, long poems and quotations from Shakespeare's plays.

My mother also knew a great deal about the opera[10] to which all the rest of us became addicted before we left school at the age of fourteen. We were fortunate in that my mother had worked in a house where operatic celebrities visited frequently. My mother frequently described her first visit to the opera, to a production of *Carmen*. She thought it was very noisy and she did not like it very much. She loved *Maritana* and *The Bohemian Girl* best and knew all the arias off by heart, so that was a great help to us going to those operas for the first time.

My father used to take a lady of independent means[11] into the city to shop. She always called at Mitchell's in Grafton Street for coffee or for afternoon tea where she bought buns for my father to bring home. As the family grew larger, the bags of buns got larger. One day she told my mother that she would like to call in and meet his family. I recall vividly the fuss in our house in anticipation of her arrival and the warnings to us to behave. She must have been very pleased with us, because I received an invitation to join her on her next outing.

From then on, she made a great fuss over me. She bought me dresses or gave material to my mother to make dresses for me. I visited her in her own home where she lived with a widowed sister and a grown-up niece. Her sister's name was Sara, so I was called 'Little Sara'. I probably chatted a lot to her and it was likely that she had a great longing for someone young around the place.

My lady also took me on trips to Dún Laoghaire when she went to visit friends. I did not go into their houses, but if her visit was to be a long one, she would give my father money to get himself tea and something for me to eat. In that way I soon made the acquaintance of the Purty Kitchen in Dún Laoghaire. One day I tried climbing up the dresser to get a closer look at the pewter plates and the whole top tumbled down with a terrible crash bringing the barman and all the customers in to see what happened. I need hardly tell you that I was pretty silent on my homeward journey that day. I am sure my father did not say anything to me; he was that sort of man - never scolding, always rather silent. He was, of course, glad I was not hurt, but he would have also been glad that no one found out he had taken me into a public house.

While thinking of outings with my lady, I remember our wonderful trips by jaunting car to the pretty little village of Lusk in north County Dublin where my mother was born. We often went there by train but it was the journey by jaunting car that was the great joy. We left early on a Sunday morning and a grown-up friend would go along with us. She sat on one side of the car with the older boys while my mother sat with the younger boys and me on the other side.

Places of interest were pointed out on our journey from Dundrum through Dublin and north. We rode over O'Connell Bridge and passed the General Post Office, the Rotunda and Findlater's Church. We liked the big bridge across Dorset Street that had a huge advertisement for the *Irish Independent* and we liked the railway bridges we passed later. We were excited to hear we were coming to the Cat and Cage wondering whether there would be a real cat. I expect we were disappointed to find out that it was only a picture on the wall of a public house.

We did not stop at the Cat and Cage, but we did get down once or twice on the journey to stretch our legs and to ease the load on the horse when going up a hill. On our return journey, we called in at a little shop in Swords for sweets. Relations of my mother owned the shop and it was the place where she earned her first wages.

My mother always took food with us so as to avoid the trouble of cooking when we got to our grandfather's house. Her father, who lived to a good old age, was always anxious to make the acquaintance of the latest addition to our family. Another aunt who lived in Balbriggan and who had a family the same age as ours often met us at my grandfather's so we met our cousins too. They arrived by pony and cart and our horse and their pony were put in the field by the side of the house to rest. We too went into the fields to wander and play. We had the beautiful countryside to ourselves because the nearest house was about a quarter of a mile distance on one side and almost a mile away on the other. Pigs and chickens interested us for a short while; another wonder was a stream near the house. We were never bored, and while we played, our relations talked and laughed. My mother returned home with a few dozen eggs, a piece of home-cured bacon, a couple of chickens, and a lot of very tired children.

On September 14, 1900, I made my first Holy Communion in our parish church. It was the feast of the Exaltation of the Holy Cross which gives its name to our church. It was a red letter day not only for the small group of girls and boys but also for all the parishioners. We were a great anxiety to our parents and teachers who worried that we would do everything in the proper manner. After Mass we were given breakfast in our schools where our teachers looked after our interests and praised us for being so good. I recall going back to the church several times during the afternoon that day because some of the old people asked us to pray for them believing, no doubt, that the prayers of innocent children on such a day would be pleasing to our Heavenly Father.

With the birth of my youngest brother Patrick in 1901, we were a family of six boys and one girl. We were doing well at our lessons at school and finding life very interesting. Dundrum grew with the addition of council houses on the outskirts of the village and the children came to our schools. Village life got busier and there was more traffic on the roads.

My older brothers Joseph and Batty started going out to meet the 7.30 train from the city that brought the morning newspapers. They delivered the papers to the big houses for a local newsagent. In doing so, they earned a little money that went towards the housekeeping. They also made friends for themselves among the local gentry which served them well afterwards when they were seeking employment.

I was always up early, but they would not have me with them. I had to wait until my twin brother Jimmy was old enough to do this work and then I got my opportunity of going on these exciting rounds. There was, however, one little job I could do and did do: to watch for the mountainy carts on their way to market with white turnips, mangolds, carrots, orange-jellies and rabbits. When I heard the carts rumbling along the Ballinteer Road, I would run home to tell my mother who would send me back to ask the men to wait for her if she were not quick enough getting out to them. I am sure she was always in time. After buying what she wanted, she had a little chat with the drivers, generally asking about the health of someone. We were such a small community we were able to know and to take an interest in our neighbours in Ticknock and Glencullen.

Soon I was able to do all the business of buying the rabbits and vegetables on my own. The men knew me and always had a cheerful word for a child. Years later, I met the son of one of the men and was surprised to hear him say that he knew me. He remembered me as the little girl who used to watch for his father, the man who sold the rabbits. I was learning to be useful in other ways. I could skin a rabbit and pluck and clean a chicken when I was only ten.

The recollection of the vegetable and rabbit men reminds me of another of our characters, 'Red Nellie', the fish woman. She came Friday mornings all year-round and on Wednesdays during Lent. She was a very cheerful woman who knew us all by our Christian names. I think she came by train from Harcourt Street to Milltown Station and she walked from there along the main road with her basket balanced on her head calling out, 'Dublin bee-bee herns. Get Dublin bee-bee herns'.[12] 'Dublin Bay baby herrings' was what she wanted to say, but with the swaying of her basket as she walked along 'bee bee herns' was easier to say. On meeting a customer, she would set down her basket, place a board across it, slit open a fish and cut it into the required sizes. It was not long before I asked for a herring and learned to deal with it.

Lent in my youth was a season of strict fasting. My mother obeyed all the rules and expected us to do the same. On Ash Wednesday, Spy Wednesday and Good Friday, she would not give us milk in our tea or butter on our bread. For our tea she made what looked like milk by putting water on flake oatmeal and we got jam on our bread without butter. We were forbidden to eat sweets and we were not to read anything but religious books. The seven weeks took a long time to pass and I am sure we were not the little angels that we were expected to be.

At the close of the nineteenth century, in 1900, there was a church celebration, a Jubilee Year. There were indulgences granted to the faithful who completed a round of three visits to three separate churches with special prayers said each time. My parents took part in these visits with the rest of the parish. They walked from Dundrum to Kilmacud church, to Sandyford church and back to Dundrum again on three successive Sundays.

My father's sister Aunt Margaret looked after us while our parents were away and she must have been bossing us because my older brothers would not submit to her. They took the sweeping brush to beat her with it and she ran into the bedroom. They locked her in the room. I can only remember the turmoil, the crying and the general pandemonium. She must have made a truce with them, promising the world if they would only be good and let her out again. We were all pals again in a short time.

In the autumn of 1902, John Butler Yeats,[13] father of the poet W B Yeats and the artist Jack B Yeats came from London with his two daughters[14] to take up residence in Churchtown. Their house was not ready for occupancy when they arrived so they found temporary accommodation in Sydenham Villas where they remained for some months. The Yeats daughters, Susan Mary and Elizabeth Corbett, together with Miss Evelyn Gleeson[15] were about to start a small art industry for the manufacture of hand-tufted carpets, tapestries, embroideries, hand-printed books and broadsides.

Miss Gleeson rented a house named Runnymede[16] on Sandyford Road, a short distance from the main street of

Dundrum. The name of the house was changed to Dun Emer and the Industry was called the Dun Emer Guild. The two Misses Yeats had been trained[17] in the Merton Abbey Works, William Morris's famous art school.

My brother Batty delivered the morning papers to the residents of Sydenham Villas.[18] The Yeats family asked to have the newspapers and Batty was soon on friendly terms with them. The Yeatses were known for their friendliness to everyone, especially to children. They gave Batty books including an Irish phrase book[19] by Norma Borthwick, founding member of the Gaelic League, with drawings by Jack B Yeats.

Dun Emer Guild Ltd.

DUNDRUM. Co. Dublin.

MANUFACTURERS OF

Rugs, Carpets and Tapestries.
Bookbinders & Embossed Leather Workers
Vellum Painters, Designers & Enamellers.

The Carpets and Rugs are made by hand, of best Irish Wool. Designs and Estimates free. **CHURCH CARPETS A SPECIALTY.** Bedroom and Bath Rugs made in the American style. The Bookbinding closely resembles the excellent Irish work of the Eighteenth Century. The Enamels are noted for fine colour. **Secretary—Miss EVELYN GLEESON.**

Sandyford — Churchtown — Merrion Square.

Advertisement for the Dun Emer Guild from a local church magazine, 1915

There were a number of big houses in Dundrum with several acres of land attached to each. I became acquainted with a wealthy pair who lived on the Ballinteer Road.[20] They kept a herd of Jersey cows and would sell the surplus milk to anyone who collected it, so four or five of us from the village went each evening between five and six o'clock with our tommy cans. Word of the quality and good value of the milk spread, and soon I had a tommy can on each of my fingers for people who had no children to do the work for them. I was rewarded for my labour - first with a daily ha'penny which I spent immediately, later with a weekly wage. Paid weekly, I was able to save my pennies and buy something I otherwise would not have got.

In early summer we were not allowed to go up to the house for milk until the gardener returned to his house after his day's work. They kept us out because of the uncut meadow. When the hay was stacked, there were no restrictions on us. There were two avenues to the house, but we always went by the back avenue.

We use to have good fun while waiting on the roadway as the 'bogies', flat cars for drawing the hay from the fields, would be working. We would get a 'jaunt' on them and on the mountainy carts returning home from the markets. The men always brought the horses through the stream for a drink. On one occasion, when the river was in flood, the driver of one of these carts whipped five of us off his cart right into the water. He thought it was great fun, but he paid for his foolishness. Armed with wet sods, we waited for him the next time he came along and we pelted him from a safe place in the field by the river. After that, he avoided us by coming early or waiting until we were gone.

In autumn it was lovely to walk through the fallen leaves or to pick up chestnuts which we brought home and dried so that we could play a game called 'conkers.' Next to the house where we waited to collect our milk was a big cobblestone yard with houses for all the animals, a harness room and a special room for the coachman to rest. There was a spring water pump as well. The most wonderful house of all was the boilerhouse where food (mangolds, swede turnips and grain) was boiled for cows in a cauldron raised up on two large hobs over a fire on the floor. The smell of the burning firewood and of the contents of the cauldron was rather pleasant. After the herdsman lit the fire under the cauldron, he let us help keep the fire going by pushing in the faggots after the tops burned off. We ran back and forth to the cowhouse where the herdsman milked the cows, so he would know that nothing wrong was happening.

One evening I wandered away from my companions and walked toward the back gate. I stopped at a gate leading into a field and suddenly I saw what appeared to be a beautiful little dell stretching away into the distance. There was a pathway in the center of two slightly-raised banks that had bushes and trees growing on them. Although it was a dark evening, there was sunshine and shadow all around. It did not seem strange that there was such a place, but I remember wondering why I had not seen it before, or indeed why I did not even know that it was there.

I ran back to my companions and whispered to my girl friend to come quickly that I wanted to show her something. When we reached the spot, there was nothing to be seen and as the boys had followed us, I did not do any explaining. Instead I popped that experience into my secret hiding place, the place in my brain where I deposit things that are awkward or secret. (I feel this spot is located behind my left eye in back of my left ear, a place where I often experience a slight ache.)

One evening, in the early winter of 1902, we saw a house on fire as we came along the road with our milk cans. It was the out offices and goods entrance of Browne's shop. I ran to tell my mother about the fire and was kept home out of harm's way. When we heard the loud clanging of the fire brigade bell, I was allowed to go down to the main street to see the fire brigade engine rushing by to the fire. The fire engine was like a float on four wheels with centrepiece shaped like the body of a railway engine. It had several buckets hanging on it with a long ladder on each side, a lot of rope and four firemen who stood, two on each side, on a narrow platform over the wheels. They wore red jackets and brass helmets. The brigade, phoned from the Dundrum Telephone Office, arrived in the amazing time of twenty-three minutes. They kept the fire from doing much damage to the shop and dwelling house overhead and they prevented the fire from spreading to the adjoining houses.

Portrait of Lily Yeats by John B Yeats (National Gallery of Ireland)

CHAPTER THREE

(1903-1908)

Joseph begins work - Ghost stories - Local elections - Nationalist victory - Cockle-picking - Boss Croker - Outings with the 'Bun Lady' - The Telephone Exchange - Household chores - Confirmation - Batty becomes a driver - Wakes - Postal service - Browne's - Travelling theatre - Cissie arrives - Opera - Lolly and Lily Yeats.

In 1903, my eldest brother Joseph turned fourteen, left school and became apprenticed to a local painter and decorator, a near neighbour, who had two other men working with him. Joseph liked the work very much and was full of enthusiasm for it; however, he had an attack of lead poisoning. While he was recovering, the proprietor of a large drapery and hardware shop[1] on Main Street gave Joseph work to do in the garden and in the shop. When he went back to painting, he continued doing odd jobs. He was a great source of all the local happenings and was never short of a piece of sensational news, very often of a ghostly nature.

Dundrum abounded in ghost tales, some credible. There were many dark places on the different roads leading away from the main street and as there was no public lighting, many

47

people would not go outdoors after dark, but since our house was situated close to the main street, our family was never cut off from local happenings. I always enjoyed hearing different ghost stories and I believed some of them. My credulity depended on the narrator and I soon recognized the Munchausen[2] among the talkers.

Kilmacud Road and beyond, including Birches Lane, seemed to be teeming with spirits of all descriptions, including poltergeists. Few people were indifferent to walking down Sweet Briar Lane on their own on a dark night. A coach with a headless driver[3] was the favourite story about that place and it was mostly to be seen on a moonlit night, but whatever the truth of these tales, there was often evidence that something had taken place.

I remember one Christmas time hearing that a delivery van from one of the local shops had been turned over and all the goods spilled over the road. The driver was found the next morning and had to be taken to hospital. The people went around the next day with ashen-grey faces; they gathered together in small groups and spoke only in whispers to each other, and some went over to the lane to see the evidence for themselves. 'Yes,' they said when they came back, 'there was sugar lying about in blue bags, some half empty, and others barely burst open.' The same was true for packets of fruit, rice, raisins, currants and candles as well as for bottles of stout and minerals. Everything that a delivery van was likely to contain was strewn about the road. The talk of this event continued for a long time and it awakened memories of other happenings among the talkers. There were stories of such a person meeting a huge dog with feathers instead of hair that emitted a dreadful stench. There was another story of a little woman, wearing a mobcap and shawl, hurrying along and turning into a gateway that led to the avenue of one of the big houses.

We had history as well as legend in Dundrum that included an occasional election meeting in the village when a local person was going forward for a seat in Parliament or in the County Council. Meetings were held in the lane near our house at night to suit the workers who might have a long walk home after their day's work. (A day's work in my young days was from ten to twelve hours long, and in the wintertime it was from dawn to dusk.) I was too young to understand what the men were talking about at these meetings or why they were there, but I liked the feeling of mystery and unreality that surrounded men out in the darkness of night, standing on a vehicle, talking to people they could not see except occasionally when one of the lights swung in their direction. The torch lights spitted and sputtered needing the full attention of the bearers and people watched to keep out of the pathway of the sparks.

Few people had voting privileges when I was young, particularly the Catholics who generally spoke about such things with bitterness and frustration. Householders had the vote and male members of the family qualified if they occupied their own rooms; however, we heard it was easy for a Protestant man to get the vote even if he lived at home with his family and did not have a room to himself.

There was great excitement in Dundrum when a Nationalist defeated the Unionist Member of Parliament[4] for the County Dublin seat. We had great celebrations to mark the event because the successful candidate lived locally and his victory was unexpected. We had a huge bonfire in the Rocky Field on the Kilmacud Road and with it speechmaking, singing, a band playing and fireworks going off. My brother Joseph was in charge of the fireworks display. The real joy of the election was the ray of hope among grown-ups that the national spirit had re-awakened, and that a day in the not too distant future we would be 'a nation once again'. That song was sung again and again that night. Since the Gaelic League started in 1893 and Arthur Griffith introduced the idea of 'Sinn Fein,' there was a feeling of unity amongst the people and a determination to work for Ireland on every occasion.

My father often came home and told my mother to send a couple of the boys to one of the big houses to pick up the apples and pears that had fallen or to pick gooseberries and currants. Once or twice I was let go on such errands. I remember a gooseberry bush in the garden of Barn Elms[5] in Churchtown that had very large berries, almost purple in colour, with a heavenly taste.

Life was a joy in those far-off days. We loved walking and thought nothing of taking a trip to Booterstown Strand[6] to pick cockles. The boys generally took off their boots, tied the laces together and slung them across their shoulders, one foot at the back and one in the front, which made them easier for carrying. I did not take off my shoes as I feared that someone would tread on my toes, and I did not like the feel of gravel under my feet. We sang songs as we marched along; we chased one another, or we sat awhile on the pathway. Since there was little or no traffic, we had the world to ourselves. After picking the cockles on the strand, we generally hurried home with them. There they were washed free of sand, put into a pot of cold water, and when boiled - they opened. We took out the cockles and ate them with bread and butter.

It was mostly Danish butter that we ate then. Think of that! In Ireland we could have produced all of the butter and bacon we required and more, but we were not let do so by the English government who were making a profit out of the trade. It did not suit them to let us develop our country economically. Is it any wonder that we grew up with a hatred of the English government and that Ireland produced heroes and heroines who loved their native land so much that they were prepared to give up their lives that she might be free. Down the years, there have been risings and rebellions that were crushed in most brutal ways. We visualized the British government as a wicked old hag[7] floating in the air over our country, spying on us with her dreadful talons outstretched, ready to pounce down on anything that she felt might be against her interests and those of the parliamentarians who directed her in the government of Ireland and of the other countries from whom she seized power.

In 1904, Richard 'Boss' Croker[8] bought a place called Glencairn in Sandyford where he set up stud and racing stables which brought employment to our village. It brought a feeling of well-being to us that was sorely needed. The workers got good wages; the local shops benefited by their prosperity.

The 'Bun Lady' invited me on a picnic party with some of her friends to Lough Bray. It was a beautiful day and I was put sitting in the well of the jaunting car behind my father. We had to dismount several times at the very steep hills. When we finally reached the place for the picnic, my father pointed to a hillock and told me to run off there. He did not want me under foot while the ladies were getting the fire lighted to make the tea. When I got to the top of the hillock, I looked down on a beautiful stretch of land. I felt sure that nobody knew it was there because you could not see it from the road we had travelled. I was sure that I was the first person to find it and if I hurried back to the ladies and told them about it, they could climb to the same place and see that view for themselves.

I had a curious habit of identifying myself with places and people all my life. When I first read *David Copperfield*, I was Dora.[9] Later in life when I re-read the story, I considered her very silly and did not wish to be like her at all. *David Copperfield* was the first of many books my benefactress gave to me. It was quite a large book with a pale blue, stiff cover and small illustrations throughout it. I'm sure I must have told her the story bit by bit as I read it as I expected she wanted me to do. She always found time to listen as she was very fond of me.

I realize now that I must have filled a lonely spot in her heart. She sent me cards by post at Christmas, Easter, and for my birthday which she never forgot. I did a lot of little errands for her, and she always rewarded me on my return - perhaps an apple in one hand and an orange in the other. She would say, 'Which one will you have?' If I said, 'the apple', she would say, 'Eat the apple now and take the orange with you'. (I soon got to know that I would be given both.)

In the summertime, the 'bun lady' went to Howth for three months for a change of air. My father borrowed a van from one of the local shopkeepers to take her trunks and bedding. We started early in the morning so that we were back in time to take her to Howth by cab or car in the evening. I remember being thrilled with these outings, because my father drove part of the way on the seashore and this gave me a wonderful feeling of doing something unusual. I thought my father drove there just for my pleasure, but it was the usual route. I did not find this out for a long time, so my pleasure was undiminished.

One day I was sent to the local Telephone Exchange[10] with a message for a city shop. There were few private telephones in those days. I entered the Exchange by the hall door which was open to the public, and I asked for the number which was written on a piece of paper with the message. Mrs O'Gorman sat at the switchboard in the room off the hall a few feet away from me. She put in some plugs, turned a little handle and said something to me. The next thing I knew, there was a voice speaking in the little black object which I was holding in my hand. I was so terrified that I could not speak and started to cry. Mrs O'Gorman knew something was wrong and came out in the hall to tell me not to be afraid. She took my message and sent it through to the shop. I hoped that she would not tell anyone about me, and I never heard that she did.

My brother Batty had a passion for scrubbing the large tiles in our kitchen and woe betide anyone who walked on them whilst he was on the job. We all had our weekly cleaning and scrubbing jobs allotted as soon as we were capable of doing them. We had a wonderful time with the wallpaper pattern books that Joseph brought home from work. My mother let us paper the small back room from floor to ceiling with various patterns. She made us a small bucket of paste by stirring boiling water into flour until it became very sticky. We started our papering from the floor upwards. I expect my mother often came to our rescue straightening our crooked work, possibly finishing the job.

The outside toilet was another place where we were let try our papering skill. This place was always called the 'House of Parliament' and we gave plenty of thought to its decoration. We selected patterns that had trees or pasture lands on them and papered them in a straight line on the wall where we could feel as if we were out in the country. Flowers and other patterns went on the sides and back walls and it did not matter if we kept our work straight on those walls.

I had a wonderful time learning to iron clothes. My mother bought two flat irons and my father made an ironing table for me. The irons used in my youth were heated on an open coke fire. They were cleaned when taken off the fire by rubbing them on a flat board that had powdered bath brick and a small piece of wax on it. They were then wiped clean with a very thick cloth. The smell of the cleaning operation was very pleasant. A later improvement was a light metal shield or slipper made in the shape of the iron and easily fixed to it. With the shield in place, the iron only needed a wipe of the cloth.

I started first on handkerchiefs, pillow cases or any small flat articles. Then, I ironed my own pinafores. Soon I was able to help my mother with the baby clothes that she laundered for people who did not want to send such fine articles to the public laundry. Babies were kept in long clothes until they reached the age of three months, and well-to-do people had some very beautiful garments for their children. I loved ironing the little clothes and was proud of being so useful to my mother.

The year I was confirmed, the 'bun lady' presented me with the material for my dress which she let me choose. To my mother's horror, I chose grey material and white satin for a collar. I expect I was thinking of the brides that I had seen in church and I concluded that grey with white satin was absolutely correct. The satin collar never sat properly, and I have the painful recollection that my choice of material and style of dress could not have been worse. I seemed to get a leg pulling about every time I put the dress on.

My brother Batty left school at the age of fourteen in 1905. Motor cars were coming into daily use at the time and were such a novelty that all young boys yearned to drive one. Batty was fortunate to be taken on for such work by Dr Goff, our local private doctor, who could drive his own car but who wanted someone he could teach to drive so as to help him on his rounds of visiting patients.

Cars in those days were constantly breaking down, so it was necessary for Batty to learn something about their machinery. He went to a local garage that had been set up recently by a wonderful mechanic, a genius who had some inventions to his credit. Batty was with Dr Goff when he was needed and in the garage during his off-hours. The mechanic, a character of some importance, attracted some very odd people to his workshop, so there was never a dull moment.

With two brothers working in two different workplaces at the same time, it seemed as though our household had a grip on all the gossip about everything that was going on in our parish. At home we looked forward to hearing all the titbits of news about what took place during the day in the many different places, and my brothers vied with each other to tell the best story.

My mother encouraged us to tell about our exploits; however, if there were any tales of practical jokes she would lecture them on their danger. She often had to do this. She had her own stories of things that had started in fun and ended in disaster.

We were all talkers in our house except for my father who was a very quiet man. He left the bossing to my mother and if we failed to get her consent for something we wished to do on our own or to go someplace she did not wish us to go, we asked our father to make a special appeal for us. First, he always reminded us that our mother knew best and that she was the boss, but I expect he often persuaded her to change her mind. He was a very wise man to leave the bossing to her because it saved him and us a lot of bother to have just one master in the house.

My mother did not go out visiting among her neighbours because she was too busy pottering about her own house; therefore, she must have been glad of our stories. While she did not go visiting, she always called at a house where death had taken place and she always took one of us with her. On the way to the wake-house, as it was called, my mother talked to us about death - how beautiful it was and that we were not to fear it. When we had knelt down at the bedside and said our prayers for the repose of the soul of the departed one, we had to put our hand on the forehead of the corpse. At first, it was rather frightening, but after a little practice and with our mother's encouragement, we felt we were doing a wonderfully good deed. I still do it and, strange to say, it is my mother I think of while I do it. She was a remarkably good woman.

When my twin brother Jimmy took on one of the newspaper rounds, I was able to go out with him in the early morning. It was a lovely sensation to be up and about while other people were still in their beds. I had the feeling that the outside world was mine alone and the few people I met on the road were just my friends. The morning air was cool and soft and it blew gently on my cheek in a caressing manner. The crows and blackbirds swooped down to the road for the little titbits that they thought were there for their breakfast and they came very close to us, trusting us as friends. The train puffed into the station, its breast appearing to burst with pride at having made the journey successfully from Harcourt Street and announcing it would continue on bringing the newspapers, the post and the travellers to other stations along the line.

One of our five postmen arrived to collect the mail bags. The Dundrum Post Office[11] in Main Street near the railway station was ruled by an elderly Protestant lady who sat upright on a very high stool trying to look regal and very important. Since she was Her Majesty Queen Victoria's loyal servant, she felt she should look the part. She folded her mittened hands on her lap and rested her feet on a bench underneath the counter. Blinking through her spectacles, she looked down at us saying in a low voice, 'What is it that you require?' Whether or not she heard the reply, she called her assistant, 'This child appears to be saying something'. We repeated our request for one or more stamps and the assistant, who did all of the work except sign documents, sold us what we needed.

There were two daily postal deliveries at 8.00 am and 7.00 pm and one delivery on Sunday mornings. Letters were dispatched to the city on the noonday train and again at 10.00 pm. These hours will bring home the length of a workingman's day in comparison with today's shorter hours. At Christmas, the postman's work increased with the extra letters and parcels. The real bustle, however, was reserved for a few days before Christmas Day. No one wanted their cards to arrive too early so most people waited to post them until the last minute.

Few houses boasted of having a letter-box, so the postman, having knocked, waited for the door to be opened. His distinctive knock brought people running quickly to their doors. It was at this time of year that the postman was usually generously rewarded for his past year's work with money gifts which were called Christmas boxes. Well-to-do people often gave something substantial, a half-sovereign perhaps, and sweets or something for his family. Well-meaning, unimaginative friends started his day with a glass of whiskey and after a few such glasses, he was incapable of continuing his work and a friend or neighbour came to the rescue. Sometimes a wife or mother, who anticipated the situation, was ready to take over. Life was leisurely in those days and as a small community, we were always ready to take over and help when it was necessary.

The Browne brothers' provision and general store and news agency was at the corner of the Ballinteer and Sandyford Roads. Two brothers and two sisters looked after the shop which did a good business. The men took turns each week rising early to take in the newspapers which they distributed to the newsboys to deliver. One of the brothers was a late riser; consequently, there were complaints every other week. He was a bit of a joker and proposed, half-seriously, a brilliant plan. Since I was out early each morning to deliver papers with Jimmy, he asked me to cross the wall at the end of his yard, climb into the house by the kitchen window and call him out of bed when it was his week on duty. I did this very successfully for a number of years.

The Browne sisters found that I was useful for running errands to the chemist or to the drapery shop. I was allowed to help in the shop on Saturday evenings and came home very proudly with one shilling and sixpence plus a pound pot of jam every Saturday night. Between all my little jobs and earnings I did quite well and was saving to go see and hear an opera. My older brothers had been going to the opera for some time and promised to take me along.

Closer to home we were promised entertainment. Posters appeared overnight on every available spot in the village announcing the arrival of a very talented theatrical touring company called Purcell's.[12] A list of plays and a date for the opening night followed and our quiet little village prepared for an exciting experience. A formidable amount of equipment arrived including several horse-drawn drays with marquee, stage, seats, and props and a number of caravans used as living quarters. It was like a miniature village on wheels.

Purcell's arranged accommodation in Bob Doyle's field, a large field on the Kilmacud Road about three hundred yards from the Main Street, the site of the present National School. They brought the usual type of torch-lights and storm lanterns for outdoor lighting was a big problem in those days. They also had braziers for cooking and for heat. Boys and girls came in great numbers to the plays from the outlying districts. The company not only had a very profitable season, but there were also a number of romances that started at the performances and ended in happy marriages. The Purcells provided their own improvised lighting system because outdoor lighting in the village was a big problem in those days. The public lighting consisted of only two gas lamps on Main Street - one at the railway station and the other at the crossroads of Sandyford and Ballinteer roads. Although the village was very dark in winter, it did not prevent us from getting out and about. I expect that the *Old Moore's Almanac* was closely studied for the dates of different phases of the moon. A person often came into the house on a moonlit night saying, 'It's so bright out tonight that you could pick up pins by the light of the moon'.

We took a great interest in the planets in my youth. We knew the names of the different planets and could name them correctly when they appeared. We knew some of the groups of stars and the direction in the sky where they could be found.

Toward the end of September, we were on the look-out for the Aurora Borealis and we were disappointed if winter passed without our seeing it. If one of us saw it, we ran home quick with the news so other members of the family could go out and enjoy the sight. If has been many years since I have seen the Aurora Borealis and I wonder is it all the different gasses and fluids in the air that are depriving us of some of our old pleasures.

On New Year's Day in 1906, my parents went to Balbriggan on a very sad errand. My mother's sister had died after giving birth to a baby girl, leaving a family of seven children to mourn their loss. These children were the cousins we met when we visited our grandfather in Lusk. When my mother arrived home, she opened her cape proudly and showed us that she brought us a new baby sister. We did not welcome the poor infant that night, nor indeed for a long time afterwards. She was crying and it must have been a big problem for my mother who had nothing prepared for such an emergency nor any idea about bottle-feeding a baby.

Some of our thoughtless neighbours tweaked my nose and said, 'Ah-ha, my fine lady, your nose is out of joint now with another little girl in your house. You have lost your place'. There were others, thank God, who welcomed the child saying it was a wonderful gift that God had sent to our house and that my mother would be well rewarded. She was. My cousin Brigid Gaffney, whom we called 'Cissie', was a great source of comfort to her for the rest of her life.

The opera season was in full swing at the Gaiety Theatre when I was let go to my first opera. It was *Tannhauser* and I think it was the Carl Rossa Company[13] that performed it that year. In those days, the opera season generally opened on St Stephen's Day with a matinee and continued for three or four weeks with a change of programme daily for each performance. Joseph and Batty had been going to the opera for some time, and they knew the best seats in the gallery for sitting, hearing and seeing and for getting out quickly when the opera ended.

It was great fun running from Harcourt Street Station to be first in the queue. We were never far from the top of it, and we thought nothing of standing there for two or three hours waiting for the doors to open. There were always characters among those waiting to keep us amused, and we often contributed to the fun ourselves. A seat in the Gallery, affectionately known as the 'Gods' cost sixpence; a book of the words of the opera cost another threepence or fourpence, and we shared a programme between us for another penny. Metaphorically speaking, we were in Heaven!

I loved the operas and the excitement of going to them. My brothers knew most of the melodies and whistled them all day long during the opera season. The same was true of all the messenger boys in the city. 'Life was worth living,' was the feeling we had at that time and we knew we were fortunate to have such wonderful opera companies coming here year after year: Carl Rossa, Moody Manners, Joseph O'Mara, Harrison Frewen and the Quinlan Opera Company.

The Yeatses house in Dundrum

A great advantage of being in Browne's shop each Saturday morning was that I was able to observe the two Misses Yeats on their way to Dun Emer without my being seen by them. Miss Lily Yeats generally called to the shop to leave an order for goods which she wished to have sent to her house during the day. I would see her coming and go into the parlour to tell Mr Browne. Then I took my place behind the lace curtain to have a good look at Miss Lolly Yeats who generally stood waiting outside the shop.

She wore beautiful clothes, mostly Irish tweeds of rich purple or heather mixture or sometimes different shades of green. She had large pieces of handmade jewelry with semiprecious stones, beautiful hats and buttoned boots. She was nice-looking, had a very trim, slim figure and was rather tall. Her crisp, curling hair was turning grey. Her neck was rather long so she usually wore a black velvet band on it or a ruffle of lace in a high, upstanding collar fashion. When she walked she took short steps giving the impression of a slight rocking movement. The local people called her the Purple Miss Yeats.

Miss Lily Yeats always wore clothes of a fine material in shades of blue, fawn or grey. She was very good-looking with a trim square figure and she moved smoothly when she walked. She was known to the people as the Blue Miss Yeats. Both ladies had good complexions and never wore make-up. They were very popular with the village people. My mother was promised a place for me in the embroidery section at Dun Emer when I was ready to leave school, so naturally I was interested to observe the Misses Yeats whenever I had the opportunity.

Browne's Shop had another advantage for me. I was very fond of reading and I could take a book or a newspaper up to the hayloft or to the storeroom where I made myself comfortable sitting on a pile of empty sacks or indeed on a full sack of chicken meal. Anyone looking for me knew where to find me, even in wintertime. It was there that I was able to read the concluding chapters of a serial called 'Love's Thorny Path'[14] which ran in the *Saturday Evening Herald*. It was not finished before the season of Lent began and my mother would have been horrified if she had known what I was doing. I thought it was great fun to get to the end of the story without being caught and doing what I ought not to have done.

Outside the Cuala Industries

CHAPTER FOUR

(1907-1909)

Sara goes to Dun Emer - Boss Croker's Orby - Cuala - Bun Lady's funeral - Lily's stones - Local folklore - Cuala visitors - Susan Mitchell - Cuala socials - Christmas.

Jimmy and I left school on the same day in April, 1907. He went to the Post Office to be a telegraph messenger boy, with the chance to be a postman later. I went to the Dun Emer Guild[1] to become an embroideress under the tuition of Miss Susan Mary Yeats who was better known as Miss Lily. Her sister who managed the hand printing press was known as Miss Lolly.

Dun Emer House was big with some very large rooms, and the room where Miss Yeats did her embroideries also contained the looms for the tapestries and carpet-making which was under the supervision of Miss Gleeson. There were three grown-up girls[2] at the embroidery when I started, but I did not know them. They did not live in Dundrum and had not attended my school. Fortunately, I knew some of the girls who were at the carpet making, so I did not feel lost among strangers on the first day when I was launched on the career that I was to follow for the rest of my life.

I learned the work very quickly as I had a good knowledge of stitchery from my mother, but this caused some uneasy moments with my fellow workers. Another mark against me was that I had appeared in an overall made in the same style as the one worn by Miss Lily. This was pure coincidence, but it made an unfavorable impression. After my first day, I almost gave up going there, but my mother would not let me do that. How glad I am that I kept on going as I had such a wonderfully happy life with the Misses Yeats.

The walk from the village to Dun Emer took only about four minutes and it was very pleasant. The little children who lived in the various gate lodges, while remaining demurely within the heavy gates, were always eager to show their toys to passers by and they watched for us going and coming from work. In the grounds of Dun Emer our friend the Slang, the school river, flowed merrily on its way and we met it again on the Ballinteer Road. From there it wandered southward to the grounds of Dun Emer, flowed under the road and then east. It crossed under the road again where it flowed into the pond used by the Manor Mill Laundry and on below by our school playground.

The short avenue into Dun Emer was rather dark because of the tall trees which grew close together. A large sweet briar bush gave a wonderful perfume each May. The house had a good open space in front that looked out to the Sandyford Road, and the road was like a book to us workers. From the large windows of our workroom we could see everything that took place in it, and our friends could call out a greeting to us as they passed by.

From our window one day, we saw Boss Croker's horse Orby passing by on the Sandyford Road to the blacksmith's forge in the village. Orby had won the Derby in 1907 and there was a great deal of excitement in Dundrum about this event. There was also a great deal of gossip about King Edward who, it was alleged, did not shake hands with Boss Croker as was the usual custom. The people asked themselves was it because Boss Croker was Roman Catholic or was it because he was considered a commoner. Such speculations kept tongues wagging for quite a while. For us it was a great thrill to see Orby and as some of the girls knew the rider and he knew where to look for an audience, he turned the beautiful animal around and paraded him for our benefit. We felt like very privileged people.

My work at Dun Emer kept me from visiting my benefactress the Bun Lady. My last outing with her was when she took some friends on an outside car to watch the arrival of King Edward and Queen Alexandra to open the International Exhibition at Ballsbridge in 1907. After that, I lost touch with that part of my younger life.

At the end of 1907, Miss Lily went with her father John Butler Yeats, RHA to the great New York Exhibition of 1907-1908 to take part in its Irish section.[3] Miss Gleeson went with them taking along one of her workers to demonstrate carpet-making and tapestry weaving. During Miss Lily's absence, Miss Ruth Pollexfen[4] returned from Germany to take charge of the embroidery department. She was a much younger lady who lived with them in their house in Churchtown.

At this time Miss Lolly was considering a move from Dun Emer to some other place for the purpose of extending the work of her hand printing press. A four-roomed cottage[5] with an acre of land attached became vacant in the Churchtown area, and it was very suitable for an art industry. We moved in during Miss Lily's absence in 1908.

After a good deal of consideration and consultation with her many Irish friends, Miss Lolly chose the name Cuala[6] for her hand printing press. Cuala was the name given to one of the five great roads that led from Tara throughout Ireland. History tells us that the Cuala road came through Churchtown and continued south toward Wicklow and Brí Cualann or Bray Head.

Walking to Cuala from my home in Dundrum was a big change. It took fifteen to twenty minutes to get there and the longer walk was full of excitement and pleasure. Going down the village street I met friends and acquaintances as I passed the different shops and the railway station, so I saw more of the day-to-day life of my neighbours.

I made new friends along the Churchtown Road where I enjoyed, to the fullest degree, the changing seasons. The road was heavily lined with trees of varying size and description; there were pasture fields with hawthorn hedges, beautiful avenues to different big houses and neat gate lodges. While it would be difficult to say which season I enjoyed most, I'm sure that there was no equal to an evening after a summer thunderstorm - the perfume of the trees and grass and the sunlight dancing and glittering on the bubbles of brown water that rushed madly to the shores to get away underground to the darkness. The earth and insects conversed with each other; the birds twittered in the hedgerows and warm air, rising from the ground that had been parched before the storm, gave a feeling of relief as though Nature had ridden herself of an unwanted burden.

Cuala had a great number of advantages for us workers as well as for the Misses Yeats. We were a separate unit from Dun Emer[7] and could, therefore, develop in whatever way was most suitable. The printing press was set up in the largest room which faced south and from which we could get a glimpse of the Wicklow hills. The smaller embroidery room looked north over the Milltown Golf Course. An office and a private room for Miss Lolly were parallel with the embroidery room and opened on to the printing room.

A large kitchen down a few steps from the printing room made a rest room and dining room for the workers. There was a good-sized yard and several outhouses that were converted into cloakrooms and storerooms. An orchard, an unheated greenhouse and some small flower beds made a very pretty cottage for our Cuala Industry. There were four girls at the printing[8] and three girls, including myself, at the embroidery when we started in Cuala, and soon we were to have more. The big advantage of the new arrangement was being closer to one another and living more like a family unit.

Miss Lily was very pleased with the Cuala arrangements when she returned home. She liked to talk to us of her visit to America and of her impression of Americans and their way of life. She loved talking to us and imparting knowledge. The room in which we worked was not large but the walls were very thick. There was scarcely any traffic on the Churchtown Road which was about forty feet from the cottage. With no other work being done in the room, it was easy for us to hear all she had to say.

The two senior girls who had come with us from Dun Emer asked her many questions which she was pleased to answer. Very soon two other girls came to the embroidery section, and one to the printing. Miss Pollexfen had a lot of young friends who called from time to time to have a chat with her. There was always a good deal of fun amongst them. It was not long before they organised the reading of poetry and books for our benefit. They came regularly and were delighted to get such practice as most of them had an interest in amateur theatre clubs. We were allowed to choose the books or poems we wished to hear and whenever we insisted that Miss Lily should have her choice she always selected Tennyson's 'St Agnes' Eve.'[9] We heard it and 'The Lady of Shallot' many times and other poems both ancient and modern.

My friend the 'Bun Lady' died in 1908. I did not see her corpse and never knew just what caused her death. My father took me and an elderly person to Mount Jerome Cemetery where she was buried after a Church of Ireland service. I was so bewildered at having to take part in the funeral, practically on my own, that I did not see where I was going until I heard or felt the church doors close behind me. I was almost distraught with fear that I would lose my religion and that when I came out of the church, people would see a difference in me. I tried in vain to repeat the Lord's Prayer as I felt it would help me, but I kept getting it all mixed up. I was fifteen and ought to have had more sense. Miss Lily must have often been amused at my attitude toward religion. She often smiled and said, 'Sara, In my Father's house, there are many mansions'.[10] She was so tolerant and understanding.

Miss Lily told us about her work with William Morris[11] who developed a type of embroidery from old tapestry for his wife's pleasure. Mrs Morris was an expert embroideress. It was this type of stitching that Miss Lily used in her different designs. Over the years when a remark, a poem or a newspaper article would bring something about Morris to mind, she would tell us about him. He was a Jew[12] with wonderful red, grizzly hair and whiskers and blue eyes. He was good looking, powerfully built and had a very broad forehead. He showed his first impressions of art in his poetry. He was rich and used his wealth to satisfy his craving for beauty in everything around him. He was a decorative arts designer. Generous to his fellow men, he had great friendships with Christina Rosetti[13] and Edward Burne-Jones.[14] His marriage in 1859 was the result of a whirlwind romance. One of his friends was extolling the grace and beauty of an ostler's daughter whom he had seen and

Morris decided he would see this creature for himself. On seeing the girl, Morris fell immediately in love with her. He obtained her father's consent and they were married after a brief courtship.

William Morris was interested in every type of handwork, so he set up an Arts and Crafts Centre in London. In a short time, however, the place was too small for all the work he wished to do, so he found a much bigger place in beautiful surroundings near a lake, which he called Merton Abbey.[15] This was his famous Arts and Crafts Centre[16] where Miss Lolly was trained in hand printing and Miss Lily was trained in embroidery.

William Morris evidently talked to his workers in the same friendly way that Miss Lily later had to entertain her workers. One story told of him described him as a young man taken to see the London Exhibition[17] which was called the wonder of the world. He was so horrified at what he saw that he spoke of it as being 'wonderfully ugly' and decided that he would have to do something to counteract any ill effect that the Exhibition might have on Art. He used to say to his workers, 'The greatest pleasure in life is the pleasure of creating beautiful things,' and Robert Browning said something similar when he wrote, 'If you get simple beauty and nought else, you get about the best thing God invents.'

The cottage where we worked had just that character with its solid walls, nicely-proportioned rooms, shapely windows, small lawn with flowering bushes and low wall which separated it from the Classon's Bridge Road, or the Dartry Road, as we called it, because it led to the Dartry train which we used quite a lot. The cold greenhouse faced south and the orchard, which also faced south, had plum and pear trees most of which had to be cut down because of injury or neglect. The plum trees near the cottages were left standing. Being shapely, they hid the uncultivated portion of the orchard from view and they provided us with shade when we were sent out to work in the open air.

Each worker was allotted a small daily chore, such as lighting fires, cleaning and filling the paraffin oil lamps, sweeping up the fallen leaves about the porch and polishing the brasses. We did these little jobs cheerfully and took a great pride in keeping the place spic and span.[18] A woman came each week to do the scrubbing and polishing and a man came each week to keep the grass and surroundings tidy. We were a very happy community.

One of the two senior girls who had come from Dun Emer with us had arranged to get married as soon as Miss Lily arrived back from America. When she was prepared to leave, we arranged a little party to say farewell to her and this was the first of many parties we were to have at the cottage. After she left, another girl came to take her place. We were now five girls and Miss Yeats and Miss Pollexfen and we were embroidering all kinds of articles for sale and executing orders as they came in. It was a very happy and interesting life and never a day passed without bringing some wonder with it.

It was a pleasure beyond all telling to be in the same room as Miss Lily who was so kind and so good to look upon. She looked very handsome with her head bowed down whilst plying her needle. She wore her hair piled high in a crown on the top of her head and it was kept in place by a large ornamental back comb. We were always treated in a most considerate way and spoken of as Miss Yeats's girls, even by her relations who took a personal interest in each one of us.

Margaret, the second senior girl who lived in Ticknock and cycled to work each day, had a wealth of folklore and fairy stories. She vividly described an afternoon she had spent on the hills listening to fairy music and trying to find where it was coming from. She had many stories about the individual characters who lived in the few cottages that were on the hillside and about the writers or folklorists who visited them hoping to obtain knowledge of their ancient customs and superstitions.

Miss Pollexfen often took her literary friends to visit these people and they walked there or went by bicycle. She had many amusing tales of these outings and sometimes her friends were lucky to hear part of a story that fitted in with some knowledge they already had. They felt their journey had not been in vain and it could never have been a waste of time because of the beautiful scenery that enchanted them.

On the first Thursday of each month at four o'clock the Misses Yeats held an at-home at their house 'Gurteen Dheas' in Churchtown where a number of distinguished people came to visit them. We knew whom to expect and looked out to see them passing the cottage on their way from the Terenure tram. We did not see those who travelled by train since they travelled by a different road. Once we saw the portly figure of GK Chesterton[19] accompanied by Katharine Tynan.[20] Katharine Tynan was a particular friend of Miss Lily's and Miss Lily used to go to Templeogue on Saturday afternoons to have talks with old man Tynan.

Another constant visitor was Susan Langstaff Mitchell.[21] Miss Mitchell was very like Miss Lily in appearance and in manner and she was also from Sligo. She was secretary to Sir Horace Plunkett[22] who introduced the co-operative movement to Ireland. She was also a great friend of George Russell's (AE)[23] and she contributed articles to the different Irish papers. She came to all our parties and sang pretty songs. She even composed a rallying song for us workers to the air of 'O'Donnell Abu'.[24] She was very witty and had plenty of Dublin gossip.

In the autumn of 1908, we had the first of our yearly Halloween parties[25] to which the girls of Dun Emer came. It was a great reunion of young people and we had games and fun of every description. Friends of Miss Lily and Miss Lolly also came to enjoy their company.

Autumn was a very pleasant time of the year to walk back and forth to work on the Churchtown Road. We had some very beautiful sunsets and there was beautiful autumn colouring in the great variety of trees that bordered the roads and in the many bushes with brightly-coloured berries lining the long avenues to the different houses.

New houses had been built in the area so there were more people to greet on the journey. At that time there was a main drainage scheme for the village in operation where the workmen had to work very hard with pick and shovel. They encountered a considerable amount of granite in the main street and it took them a few years to complete the job.

New families came with the workmen and they settled down and made their homes in Dundrum. The population increased slowly but surely. We had some girls from the Churchtown areas working at the Industry and this brought a great change. Those of us working in the embroidery section were about the same age and we all had younger brothers and sisters. We went to each other's houses on different Sunday afternoons for tea and games, and we arranged outings, picnics and small dances. One of the mothers, who made beautiful tea cakes, was delighted that her daughter had such nice new friends. She enjoyed the Sunday tea parties as much as we did ourselves.

Christmas time was a busy time at the Industry. We made hand-printed and coloured Christmas greeting cards[26] designed by Jack B Yeats and other famous artists. We also produced small, framed pictures and embroidered articles suitable for Christmas presents. We had a stall at the Christmas Aonach in the Round Room of the Rotunda, and each girl had the pleasure of spending one or more days with the head girl, usually Eileen Colum, sister of the poet Padraic Colum. Eileen, who started with Miss Lily at the foundation of the Guild at Dun Emer, later transferred from embroidery to hand-printing. Eileen's companion at the embroidery was Máire Walker[27] who was very good looking. She later became the Abbey actress Máire Nic Shiubhlaigh. There is a nice photograph in the Sligo Yeats Museum that shows these people at work in the Dun Emer Guild.

The Misses Yeats had little wealth in the sense of money, but what little they had, they shared in a most generous manner. While they lived very frugally themselves, they made a great fuss of the season of Christmas giving presents even to children they knew only from meeting them on the road back and forth to the Industry. They remembered the sick and the very poor as well.

*Lily Yeats and her girls in the embroidery room at the Cuala
Industries*

CHAPTER FIVE

(1909-1913)

Yeats family history - Sun dancing at Easter - May comes to Cuala - Batty's gramophone - Aeroplane - Dublin sights - The Abbey - Ruth Pollexfen's engagement - Melodrama at the Queen's Theatre - Ruth Pollexfen's wedding - W B Yeats - Monica Orr - Old Age Pensions - The Titanic - Lord and Lady Aberdeen - Death of Joseph Hyland.

After Christmas, in 1908, Miss Lily went to England[1] to stay with friends where she gave lessons in embroidery at a high-class girls' school. While she was gone, once again Miss Pollexfen was in charge of the embroidery section at Cuala. Her young friends came regularly to visit her and they continued to read poetry and novels to us.

One of the friends was adept at reading in the Scottish dialect which she brought to perfection in the reading of *The Little Minister*.[2] She also read in the accents of north and south Lancashire. Another friend worked as a lady gardener. She told many amusing stories of the many mistakes she made. She loved her work and described her feeling of ecstasy on meeting a cartload of well-rotted manure being taken to a garden - how she sniffed the air with enthusiasm and longed to steal the stuff.

71

Margaret,[3] the senior girl from Ticknock, was married immediately after Easter in 1909. She gave all of us invitations to visit her, as often as we liked, in her new home on the hillside near the Three Rock Mountain. We enjoyed visiting Margaret as we loved walking and having our tea out in the open.

When Margaret left, I became the senior worker at the embroidery but this did not make a difference to me as Miss Lily treated all her workers alike. She never showed preference for one girl over another though I'm sure we each cherished the hope that we were the favoured one. She was such a perfect person to be with and she had a great wealth of knowledge that she liked passing on to us.

She told us of her childhood days in her grandparents' house in Sligo. Her grandfather was Rector of Drumcliffe and lived in the Rectory, now an orphanage called Nazareth House. Her great-grandfather died of cholera[4] which he contracted working among the very poor people of all denominations in his parish during the famine years. She told us of the dreadful poverty and hunger of the poor people and how they came to the Vicarage windows and pressed their pitiful faces against the window pane appealing for food.

She described to us the journeys her father made from Sligo to Dublin, first by coach or horseback to Athlone and then by canal boat to Portobello Harbour in Dublin. We heard a lot about her life in Sligo and the beauty of the countryside there. We heard, too, about her many cousins who lived there, cousins we were to see from time to time when they came to Dublin and called to see her at the Industry.

It is my firm belief that Miss Lily said that her brother William Butler Yeats, the poet, was born in Sandymount Castle.[5] I have since read in the newspapers that the Yeatses were living on Sandymount Avenue at the time, but since they would be visiting their relatives in the Castle, it would not be out of the question that their first child be born there.

One day at the Industry Margaret was speaking of a wonderful sunrise that she had seen from her home in the Dublin Mountains. She gave a breathtaking description of its beauty and continued on about the sun dancing always on Easter Sunday morning.[6] She cautioned that it was important to look at the Easter sun through a white silk handkerchief. We believed all she said and arranged with others, five of us in all, that we would get up early and go to the Bottle Tower[7] in Churchtown from which we would have the height to view the sunrise. Since most of the girls lived in the Churchtown area, it was natural that we chose the most convenient place to suit the majority of us. There were a great many places that would have been better choices.

The morning turned out to be very dull and only one girl and myself went out in great expectation of seeing a wonderful sight. When we met each other we had a little chat about the lazy ones who did not come; then, we returned to our homes. During the following week, and for some time afterwards, we had to put up with a good deal of teasing over our foolishness in getting out of bed so early, and, 'had we taken a silk handkerchief with us?' It was a big joke for many a long day.

Sara and two friends from the Cuala embroidery room

By this time, the phonograph had been invented and was being improved almost daily since its first appearance on the market. We were now calling it a gramophone. One of the small shopkeepers in Main Street purchased a machine with a very large, garishly-coloured tin horn and loud sound-box. He placed the gramophone in the parlour window, opened the window wide and treated the public to a very strong voice. I think it was Peter Dawson singing 'The Holy City' and 'Come Back to Erin'. It was almost ear-splitting to be near the machine when it was in action, but still it was a novelty and we enjoyed it. The owners were proud of being first in the field with this type of entertainment. After a little while they got a second record, 'Stop Your Tickling, Jock' and 'I Love a Lassie' by Sir Harry Lauder. At this time my brother Batty left his employment with Dr Goff and went to work in the city for much higher wages. My twin Jimmy also changed his work and he took over from Batty with the doctor. My younger brother Larry left school and got a position as a boy clerk in the local Criminal Lunatic Asylum in Dundrum.[8]

There were changes at the Industry as well. When Margaret, the senior embroideress left the Industry to get married, May[9] came to take her place. Her coming was to have a very marked affect on my future life. Her father had died recently and her mother, who was a professional nurse, had taken up work again in order to support her young family. May was the eldest of the four children. An uncle took one of the boys to live with him in England, a sister went as a boarder to a convent school, and May and a younger brother stayed with their mother in their house opposite the Industry in Churchtown.

I cannot now recall exactly what it was that attracted me to May. She was two and a quarter years younger than I was, and I was in the habit of looking for companionship in older people. Perhaps it was that she gave all her attention to listening to the poems when they were being read. One of the other younger girls paid scant attention to the reading except when the poem was a short one, 'The Goose' or 'The Lady of Shallott'.[10] Because of her giggling habit, she was often sent from the room during the reading, and she had to take her work with her.

I remember hearing May repeating to herself some of the couplets of 'The Lotus Eaters', and they were the same that had attracted my attention. It may have been a marked inflection in the reader's voice that had registered itself on both our ears. I soon found that May was a veritable bookworm and that she had been taught a great deal by her mother in much the same way as I had been.

May was lonely on account of her father's death and the separation of her family. I was ready to give her sympathy and comradeship. However it came about, we became firm friends and our friendship lasted to this date. We must have both used the proverbial hooks of steel. Our friendship was a real matter of fact, no demonstrations of affection, but a true feeling of reliability and trust in each other. We never questioned each other's action and both of us made other friends, but that did not intrude on our companionship. I will have something more to tell about the outings we took together and how much we learned about the history of our native city, mostly guided by the advice of Miss Lily.

That year we got an invitation to visit the Zoological Gardens and afterwards to have tea in the house of Dr Gordon, Medical Advisor to the Royal Irish Constabulary Force, who lived in a spacious house, situated in the Barrack Square of the Phoenix Park depot. Dr Gordon was married to an aunt of the Misses Yeats and they had three pretty daughters who made us very welcome and entertained us most royally. This was one of the many favours given to us by relatives of the Yeatses.

One day my brother Batty came home from his work in the city and told my mother that he had bought a gramophone. She was horrified. First, the gramophone, which was costly, was bought on the hire-purchase system which required the signature of a guarantor. My mother felt that she could not stand such a noisy instrument with its dreadful metallic sound in the house.

Batty, however, had an answer to all her objections. The gramophone he selected from O'Neill's Shop opposite the Gaiety Theatre in South King Street was a 'His Master's Voice' production. It was made of mahogany wood. The sound-box was lavishly embedded in wax and gave an almost true reproduction of the human voice. Batty was such a good worker and so earnest about wanting the machine that my mother agreed to go to O'Neill's Shop and sign the forms for him to get it.

It was a great day in our house when the wonderful gramophone arrived with its one solitary record, 'Oh Star of Eve' from Wagner's *Tannhauser* on one side and 'The Pilgrim's Chorus' from the same opera on the other. To my mind, Batty's choice of a first record could not have been excelled. The great music gave us a feeling of sorrowful, yet hopeful, imploring with the opening words of the song:

Like Death's dark shadow

Ev'ning is descending
O'er all the vale
Its sable robe extending.

I had seen *Tannhauser* so many times that it was easy to re-live it again in my imagination and our whole family was almost intoxicated listening to the record over and over again.

From that day on, while my brother continued to pay his weekly installments, each member of the family saved and scraped in order to buy more and more records. Never did an instrument give more pleasure to its owner. My father was not high-brow in his choice of songs, so he was catered for by his children from time to time by such records as 'When Father Papered the Parlour', 'I'll Tell Tilly on the Telephone' and 'Bonny Mary of Argyle'. The first of our many records sung by our Irish tenor John McCormack was 'Has Sorrow thy Young Days Shaded'; later, we bought his own favourite, 'I Hear You Calling Me'. Miss Lily took an interest in hearing about our gramophone and about our choice of records, so Batty, on hearing this, brought the gramophone with a selection of records to the Industry one day and left it with us for a short while.

Another new invention of the time was the aeroplane. There was an announcement that an aeronautical display would take place on the Leopardstown Racecourse one Saturday after-noon. This would be a wonder-of-wonders, so everyone who could do so travelled by train, bicycle, pony-trap, cart or came on foot. Such a gathering of people had never before been seen in Dundrum making their way to the Racecourse. I myself went with friends in a pony and trap.

My recollection now is that due to poor visibility or adverse winds, the planes did not leave the ground that day. Perhaps I got more interested in the company I was with and the arrangements made for our return journey to be quite sure about what happened to them. It was a long time afterwards, in 1927, that I had the opportunity to take a short flight in a plane with an open cockpit. It was in Southport, England and the pilot took two passengers for a short trip and used the price of the tickets for some charitable purpose.

May and I explored the secrets of our city. We started by taking Sunday afternoon walks from Dundrum to O'Connell Street window-shopping en route. We usually walked as far as

Clery's in O'Connell Street before turning back. When Miss
Lily got to know what we were doing, she immediately directed
our footsteps to things more worthy of our efforts. We spent
our next visit to the city in the Municipal Art Gallery[11] in
Harcourt Street.

Miss Lily said we should be very proud of the Gallery
because it was the only one in the British Isles. A friend of the
Yeats family, Sir Hugh Lane,[12] had a great deal to do with it.
Miss Lily told us about the pictures that were in the Gallery and
picked out the ones we were to look at with particular attention.
We went there quite frequently and spent other Sundays in the
Museum. On Saturday afternoons we visited churches old and
new. We looked at Georgian doorways and saw beautiful
plaster-carved ceilings and marble fireplaces. The fact that we
got a thirst for knowledge and still more knowledge was due to
the educational instinct of the Yeats family.

One Saturday afternoon we arrived at Christ Church
Cathedral when the crypt was open to the public.
Unfortunately, they charged an admission fee of sixpence and
we did not have that sixpence, or if we did, we did not think it
right to give money to a church that was not of our religion. We
probably were looking very disappointed because the Verger
spoke to us. I, being the older, told him we would like to see
the crypt but that we did not have any money.

The kind-hearted man said, 'Come along, I will show you'.
If we had been the children of the highest in the land, he could
not have shown us more courtesy. He put us on the stocks,[13]
fastened the bolts, told us about the people who had been
punished that way and explained the use of every old item that
was lying about the floor. He even told us the tale of the cat
who chased a mouse down a narrow tunnel from which she
could not return. Years later, workmen repairing the street
outside the cathedral dug up her skeleton and that of the mouse.
This story now appears in many of the books written about old
Dublin, but we heard it first from the true gentleman verger.

Miss Lily, seeing that our parents trusted us to go into the
city, and no doubt feeling that we were a reliable pair, got their
permission for us to go to plays at the Abbey Theatre.[14] At first
it was an occasional visit, but we were soon going there
frequently on free passes to seats in the balcony. We always got
there early to see the ladies arriving in their beautiful evening

dresses of pretty coloured satins and silks and cloaks of velvet or other rich material. People dressed in their party clothes when they went to the theatre in those days. Miss Lily had a beautiful black cloak which was called a 'burnous'. It was fashioned from one straight length of material and folded at the centre-back to form a hood with a very long tassel. A pretty design of large embroidered roses made a clasp-like fastening in front.

There were some rather eccentric Dublin characters who patronised the Abbey Theatre in those days. If we saw them, we delighted in giving an account of them on our return home. From the entrance there was a short stairway with a little platform into the Parterre of the Theatre. Visitors liked to stand there looking about them and chatting to their friends before taking their seats to watch the play. At the intervals we got a second look at the patrons when they left their seats to go into the Green Room for tea or coffee or to meet the actors and actresses. May and I were a fortunate pair to have seen the Abbey Players at the height of their glory.

In January, 1911, Miss Pollexfen announced her engagement to Mr Charles Lane-Poole, a native of Dundrum who was working in Sierra Leone for the British Government as head of the Forestry Department. He gave her a magnificent sapphire and diamond engagement ring. The wedding was planned for the following June in the church of St Columba's College where Mr Lane-Poole had been a pupil. He was born in Glen Southwell, the house adjoining the College. All the girls at the Industry were invited to attend the wedding and were asked to dress in white. Miss Pollexfen planned to present each of us with a pretty straw hat of similar design in our own sizes. They were to have small bunches of blue flowers that we would place according to our own ideas. That way the hats would be alike but not uniform.

Miss Pollexfen treated us to an engagement party at the Industry, a truly enjoyable affair which included a secret that was not divulged until near the end of the party. The secret was ice-cream, common enough today, but not known of here much before that time. The story of its origin is, like many discoveries, mainly one of pure accident. A cook in New York, while preparing a dinner for a large number of guests, prepared the sweet dish early and accidently placed it near an ice-cold container. The sweet was made of fresh cream and, to her horror, when she was ready to serve it, she found it frozen stiff. Not having anything to serve in its place, the mistress told her to send it to the table without any apology. The guests were so intrigued and thrilled with it that the sweet became a firm favourite. This was the beginning of what we now enjoy almost daily if we wish it.

Miss Pollexfen got great enjoyment out of her secret and her experience in the making of ice-cream which she did very successfully. She whipped fresh cream with fine sugar, adding a flavour and putting the container into a deep bucket surrounded by large pieces of ice which she got from a fishmonger's store. The weather, being frosty at the time, was a great help in the operation.

May and I had an unusual experience in our adventures that year, an adventure that was to supply us with much secret enjoyment for the rest of our lives. Even to this day we recall the event with amusement. It started when May went into the city on an errand for the Industry. She saw a large, beautifully-coloured poster on the advertising site on the corner of Hatch Street announcing that a drama titled *Sins of the Rich* would be performed at the Queen's Theatre during the coming week. When she told me about it and evidently longed to see it, we decided to go there. We had a lot of thinking and planning to do in order to avoid arousing suspicion as we both knew that if we asked for permission to go, we would not get it.

We made our plans and off we went. We knew nothing about the interior of the Queen's Theatre so, as we were in the habit of going to operas in the Gaiety or in the Theatre Royal and getting our seats in the gallery, we decided that that was the best place for us. We were early and when the ticket office opened, we got our tickets - fourpence each, a bargain indeed, but what a difference to other theatres!

The walls on the stairway to the seats were filthy and the place smelt of at least one hundred dirty odours, and when we got down to the seats in the front row, with very dim lighting, we were almost afraid to put our hands on the surround. We decided not to sit in the centre seats, and sat well over to the side we had entered. This was a lucky choice for the events that were to follow.

Some time elapsed and the awful thought struck us that we

were to be the only occupants that night. Where had we gone wrong? It was with great pleasure that we heard voices, laughter and noise of many footsteps approaching the stairs. A considerable number of people arrived together and took their seats in the centre. If we had stayed there, we would have been hemmed in by them and would have missed a priceless experience. There was a rustling of paper bags being opened and the pleasant smell of oranges being peeled. It was truly a Dublin crowd of newsboys, barrow-boys and stall-holders with sweethearts and families.

Very soon after the play started, there was a commotion in the gallery. A young man stood up with his fists clenched above his head shouting in a very loud voice to the players on the stage, 'Let her go ya-brute-ya'. A young woman who popped up beside him shouted in an equally loud voice, 'Oh ya-murderren villen-ya'. The young woman, not to be outdone, shouted, 'If I could only lay me hands on ya'. A woman whose shawl had slipped off one shoulder was clutching at the young man in order to restrain him and he looked as though he might try to lean from his seat to get at the villain on the stage. What an unwittingly supreme tribute to the acting and also a tribute to the stout hearts of the city folk.

The curtain fell on the first scene and with the little extra light, we made our way out feeling quite satisfied with ourselves at what we had witnessed. Although we missed the rest of the play, we had been well entertained. We were walking towards the Mansion House to get on to a Dartry train when I saw my twin Jimmy who was looking for us at the Engineers' Hall, the place where we were supposed to be. My mother told him to call there on his way home and take us with him. I told him where we had been because I knew that our secret would be safe with him, and it was nice to be able to share our joke with someone. Our secret never leaked out.

During the spring of 1912,[15] Miss Pollexfen was busy preparing for her wedding in June. On Saturday afternoons in fine weather, the girls from the Industry held sewing bees to help with the bride's trousseau: embroidering initials on garments, sewing on tabs or doing any little jobs that had to be done by hand. For this work we were given a sumptuous tea and we had much fun. It was quite a usual thing in my young days for people to hold garden bees. A person moving to a new house that had a neglected garden would organize a garden bee of about twenty friends. Working under the direction of their host and enjoying themselves as well, the young friends would transform a wilderness to a thing of beauty in just a few weeks. They were rewarded for their work with tea parties and dances.

We girls were in a great whirl as Miss Pollexfen's wedding approached. Our hats arrived and each of us selected the hat that fit. We had our quota of blue posies to arrange and to sew into place. Our white dresses were ready and we were told that we would be taken to the wedding in the St Columba's College wagonette. The wedding reception was planned to be in the College and we were each promised a glass of champagne.

We knew by sight the majority of the guests who had been invited and we were going to be looking out for the unknown ones. Mr W B Yeats, cousin of the bride, was to be her sponsor as her father, who lived in Sligo, was in very poor health and could neither undertake the journey nor the strain of the event. Captain Dick Lane-Poole of the British Navy, only brother of the bridegroom, was best man and the bride's sister and four friends were the bridesmaids.

We hoped for a fine day, but it dawned a wet morning. It was a great disappointment to us since we were to have travelled from the railway station to St Columba's in an open wagonette; however, the sun later came out in all its glory, dried up the little pools and it was a fine afternoon.

The bride looked bewitching in her white satin gown. Her five bridesmaids dressed in white, the officers in their colourful uniforms and the varied and beautiful dresses of the guests made a pretty picture on the grounds of St Columba's College that afternoon. The ladies' hats were very large with quantities of trimmings. I recollect seeing Miss Sarah Allgood, the Abbey actress, exquisitely dressed in flowered satin and carrying a parasol. She was wearing such a large hat that it looked as though she would have to remove it in order to enter the door of the chapel.

This was the first time that I was near enough to observe Mr W B Yeats closely and to try to estimate what type of person he was. He was a magnificent figure of a man in an immaculate white, white suit of very fine material. He held his head high and he moved about effortlessly in a gliding, swan-like manner. His body gave the impression of having been sculpted by a first-rate artist and he was good-looking with his lock of dark hair falling carelessly over his left eye. He had a kindly countenance with a dreamy far-away look and he would not see you staring at him.

We had a very enjoyable day at the wedding and when the feasting was over we were taken by wagonette back to Dundrum. We had a lot to talk about for some time afterwards, and Miss Lily liked to hear our impressions of the events and our opinions of the clothes of the different guests. On returning to work the week after the wedding we were all very lonely and wondered how we were going to get on in the future without Miss Pollexfen and her friends who came so regularly to chat with her.

Two new workers came to the embroidery department in 1912. One came from the Rathfarnham area near St Enda's College. A younger sister of Eileen Colum's[16] also came to the Industry to work with Miss Lolly in the printing department.

May and I continued to explore Dublin and its history. We went more frequently to the Abbey Theatre and made new friends as well. Two of our new friends came from County Wexford to work for a wealthy lady and her doctor husband who had moved from a house in Merrion Square to a large residence in Dundrum. The wife of the pair was employed as a dairy maid while her husband served as chauffeur to the lady of the house. They lived in a commodious house in the yard, some distance from the main house.

My brother Batty was chauffeur to the doctor and he liked the idea of working in Dundrum again. He brought these friends to our house and they were eager to be acquainted with his family. We discovered that they had a good knowledge of opera and had attended many of the same performances that we attended so we had that strong talking point. We played our gramophone records for their entertainment.

Their kitchen was very big and ideal for dancing, so some gramophone records with tunes suitable for dancing were purchased. May and I were launched on a new phase of life with more and more new friends. We got invitations to dances in the city where we heard Moore's melodies played on an accordion in waltz time. Dancers whirled around singing as they danced to the tune of 'Be-e-lieve Me if All Those Endearing Young Charms' and other songs.

One day Miss Monica Orr,[17] a cousin of the Misses Yeats, came to visit them at the Industry. She was a violinist and she promised to bring her violin with her on her next visit. She did so and returned on several occasions to thrill us with her playing. She was pleased to find that we workers had such a good knowledge of music. After a few months in Dublin, Miss Orr was called to take a place with the Halle Orchestra. She was quite young to have that honour bestowed on her.

In 1912, the National Health Insurance and Old Age Pensions were introduced into Ireland. The Health Act was looked on favourably from the beginning. The Old Age Pension was a different matter. Here was something for nothing - or so the old people thought - and very soon some farmers with small holdings were signing over their property to their eldest sons in order to draw the Old Age Pension of five shillings per week. In a great many cases, the handing-over of the property had disastrous results and often ended in a court of law with the pensioner trying to recover what he had signed away when he felt that he was not getting a fair deal from his family.

The *Titanic* was sunk in the Atlantic by a submerged iceberg on her maiden voyage to America in 1912. She had been built and launched in Belfast. It was alleged that there were some very bitter anti-religious remarks made by the dock workers. The whole world was aghast at the tragedy that could have been avoided with a little care.

Our friends who worked at the big house in Dundrum left that employment and went to live in the city. It was a great blow to us as we had become great friends and had hoped they would be with us for a long time to come; however, the wheels of fortune kept turning. My eldest brother Joseph was going through a very lean time at the painting and decorating so he decided to change his work to driving and to take over where his friend left off as chauffeur to the doctor. He had no difficulty in obtaining the job. The car he had to drive was a beautiful Minerva and he and the car were to see some exciting times during Ireland's fight for freedom.

In 1912, Lady Aberdeen,[18] the wife of the Lord Lieutenant, opened a hospital in Beaumont for the care of victims suffering from tuberculosis. Lady Aberdeen was a great friend of Miss Lily's and she and her husband came regularly to the Industry. Lord Aberdeen took great pleasure in telling us amusing stories of the Irishman, Scotsman, Englishman type. He always brought out the 'canny' character of the Scot, for being a Scotchman himself, he probably felt entitled to poke fun at his own clansmen.

1913 began sadly for us. My father died on March 28, 1913, in the same quiet way as he had lived among us. Our family was stunned at the cause and at the suddenness of his departure from this life. He had what was known as a blind boil on the back of his neck which always looked like it troubled him because of the stiff collars men wore in those days. The local medical dispensary doctor advised him to have it removed saying that it would be simpler to do than to extract a tooth, so on Good Friday, 1913, my father agreed to have the boil removed.

The operation was so painless and took such a short time that he wondered why he had not had it done long ago. On Easter Sunday he fulfilled all his religious duties. Monday, a Bank Holiday, was not a working day for him. He seemed to have a cold on Tuesday and decided to stay in bed, but he became worse and on Wednesday morning my mother became alarmed and asked for a second opinion.

The truth was that his heart was in such bad condition that there was no hope of saving his life and he died the following Friday. My mother's grief was so terrible that it frightened all her family. She blamed herself for not advising him to leave well enough alone. Fortunately most of the family were grown up and in fair employment, so we were able to manage. I don't know how my mother did not die from grief at the loss of her companion and from her regret that she had not foreseen the possible consequences of his operation.

CHAPTER SIX

(1913-1918)

Sara's dreams - Yeats and spiritualism - A visit to Jack and Cottie Yeats - Lucy Middleton - Fortune telling - Jack Yeats entertains the Cuala girls - Early cinema in Dublin - Sara visits Manchester - An uncle's funeral - The Carnegie Library in Dundrum - World War I - War restrictions and shortages - Sara to Liverpool with Larry - Cuala's Irish patrons - Alice Furlong.

After the marriage of Miss Pollexfen, there were some changes in our conversations with Miss Lily who had more opportunity to chat with us. She was very interested in my dreams,[1] and, of course, I took great delight in relating them to her. She often tried to interpret their meanings for me, but of course I did not pay any attention to that side of them. One aspect of my dreams that intrigued her was the fact that there was so much colour in them. I understood from her that seeing so much colour in objects in dreams was unusual and of course I liked the idea of being unusual.

My dreams were a nightly occurrence over a long period of time and they were generally very detailed. Each day I had a story and on Monday mornings, I had two. I can still remember some of my dreams very vividly after nearly sixty years. One dream, a dream that continued for three nights, excited Miss Lily very much. In the dream I was attending a big funeral in the darkness of the night. The altar boys, dressed in their soutanes, carried huge lighted candles that did not blow out in the wind. There were a lot of clergymen and people - young and old - in the procession. I did not know who was being buried or where the graveyard was.

We entered a narrow pathway by a revolving gate like that on our railway accommodation walkway on the Upper Kilmacud Road. We could only walk in single file. I saw the coffins on the shoulders of the men in the distance getting farther and farther away from me till I lost sight of them.

The following night I was at the same funeral but there were no lighted candles. We started off on a different road and all went well until I saw a loaf of bread on the roadside. I picked up the loaf and spent such a long time trying to get the bread to stay on a low wall that I lost the funeral again.

On the third night, I was back at the same funeral and the large crowd of people started off from the same place as they had done the two previous nights. It was a pitch dark night and dreadful wind and rain beat us back two steps for every step we took forward. We made no progress and that was the end of the dream.

When I dreamed of fish in a stream or a fish on a string, Miss Lily got really excited. She told me that she believed that fish had a meaning for her family.[2] You can imagine her surprise one day when she told me that I had told her a dream that was so similar to one that her brother the poet W B had told her a long time previous to my dream. He had written a play on the theme of that dream.[3] I realised then that Miss Lily had been telling him about my dreams. There was great comradeship between Miss Lily and this brother.

W B Yeats's name was very much in the news concerning spiritualism and séances. There was a lecture given on the subject[4] one Sunday night at the Abbey Theatre and, in our secret way, May and I attended. The only thing we got out of the lecture was our surprise at seeing so many of our priests in the audience. As a result, we felt that we had not done anything wrong in attending.

Miss Lily never encouraged us to take part in anything that was far beyond our understanding or in anything that would be forbidden by our religion. She was always very considerate. When we showed an interest in her brother's work, she told us stories of things that had been said to him, or about him or unusual remarks that he had made himself. For example, when a friend of theirs was playing the violin, he said that it was a pleasant way of making noise. Another time he was very amused when a teacher of elocution, after hearing him reading one of his own poems said, 'That is not the way to read poetry'. She also told us he got the inspiration for the 'Lake Isle of Innisfree'[5] from watching water rippling down on the inside of a pork butcher's window in London. It was a very warm day and the water flowing on the inside of the window was to keep the shop cool.

In 1913, Mr Jack B Yeats and his wife came back to Ireland to make their home here. They rented a house in Greystones,[6] County Wicklow, and in truly benevolent Yeats manner, they invited us work girls to visit their new home for afternoon tea. Accompanied by the Misses Yeats we went on a beautiful Saturday afternoon in June. We took the train from Dundrum to Bray where Mr Jack waited to welcome us. He had engaged four outside cars which took us through the Kilruddery Estate to their house.

When we reached the house after this beautiful drive, we were given soft drinks, biscuits and fruit. The lawn had been prepared for croquet and winners of the games and performances arranged by Mr Jack received small prizes that he made himself. He used fir cones, acorns, sea shells and other little things for prizes and each of us received one. I won a dice container fashioned from a large cork ingeniously cut to form a box containing two dice cubes. The lid slipped into place over the cubes and could stay closed because of the clever way it had been cut. The amount of thought and trouble he took with the prizes was typical of the Yeats family's perfection in all of their undertakings. After a beautiful tea we returned to the Bray railway station by another route in the outside car.

That year Mr and Mrs Yeats came to our Halloween party at the Industry in Churchtown. Miss Susan Mitchell and some of the Yeats cousins usually came to these parties. Miss Lucy Middleton,[7] an elderly cousin who had lately come visiting at the Industry, received an invitation to come to the party. She was very interested in fortune-telling from cards, a different kind of fortune-telling than she found amongst Miss Lily and her girls. One of our workers was reputed to be marvellous at deriving the meaning conveyed by the position of the cards as they followed one another in an ordinary pack of cards and we had a great deal of fun with this practice.

Miss Middleton generally carried a large-sized handbag, like a miniature Gladstone, into which she dived to bring forth a pack of Tarot cards which were quite large and had curious drawings and devices on them. They were not used in any card game as far as I can remember, and she spoke of the cards in an almost unhuman voice.

Miss Lily generally chuckled at the fuss we made of all the fortune-telling, but she liked looking at the different drawings on the cards which I think were made by an artist whom she knew personally. In those far-off days, fortune-telling by the reading of cards, the lines on the hands, the shape of tea leaves in cups and horoscopes was a great pastime. A pack of cards was often referred to as 'Satan's Prayerbook' by those who looked with disfavour on such frivolity.

While the fortune-telling was taking place in the sitting room, Mr Jack was entertaining us with a wonderful display of his ability to make an amusing game with his chalk-drawings on a blackboard which was placed on one of the walls of the embroidery room. With chalk and a duster he lost no time in making a beginning of what he called 'Moving Day' by drawing a cottage on the top right-hand side of the board and a horse and cart complete with driver on the bottom left-hand side.

Next a woman handed a parcel over the half-door of the cottage to a little girl who, after being rubbed out, reappeared to give the parcel to the cab man who deposited it in the cab. Soon the girl returned to the cottage door, and the woman appeared again to hand out another parcel of a different size and shape. The transportation of packets and parcels continued until the cab was almost filled inside. Then they were packed on to the cab roof: pots, pans, sweeping brushes and finally the child's toys.

Finally, the woman appeared in her cloak and bonnet with a few last articles, locked the door behind her and got to the cab to start on her journey. As she stepped in, the parcels tumbled off and the cab collapsed to the ground. At this point, the horse looked back over his shoulder to see what happened. Mr Jack, with a very broad smile and one large wipe of the duster, finished the amusing episode.

Our friends who had moved from Dundrum to the city moved on to a wealthy family who lived in a big house near the seaside in south County Dublin. The house had the usual cobblestone yard with a water pump, outhouses for cattle and poultry, a dairy, and living quarters with running water and good heating arrangements. Our woman friend managed the dairy and the poultry and kept the accounts. She received a salary for her work and, in addition, she was permitted to sell the surplus milk, butter and eggs. Her husband's work as chauffeur was very light. He drove the elderly couple to visit their married children and their friends and he took the old gentleman out for airings in his wheelchair. This was a splendid job for a childless couple and it held great possibilities for plentiful entertainment.

I cannot say where the first moving pictures or cinematographs[8] were shown in Dublin or how soon my brothers became interested in them. One evening my twin Jimmy took me to a small cinema in Lower Camden Street. It was very dark inside. We walked in by the side of the screen; then, we had to turn around to take our seats to view the pictures. This picture house quietly became known as 'Flay Park' on account of the number of fleas that we encountered there.

The pictures shown were called the 'movies'; however, it was we, the audience, who did a lot of moving every time we got a nip from one of the flea family. There were numerous remedies for fleas. One was to put paraffin oil on our legs. Another deterrent was to shake Keating's Powder on our person, but I don't know whether that worked or not. The excitement of seeing people moving about in pictures and looking so alive made us forget our discomforts and we became immune to the flea bites. Air conditioning was also a problem for the proprietors of picture houses, and men with containers moved constantly about spraying a chemical mist on the audience.

The first picture screens looked very unsteady and we saw the pictures through, what appeared to be, a continuous shower of heavy rain. We saw Charlie Chaplin with his funny little moustache wearing his bowler hat, reaching his hands into his trouser pockets and extending the pockets to make them look like wings while he strutted around in his own inimitable way. There were many other funny characters as well.

The moving pictures were a new and very wonderful invention and we thoroughly enjoyed them and the jokes about the fleas. That reminds me of a story Miss Lily told us about a local man in the County Council who, when he spoke at a meeting, wished to impress his listeners with his intimacy with the notable people of the district. He said, 'The same flea that bit me also bit his Lordship's shoulder'.

In May, 1914, I visited England for the first time. I travelled on the boat from Dún Laoghaire to Holyhead with Miss Lily who was going to visit the home of a friend who had organized a sale of Industry products.[9] The Industry had some very good patrons in England, wealthy people who liked to promote the arts. Miss Lily made these visits a couple of times each year and they were the mainstay of the Industry. Miss Lily also had a holiday with her friends, met other old friends and made new friends.

On this occasion, Miss Lily was going to London whereas I was going to a suburb of Manchester to visit my uncle, my mother's eldest brother, who was very ill. He had expressed a wish to see her, but my mother, who had never travelled more than a few miles by train inside County Dublin, could not think of undertaking such a journey so I, being her brother's godchild, took her place.

When we reached the railway junction at Chester, I had to change to the Manchester train. Miss Lily walked with me to the train and asked the guard to look after me. This was yet another example of the thoughtfulness and thoroughness of all her undertakings. For many years afterwards, I made myself known to the guards and always took a seat in a carriage near the luggage van, so I could have a chat with the guards at the different stations.

On my midnight journey from Chester, I noticed a great change in the landscape. It was a moonlit night and the houses were numerous and close to the railway line. They were black and grimy-looking with the smallest of backyards. Then I saw Warrington with its large and small factories jumbled together with their chimneys - short and stout or tall and narrow - belching smoke of different denseness and shades that varied from grey to heavy blackness. It was like a horrible nightmare to see so much life going on when people should have been in their beds. At home in Dundrum we had only one tall chimney that belonged to the Manor Mill Laundry which did not work at night and which seldom had any black smoke pouring from it.

When the train arrived at Manchester, the guard told a porter to take me to the waiting room and he further instructed him to put me on an early train going to my final destination, Ashton-under-Lyne. My uncle was very pleased when I arrived at his house as he had been going through a period of restlessness. He asked me questions about Lusk, the village where he was born and learned the trade of tailoring some forty years before.

Fortunately, I was able to satisfy him with my answers for I was very familiar with Lusk and its inhabitants. He said it cheered him up to hear an Irish voice and to get such detailed news of his former neighbours. Although the craft of tailoring was no longer taught in Lusk, he was happy and appeared to be reliving his youth. He had not been to Dublin for a number of years and had almost lost contact with his people.

My first day in Ashton-under-Lyne was completely bewildering. I scarcely understood what anyone was saying because the Lancashire dialect was strange to my ear; however, I thought the accent was rather musical. I liked it and I liked the people who were very friendly and warmhearted. I was not surprised to learn that most of them had Irish parents or grandparents, some of whom had visited Dublin when they were younger, and they wished to recall their pleasant memories.

I lost no time in asking whether it would be possible to see the inside of one of the cotton factories while the machines were working. A neighbour agreed to take me to one on the following day. When I awakened early the next morning, I heard a queer noise I had not noticed the previous day. It was the sound of pairs of clogs on the cobblestone streets. I also heard another sound, a small sound, accompanied by a few words in a chanting manner.

I got out of bed quietly to look out of the window. I saw people hurrying to work and an elderly man with a long cane with a bunch of lead pieces fastened to the top. He knocked with the cane on the top window panes of certain houses in the street calling out, at the same time, in a sing-song voice. My cousins told me that the man was called 'The Knocker Up' or 'The Window Tickler' and that he received a weekly salary from the factory owners for his services.

After breakfast I talked with my uncle whom I could understand since he had not lost his Irish accent. He described his work and the benefit of the sewing machine; however, he preferred to work by hand and let the younger men work the machine. In the afternoon the neighbour took me to see a cotton factory where I saw machine reels of all sizes whirling around on different machines while being filled with threads of varying thicknesses.

I thought of the boy Elias Howe who was born in Massachusetts less than one hundred years earlier and who had invented the sewing machine in order to help his mother with her sewing. She had to sew late and early in order to make a living for her orphaned family. They were very poor and he was desperate to help her. He watched the movement of her hands while she was sewing and he especially noticed the position of her hand that held the needle. After a lot of trial and error, he realized that the thread had to be close to the point of the needle in order to get it to work properly. From that moment, he had success and he perfected the machine about the year 1850.

I was very excited about my visit to the factory and the different life in that strange place. The women's clogs and shawls fascinated me. I was anxious to get back to my uncle and talk to him about the wonders I had seen but alas when I got back to the house he was not well enough to talk with me and he passed from this world during the night. The next day was very mournful and upsetting and I suddenly felt very homesick. I got a dreadful pain around my heart that was so intense I thought it would surely burst.

Everything that took place after my uncle's death was so unlike our Irish custom that I was almost shocked. The undertaker, a near neighbour, came to the house and took charge. He seemed to do all the necessary things without consulting anyone. The bedroom door was locked and no one entered till a short time before the funeral on the following day when the undertaker's men arrived to make the final arrangements. They carried two black bags, one containing black silk tall hats and the other containing black leather gloves for those who might be without them.

The men invited to attend the funeral wore long-tailed coats and striped trousers. The children of the house, all girls, wore white dresses with large black sashes. The hearse was like a huge glass casket, very ornamented, drawn by two horses draped in black loin cloths of velvet with fringed edges that almost touched the ground and black plumes on their heads. It was a very silent and spectacular event. When we returned to the house an elaborate meal of cold meats and savouries had been prepared for us during our absence and this we took in deep silence. My homesickness steadily increased after my two sleepless nights and my wondering whether my heart would burst from exhaustion. I returned to Ireland feeling that I never wished to leave home again.

In 1914, as I made my way to and from work at the Industry, I watched the progress on the building of the Carnegie Library[10] located on the Churchtown Road close to Main Street. The plot had been donated by the Select Vestry of Taney Church, for it was stipulated by the Carnegie Trust that the ground had to be free to get their grant for the building and books. The large, two-storey library was planned to include a lecture or concert hall upstairs, a book room, a reading room, a recreation or games room and a suitable cloak room. The Library opened in the autumn of 1914 and with it a wonderful world to the inhabitants of this village.

This was the year I was fortunate to become the owner of an almost new bicycle[11] that had every possible accessory including an acetylene lamp. I was able to purchase it at a small cost from a friend who was leaving to make her home in America. It was like a wonderful dream come true and the bicycle took me to places I had not hitherto been able to reach.

In the autumn of 1914, the world was shocked by the outbreak of war in Europe, a war that involved many countries and became known as 'The Great World War'. The War had a marked effect on Ireland. It made some of our unthinking people realize how much we Irish depended on Britain for essential foodstuffs which came to us from foreign countries on British merchant ships and for which we paid a substantial carriage charge. At the same time it opened our eyes to the fact that our country was able to produce in abundance and in superior quality much of the butter, bacon, animal feed and other products that we were importing.

As soon as Britain became involved in the War our food was rationed and our men were called on to join the British army and fight as British citizens for the freedom of small nations. We realized the incongruity of this British recruiting slogan for we Irish had been agitating peacefully and in arms for a period of almost seven hundred years after our freedom had been filched from us by Britain in the thirteenth century. From that time onward, English families of the Protestant faith had been systematically planted on our best lands with the purpose of breaking our spirit, changing our faith and generally making us slaves. At the same time, they established a large number of loyal subjects who could act as spies and who could always be ready to support the government in any action it wished to take against us.

Fortunately, at this time there were Irish men and women well organized and well prepared to make another attempt for freedom when the opportunity would arise. They had studied the reasons that previous uprisings had failed, and they were determined to profit from the knowledge that they had gained. We will hear about those valiant people later in my story.

The effect of the War on our everyday lives was remarkable. We felt that we were abandoned and that we had to think for ourselves and that we had to provide food for ourselves. Landlords removed restrictions against their tenants keeping pigs and poultry in the outhouses of their premises. County Councils procured land and leased it in small plots for little rent to those interested in raising vegetables. The Misses Yeats gave land behind the Industry to us and we started, without delay, to sow cabbages and other greens before the winter of 1914 came down on us.

Men, young and old, joined the British Army for various reasons. Some believed our country would be given a measure of freedom and the Home Rule they had been promised if they joined; others joined in a spirit of adventure. Most joined because they had lost their jobs and could not find other work. They knew that if they joined the Army, they would have employment and could provide for their dependents.

Life became very confusing with so many changes and the loss of employment. Motor cars, other than those used by doctors and business people for essential services, had to be stored away for the duration of the war, because oil and petrol were severely rationed. As a result, my brother Joseph had to find other work.

My younger brother Larry,[12] having passed a civil service examination, was appointed to the Customs and Excise Waterguard Department. I made my second trip across the Irish Sea with him to the house of a relative where he stayed which was convenient to his work in Liverpool. We travelled by the night passenger and cattle boat from the North Wall to Liverpool. It was shortly after the War started, and it was a very interesting journey. At Dublin all the passengers had to walk aboard the boat single file and pass through a narrow passage where we were scrutinized by members of the British forces. Each person was asked to state his or her nationality. I remember noticing that most travellers answered 'British' automatically just because the preceding person gave that reply. 'Irish' would have been the correct answer in most cases.

It was a beautiful September night, and we stayed out on deck for the whole of the crossing, walking about looking at the stars and the sea, chatting to fellow travellers and occasionally looking down on the cattle in the holds, all very restless, who bellowed their way from one port to the other. Dawn was breaking as we entered the Mersey and we noticed a great difference in the sound and the feel of the water's action on the boat. The cattle noticed the difference and became silent and easier with each other until they were unloaded at Birkenhead where they rushed madly up the slipway to the shouts and to the whacking sticks of the drovers.

Bells rang and ships sirens sounded when the boat crossed the river to the Liverpool landing stage. On our approach, two cross-beam searchlights swept the deck with such brilliance that one could have found a lost pin. This was a sign that the War had started. The clock on the great Liver Building showed the time which was twenty-five minutes ahead of Irish time. It was necessary, in those days, for travellers to adjust their watches on entering or leaving England.

At that time in Dublin there was a great deal of whispering and speculation about things that might happen. Young Irishmen, mostly civil servants and bank clerks, left their employment in England and returned home. They feared if they stayed, they would have been called upon to join the British Army, something that was abhorrent to them. They were warmly applauded by their fellow Irishmen for their actions.

Feelings were very high on both sides of the Irish Sea, and at the Industry we had an uneasy feeling of difficulties to come. Some of our English patrons lost no time in writing bitter, abusive letters about the ungrateful Irish. One would think that the Misses Yeats were responsible for the whole unhappy affair, for they were asked, 'What are you going to do about the situation in your country?' Shortly afterwards, these people relented and wrote more friendly notes.

The Irish Nationalist leaders called on their members to join the British Army and not to wreck our hopes of obtaining the measure of Home Rule promised when the War ended. The Irish Republican Brotherhood counselled Irish youth to remember past history and how often we had been tricked. They were asked, therefore, not to give any help.

There were meetings and demonstrations and counter-meetings; otherwise, life just jogged along with grumblings about food shortage and general bewilderment. There was a great shortage of tea and sugar, and our weekly ration seemed very inadequate. Some people tried drying used tea leaves with the expectation that they could obtain a second brew from them. Cocoa beans were introduced and some children as well as grown-ups liked them. Special lightweight tin kettles were used to boil the beans but the cooked bean husks were bulky and to dispose of them was a nuisance.

Butter was also scarce and almost unobtainable. Small farmers in country places started making an extra supply of butter by churning all the milk instead of just the cream. They advertised the butter to customers who were willing to pay the price for the butter and for the shipping. Farmers found a ready market and postmen were kept busy. Alas, this type of butter sours quickly and postbags were ruined by the smelly butter which was often so badly packed that it fell out of its wrapping. We joked about smelling the postman from afar and held our noses when he passed on his way.

We were kept busy in our garden plots behind the Industry, enjoying ourselves in the fresh air, working the soil and comparing our results with our neighbours. At our homes most of the small cottage tenants kept poultry in their backyards and this gave us the benefit of fresh eggs and an occasional cockerel or young hen for cooking. A good deal of the poultry feeding was provided by our land allotments.

Life was not too miserable and we read the daily papers avidly for news of the War and for what secrets the papers might give us about our own internal situation which appeared to be at the boiling point. My eldest brother married this year[13] and went to live on the north side of Dublin. He was employed by a firm of taxi drivers and had to live near to his work.

The Yeatses found Irish patrons[14] to keep the Cuala Industries busy and we started making and embroidering baby clothes in Irish materials. We also made dresses for grown-ups. One lady had the wonderful idea of having a dress made with a rose-bordered hem; this idea was inspired by a line of a poem by W B Yeats.[15] It was a most unusual style of garment at that period as we did not have fashion designers in those days.

We also got a lot of work from the Masonic lodges[16] embroidering beautiful banners on handwoven Irish poplin materials.[17] Each lodge had a standard design. The Grand Masters of different lodges had their coat of arms or historical events embroidered on their own personal banners. These were designed by an expert, and the finished articles, which were beautiful, were trimmed with a heavy silk cord, large tassels and a fringe of matching colours manufactured especially for the Industry by a Dublin firm. We also made other articles for these Lodges which kept the Industry in full employment and enabled us to have our yearly outings and parties.

Miss Alice Furlong,[18] poet and ardent language revivalist, came to the Industry each week to teach the Irish language. She brought figurines of birds and animals and small pictures with her. She was a very frail and lovable person, but alas, her health was very poor at the time and the journey from her home in Templeogue to the Industry was a tiring one, so we did not have benefit of her teaching or the pleasure of her company long enough to make much headway with our lessons.

Lolly Yeats and her girls in the Cuala printing room (Cuala Archives, Trinity College, Dublin)

CHAPTER SEVEN

(1916-1922)

The Easter Rising - Joseph acquires a Minerva car - Cuala printing - Gaslight comes to Dundrum - Suffragettes - Joseph O'Reilly - Michael Collins - Joseph joins Collins's staff as driver - De Valera in America - Sinn Fein courts - Cuala's garden - Lily Yeats's health - Black and Tans - Sara bids at a local auction - Auxiliaries - The Truce - Bonfire in Dundrum celebrates the Truce - Treaty negotiations - Sara studies Irish - Treaty debates - Death of John B Yeats - Civil War - Death of Arthur Griffith - Death of Michael Collins - Cuala prepares to leave Churchtown - Ruth Pollexfen Lane-Poole goes to Australia - Auction cover-ups.

On Easter Monday, 1916,[1] we were at work in the Industry as was usual for those of us who wished to work on a Bank Holiday and to have some other day free. The Misses Yeats liked to work on such days. I walked home for my midday meal at one o'clock to find that my young cousin Cissie had been left in charge of the house. My mother had received a telegram announcing the birth of her first grandchild, Joseph's daughter May, and my mother left immediately to visit them in Glasnevin.

She had intended to travel to the city on the noon train so that she could return home early; however, it was almost a week before we saw her again. The noon train never arrived in Dundrum and no reason was given because no one knew what happened to it. My mother, not wishing to waste any more time waiting for a train, asked a friend who had his horse cab at the station to drive her to Joseph's house in Glasnevin.

On reaching O'Connell Street, the cab was stopped by a group of nationalist volunteers and turned back. The now famous Irish rebellion of Easter Week had started about eleven o'clock that morning with the occupation of the General Post Office and the reading of the Proclamation declaring Ireland a Republic. My mother, not realising the significance of what was taking place, continued on to Glasnevin on foot where she had to remain until the hostilities ended. It was late in the afternoon of Easter Monday before we had any news of what had taken place in the city. People passing back to their homes in Churchtown had alarming stories. At first, we were not inclined to believe them. When we did understand what happened, we were stunned and we pitied the unfortunate men who were attempting to measure their strength against the strength of Britain. We stood in groups late into the night wondering what would happen.

On the following day there was some slight panic because communication between city and country was non-existent. Joseph cycled from Glasnevin to our house that evening to say that they were well away from the centre of trouble. He came a round-about way through Phoenix Park and Terenure. On Wednesday, there was real panic. Shops were closed; no bread cars arrived, and food was running out. The brave ones who walked into the city each day brought home the news of the daily happenings. They also brought the good news that the bakeries on the outskirts of the city were working and that bread would be rationed out to those who would go to collect it. Groups of people pushing prams or carrying baskets were seen on all the roads leading to the bakeries. Our supply of milk was safe since it was delivered twice daily from the large or small suppliers in the area.

We managed to get along although we were in a state of great anxiety and bewilderment. Boys who went to the city each day seeking news were a source of worry to their parents.

100

Fortunately, the conflict did not last long, but the aftermath was so appalling that timid people became strong and the strong vengeful on hearing the punishment meted out to the freedom fighters and to their unfortunate families. As W B Yeats said, 'A terrible beauty is born'.[2]

In 1917, the poet W B Yeats married in England[3] and came home with Mrs Yeats to live permanently in Ireland. The same year a strike at the firm of taxi proprietors where Joseph was employed caused him and his fellow workmates a lot of concern as it did the customers for whom they catered. Joseph was in the habit of driving a wealthy English businessman to the Curragh training stables once a week and more frequently in the busy season.

This man was very upset when he learned of the taxi strike because it was impossible for him to obtain alternative transportation. He arranged with Joseph to purchase a car that had been put in storage and he made Joseph its owner by accepting repayments from him over a period of time with the guarantee that Joseph would drive him when required to do so. A car proprietor in Dundrum generously acted as guarantor; thus, my brother became the owner of the beautiful Minerva car that he had previously driven for its wealthy owner. Most of his fellow workmates were equally fortunate in procuring cars, and they formed an association and rented a city garage. I don't have many memories of this period. It is likely that we were so stunned with the condition of our country and the world that we went about our work in a listless and benumbed manner.

The friends of the Misses Yeats continued to call at the Industry to see our work. We had some very nice prints of illustrated verses from the poems of W B Yeats done on the hand press by Miss Lolly and her girls. After the sheets were printed, they had to be allowed to dry before the illustrations could be hand-coloured. It was interesting to read the verses and very easy to commit them to memory since the printed sheets lay on the work tables for several days awaiting completion.

There were some verses in which I took a special interest. I had a great liking for 'Still Waters'[4] which conjured up a whole world of meaning for me. I was sure that I could feel the 'Beings' spoken of in the poem actually gathering about me as I read the verse. This secret and many others I kept to myself, because if Miss Lily had known of it, she would have questioned me and I would not have been able to explain. I would have felt foolish. Miss Lily was always interested in our thoughts and problems and I am sure that we often amused her with our outspoken opinions of people and problems, but if we had any real difficulties, we could be sure of good advice or material help from her. She was just like a good mother.

About this time a gas main was laid in the Churchtown area. From it, private houses in the area could be supplied, so we had very good lighting for doing our work. In addition to the lights, the Misses Yeats had the Industry fitted with a cooker for the girls to use to make their lunch-time meal. We were not sorry to be finished with the smelly paraffin lamps and we greatly enjoyed the benefit of the good light and the cleanliness of the gas. A gas main had been laid in Main Street in Dundrum, so all the houses in the village derived the benefit of easier and cleaner ways to cook meals.

During these years the suffragette movement[5] was growing strong and receiving support from unexpected places. More and more women joined the movement and wore the distinctive dress colours of mauve and green. Success seemed near. The militant sections of the movement became more daring and admirers grew more sympathetic. This is all past history now, but one wonders whether we women have done all that we should have done with this right that was so diligently fought for and so begrudgingly given to all women over thirty years of age in the year 1918.

My brother Batty was introduced by a mutual friend to a delightful, interesting man named Joseph O'Reilly[6] who was 'on the run' from the British military in his home county of Cork. He was living with Batty's friend in the Ballinteer district. There were many young men like Joseph who were known to have or suspected of having taken part in the Easter Week rebellion and they had to flee their homes and families and remain away from the surveillance of the Royal Irish Constabulary who had a great knowledge of the inhabitants of every district of this country.

The RIC were spoken of as the eyes and ears of the British government. Now they were held in great contempt by a majority of the people for things that they themselves never realized could happen when they joined the force. A number of

RIC men resigned when asked to perform certain duties; others remained hoping to undo some of the damage done by their vigilance. Others stayed because of their families and their fear of unemployment while still others stayed as a matter of loyalty for they had no sympathy with their fellow countrymen who were fighting for freedom from British slavery.

Many men and boys who fled a nice, comfortable home found on their return that the house they once loved was no longer there. It had been destroyed by British forces or an unsympathetic neighbour. This was the pattern of events in most of our counties after the Easter rebellion.

Joseph O'Reilly was only one of many boys looking for and needing new friends. We accepted him as a lonely and pleasing character and we called him Reilly because we had a Joseph in the family. Reilly, who was very fond of music, was in the habit of attending the Sunday afternoon concerts in the Antient Concert Rooms in Great Brunswick Street, now Pearse Street. These performances were a feature of Dublin life. Reilly had many friends like himself who were 'on the run' from the enemy and they met each other each week in the pleasant surroundings of the Concert Room. Batty also patronised these concerts and was glad to have such an agreeable companion as Reilly who introduced him to a number of dedicated young men that were giving up their freedom for Ireland's sake.

One of these remarkable men was Michael Collins whom Reilly hero-worshipped. Michael Collins had taken part in the capture and in the fight at the General Post Office during Easter Week and he had been imprisoned and released with some of his comrades. Little did the British know the damage he would do in a short time to their secret service system which was their real grip on our country.

Of all the insurgent leaders that Ireland ever had, it was he, Michael Collins, who realized that to have a successful rebellion, the British spy system would have to be smashed. He set about doing this work in a most determined way. He knew that Dublin Castle was the heart of that work and finding some sympathetic friends amongst the workers there, he planted counter spies in important positions. He controlled the ways and means of doing this work himself with astounding results. He also remembered that the country was populated by the descendants of loyalists who were planted there centuries ago.

Their movements were carefully watched by the IRA under his supervision and some of them paid with their lives for the information they were giving to the Castle.

Michael Collins had remarkable brains and he had a love of hard work. He also had an engaging manner that could get people to do things almost against their own wishes. Joseph was fascinated by his character and met him several times in Reilly's company. One day Collins said to him[7] that he had acquired a second-hand motor car which he wished Joseph to take into his care, to repair it and to keep it in good order and ready for immediate use. He wanted the car for transporting members of the organization from place to place on IRA business. Joseph, on account of his work, had an official permit to be out during curfew hours and it was a useful document to have.

1918 was a very difficult year for most Irishmen because of the fight against conscription. Fortunately, except for a small minority here and there, the country was united in the campaign. Trade union members, to show their solidarity, decided to have a twenty-four hour strike to coincide with the second anniversary of the Easter rebellion and this proved very successful. Everything was at a complete standstill on the appointed day, and the British government was very angry.

De Valera, one of the leaders who had taken part in the rebellion and escaped execution by claiming American citizenship, was the recognized leader of the IRA. He was arrested and cast into prison in England. He had been busy preparing a statement on conscription in Ireland to send to America. Others took his place, completed the document and sent it to America as he intended doing. History's pages give a full account of these acts and tell in detail about de Valera's sensational escape from prison, his subsequent arrival in America where he found sympathy and funds for the cause of Irish freedom.

At home Michael Collins and his fellow workers continued the struggle with renewed vigor and hope. Although Collins was a very busy man, he found time to look after the welfare of de Valera's family while he was in prison and later in America for a considerable length of time.

To disrupt and undermine the British government here, Sinn Fein courts, law courts established by the IRA, were now operating in small towns and villages. Litigants took their cases to the Sinn Fein courts and abided by the judgments given. Most of the people favored these acts which helped the morale of the insurgents by showing them that we were behind them in their struggle. Punishment of the culprits was often difficult as imprisonment was almost impossible. Sometimes they were chained to the church railings or gates late on a Saturday night to be a spectacle for the Sunday worshippers. This was considered a very effective punishment.

The country was in a state of guerilla warfare and the British forces were being harassed everywhere. Britain was very worried about the number of soldiers she was compelled to keep on the European battlefront and the number she had to keep in this country to try to control the 'terrible Irish'. She also had trouble in England with the conscientious objectors who refused to join the army. Some of them came to Ireland where they were known as 'fly-boys'.

We non-militant ones attended to our work in the normal way and in the evening attended to our garden allotments. We had advanced to growing carrots, beetroot, onions and vegetable marrows along with our supplies of cabbage and potatoes. A glass bell covering protected our seedlings from frost and this device was both useful and stylish. We sowed flower seeds for our home gardens and we shared plants with each other. A water supply had been laid on for the plots and with the extra hour's daylight, due to the Daylight Saving Bill, we got a lot of work done with time for a gossip afterwards.

A giant-sized cabbage or vegetable marrow or a freak-shaped potato kept us in talk for a long time. We discussed our national affairs and listened with bated breath to the tales of heroic deeds performed by the insurgents and of the vile acts of treachery by the British forces. Plenty of people were talking and deciding how it would all end and they helped pass some of the weary time away as well as giving us food for thought.

Our work at the Industry continued fairly evenly except for anxious moments when supplies of required materials were not available and substitutes proved difficult to handle. Miss Lily's health[8] was now causing some concern to her and great anxiety to us. Her condition was probably due to the turmoil in the country and to the anxiety about the future. Her loyal and dear friend Helen, a former Abbey actress, took her home where she could nurse Miss Lily back to health by giving her a change of air and a rest from some of her difficult problems. Miss Lily made good progress with Helen's devoted attention and returned to us completely recovered after some weeks.

Alas, the condition of the country grew steadily worse. The World War ended in November, 1918, and then we Irish felt the venom and hatred of the British Prime Minister and his cabinet. Decent British soldiers who had finished their war service refused to come to Ireland when asked to do so. As a result, British jail gates opened and from the criminals an army was formed to come here and wage war. They did not dress in the regular army uniform or in the uniform of the police force; they dressed in a mixture of the two uniforms: a black tunic and khaki trousers (or vice versa) and a tam-o'-shanter.

The Black and Tans were a ruthless and undisciplined lot, born of hate, who put fear and terror into the hearts of young and old, but not cowering submission. They paraded the city streets and county roads in armoured cars and lorries particularly during curfew hours. Their misdeeds were a blot on even the lowest of corrupt governments. Some Black and Tans were known to be of Irish nationality and this added bitterness to our already overflowing cup of sorrow.

In 1919, Anne Yeats was born to Mrs W B Yeats,[9] an event that gave the Yeats family much pleasure and great rejoicing at the prospect of a new generation. About that time it was announced that the contents of an old, dusty, musty house near our Industry would be auctioned and we longed to go. We regarded the house, hidden from view by overgrown bushes and trees, as a replica of Miss Havisham's house in Charles Dickens's *Great Expectations*. The house had also been occupied to the end by a maiden lady, the only child of the family.

When the great day arrived, Miss Lily gave permission to some of us to attend the auction. I was one of the lucky ones to see the house with its massive furniture, heavy curtains, large pictures and quantities of knick-knacks. When some pretty coloured fruit dishes were offered for sale, I made my first auction bid and was surprised at my success. A clerk recorded my name and address and the amount I was to pay in a book and told me to call the next day to collect the goods.

Flushed with my daring, a little later I was examining and

admiring the bindings of a very large and dusty set of Encyclopedia books, apparently never opened. When the auctioneer said, 'Who will bid me ten shillings for this wonderful set of books?' I looked around and smiled at him and as nobody made him an offer, he evidently took my smile as an acceptance of his price. I was not aware what had taken place until one of my companions told me I had got the books. She had been very close to the auctioneer when he had pointed me out to the clerk and said, 'You have her name already.'

I was aghast. What was I to do? I did not want the books. I had no place to put them and I could not afford the ten shillings along with the money I had already spent. My world collapsed around me. The next day when Miss Lily heard about my dilemma, she told me not to worry, that she would pay for the books and make a place for them on the Industry book shelves. This action was typical of her consideration and care about another person's difficulties. We often opened the books to reveal the vast information in them, which seemed endless to us, and they were used for the purpose for which they were compiled.

We were a very contented group of workers who enjoyed our employment with the wonderful Yeats sisters and the many artist friends who visited them. On bright mornings, as we made our way to work, birds sang in the hedgerows; the bees gathered honey; the moorhen swished with a flutter and dudder as she announced her flight from one nest to another; the mowing machine whirred as it cut the ripe grass in the meadow; the corncrake incessantly chattered to her brood, and the distant dogs barked happily. These and other sweet sounds came through the open window of our cottage while we worked happily at our different tasks. Nature was in a benign mood, but, alas, our country was sorrowing.

At the insistence of our Irish party leaders who attended the British House of Commons, a measure of Home Rule for Ireland has been written into the Statute book at the outbreak of the World War but the Bill was postponed until after the hostilities ceased. A weak attempt was made to reopen the discussion, but, in the meantime, a settlement was reached between the British cabinet and a group of men in northern Ulster who objected loudly to any form of Home Rule given to Ireland. These men claimed to be Irishmen and, at the same time, loyal British citizens who wished to be governed by his Royal Brittanic Majesty.

No doubt these Ulstermen had a right to be considered Irishmen. They were born in Ireland as were their parents and grandparents before them. They were well-established and educated, wealthy landowners with a stake in the country and they would have to be consulted about any change in government. If we looked back at our history, we would find that these people were the descendants of the numerous Britons planted here by the deliberate cunning and foresight of previous British governments who had taken possession of the lands of native Irish unlawfully and unscrupulously. Unfortunately, there were some renegade Irishmen among this lot.

Despite the unease in the country, we workers lived a fairly normal life, going on our usual weekend outings and trying to live as though nothing unusual was happening. We walked to the hills or to the sea. May and I always enjoyed a trip to Howth Head on a Sunday afternoon. We generally walked into the city and then went on to Howth by electric tram car, riding on the top deck which was uncovered and very breezy on a windy day. The backs of the seats were reversible so we could turn them and sit in groups of four facing one another - laughing, talking, or sheltering huddled together under our waterproof coats from a sudden shower of rain which we had to endure. There would not have been room for us to move downstairs as the trams were always packed with trippers going to the seaside.

After a picnic tea, we walked around Howth Head and gossiped with friends. We descended to the quayside to watch the fishermen examining their fishnets, the people going out in rowboats or the IRA 'freedom fighters' who frequented the Howth district. We usually finished our visit with a boat trip to Ireland's Eye. Our visit was very exciting if we caught sight of Michael Collins, Ireland's 'elusive pimpernel', who moved about freely although there was a huge reward for his capture - dead or alive - offered by the British government.

After several months in America following his prison escape, de Valera got back to Ireland bringing with him funds, messages of sympathy and promises of further help for Ireland's cause. The Black and Tans were bringing disrepute on themselves and on the British Cabinet daily. World communications were so speedy in 1919 that occurrences here could be known about and commented on in distant countries in a matter of minutes. The British government was perturbed by the constant expressions of horror made by influential people at home and abroad about the conditions in Ireland. Sympathy was increasing for the Irish cause.

At this time England also had the problem of employment for her discharged army, particularly its officers. They now offered to re-employ these officers at an increased salary and to send them as an auxiliary force to Ireland to help the Black and Tans quell the rebellion and enslave the Irish people. Hope was high and success was certain. Many of these men were the cream of British Intelligence and it was hoped that they would find Michael Collins, capture the funds that were being used to keep the rebellion alive, restore the spy system to its former strength and generally restore the position that had been lost to England since the Easter Rising.

The Auxiliaries, reputed to be the highest paid soldiers in the world, were housed in large barracks and RIC stations. Others were billeted in hotels and guest houses or lived with relatives in order to have greater freedom of movement and to gather useful information swiftly, without any impediment, and in general to be a law unto themselves.

The Auxiliaries were a formidable challenge to the IRA. Their challenge was met with the firm determination of 'no surrender' by the freedom fighters who, encouraged by a very embittered public, prepared to give all the help in their power to crush this latest despicable attempt at English warfare. Joseph had been helping Michael Collins with transport as he possessed a permit to travel freely with his Minerva car and passengers throughout the country. This permit was issued to him by the Dublin Castle authorities after the Easter Rising when Joseph's work consisted of conveying inspectors of the Department of Agriculture throughout the country to different stations for the purpose of examining cattle and of issuing licences.

As the holder of a permit, Joseph was of inestimable value[10] to Michael Collins's work. Coupled with his vast knowledge of the Irish countryside and his reliable motor car, he was driving Eamon de Valera or other persons of authority on longer journeys to speak with influential people who were anxious to assist the cause but who could not rely on the information that they were getting through newspapers or from local men. Local leaders could now get firsthand news of IRA operations from the men my brother brought and with that information, they acted accordingly.

It was necessary for Joseph to call often at our home so mother, as of old, heard the daily exploits from her two eldest sons. Full names were seldom used[11] so we got familiar with hearing exciting episodes about 'The Big Fella' (Michael Collins) and 'The Long Fella' (Eamon de Valera), Tom C, Bill T, The Tans, and The Auxies. The same secret way of speaking existed more or less among the general public with one another, because we were inclined to be secretive or tight-lipped concerning our knowledge of people or things.

On one occasion, I was amazed to hear a woman of the organization telling her listeners that there was no such person as Michael Collins, that his name and exploits were those of a mythical figure invented by the IRA to bamboozle the British military. She spoke so convincingly, she evidently believed what she said. Although I knew she was wrong, I remained silent.

The swaggering impudence of the Auxiliaries was paraded through the streets of Dublin during working hours in military lorries that were heavily encased in steel mesh and armed with loaded guns protruding on all sides. Coupled with the noisy Black and Tans in similar vehicles, they made the lives of outraged Irish citizens almost unbearable. Innocent people were constantly being arrested and subjected to vile treatment by this infamous army of Britain. Protesting voices were raised in many places.

The British Cabinet denied these unfavorable reports and to show their great tolerance for the Irish, they made feeble attempts to reopen talks on the postponed Home Rule Bill. Irishmen everywhere, however, recognized this latest attempt as 'window dressing' meant to appease the clamouring voices of their wartime allies in the war where thousands of Irishmen fighting under the British flag lost their lives or returned crippled for life.

Talking about the Home Rule Bill was only a way for the British Cabinet to mark time while the Auxiliaries, with their limitless powers, would gain complete victory over the insurgents and make the talks of a settlement unnecessary. Many of the Catholic hierarchy who had heretofore raised their voices against members of their flocks who took up arms, and who received British applause for their condemnation, now denounced the British misrule of Ireland.

Conditions grew worse daily in every county, for as their chances for a military victory receded further, the Auxies and the Black and Tans became more and more debauched. They were meeting with stiff resistance and superior intelligence from the IRA. The British were losing top-ranking men with great frequency and for this the country was subjected to an orgy of reprisals. Regular Army officers would no longer be responsible for the lawless brigands who had been foisted on them and over whom they had no control.

The country was in a sorry mess and as protesting voices became more insistent, the British Prime Minister Lloyd George was forced to do something. He called Eamon de Valera to Downing Street for talks about a settlement. He dallied because he had rumours that the insurgents were cracking and, of course, he wanted a military victory. Finally, the situation was so bad that he was forced to concede the military victory and call a truce. A number of responsible persons here and overseas offered to mediate and there were a variety of ideas about the form and substance the settlement would take.

What a relief it was to the general public when they realized how fully they could go about their daily business without the fear of being stopped by a lorry-load of drink-sodden bullies who had the authority to ask them where they were going and why. If a question were not answered quickly or if someone failed to hide his feeling of disgust, he was sure to be manhandled by having his face slapped and his hat knocked off. Ladies' handbags were opened and their contents scattered on the ground. Even old men had their walking sticks snatched from them. Anyone might be trundled into a lorry, taken a long distance away on a country road before being released to get home as best he could.

To those of us who individually never had the chance to get even with these hooligans, the truce called for a celebration of some kind that would allow us to express our feelings of great joy. In Dundrum, as in most places, it took the form of a bonfire. Ours was held in Main Street at the cross of Ballinteer and Kilmacud Roads. First it was a small affair with dancing and singing around the fire, renewal of friendships and occasional visits to the nearby public houses. Soon the diligent housewives remembered lumber that had accumulated over the years and they brought it out to keep the bonfire going. Each addition merited loud cheers as the flames rose, but when a load of old, worn out bedding arrived - palliasses and mattresses on which the bonfire showed the dark water stains of bedwetters - the fun was fast and furious with jokes about naughty little girls and boys.

The crickle-crackle of the fire when the bedding was added was called the death-pangs of the fleas and a loud explosion was greeted by prolonged cheering as father flea met his end. We were a happy people that night as we commented on the numerous loud explosions and speculated on the type and age of the flea executed. Few people went home to bed as it had been a long time since we had the freedom to do just as we liked. We stayed out to enjoy every moment of it and in doing so, the size of the bonfire was kept under control. Next morning everyone good-humouredly helped to clear away the mess left by the fire. We were so happy and everywhere there were expressions of forgiveness and neighbourly love.

The following day and for many days afterwards we approached our work with lightened hearts and loosened tongues and it was exciting to find out how much others knew about the recent national events. There were many exciting discoveries made and new friendships formed. With the truce in operation, people made full use of the freedom it gave. It was now possible for city folk to visit the country to see their old homesteads and to talk in peace with their relatives with whom communication by letter almost ceased because of censorship by both the British and the IRA, for it was not uncommon for people to receive a letter that had passed through both censors.

The talks taking place between the Irish Plenipotentiaries and the British Cabinet interested each of us immensely whether or not we had helped in the struggle for freedom, for what was taking place would affect us individually and collectively. We had our own opinions about what was being done and what should be done.

The selection of the men sent to negotiate the settlement caused a lot of discussion and discontent. We questioned the suitability of some and wondered why de Valera, as head of the Irish organization, was not one of the party to meet the British head of state. We also argued that if the talks failed, could an armed resistance be resumed? Our soldiers, unknown by sight to the enemy for so long, were now seen in public by friend and foe alike. It was such an impossible situation we would not consider discussing such an unlikely probability.

Some members of the public believed it was a grave error to have exposed Michael Collins to the notice of the army of occupation before a settlement was reached. Collins had evaded arrest over the years without a disguise and had dumbfounded his would-be captors. He often spoke to them and wished them well when they were actually searching for him.

We understood from local gossip that much to his amazement and regret, Collins was chosen to go to London to take part in the settlement talks. Being a soldier and not versed in politics, he protested his inclusion, but as a soldier, it was his duty to obey. Thus he became one of a small party with a formidable task and without any time to prepare for the discussion of problems with far-reaching effects, a discussion with experienced, slick politicians.

The talks proceeded with occasional delays for investigation and for clarification of problems. We were kept informed about the progress of the talks by our daily newspapers. Joseph, being near the core of the organization, asked one morning how the talks were going and he was told gleefully, 'We are getting much more than we expected'. History's pages gives a full account of those happenings.

In the peaceful atmosphere and with the promise of a settlement in the near future, we were able to turn our attention to other things. A wave of enthusiasm for acquiring our Irish language struck a number of us, young and old, and evening classes formed in all sorts of buildings where teachers offered their services free. One of our local curates selected a parish group to form a committee to set up a number of classes in our national schools.

I joined a beginners' class and discovered, to my horror, that a lot of time was taken up with grammar and the explanation and exercises of guttural sounds. It was a most boring and unattractive class, so I left after a short time to join class number two, a class for those with some knowledge of Irish. By the time I arrived, the class had turned into a debating society. It was interesting but little was done about the teaching of the language. Class number three was for more advanced students. I hesitated before entering this one because I had only a slight smattering of Irish phrases and rhymes.

The first night I attended the class we were told that the teacher in charge was ill and would not be returning. The committee was in touch with the Gaelic League headquarters in Parnell Square who promised another teacher the following week. We were asked to pay a small fee and to promise we would attend the class regularly. The next week a young man appeared. He had a nice speaking voice and a fine flow of Irish that sounded distinct and musical. He chatted in Irish with those who had some knowledge of the language and accepted a shake of the head from those who did not. He did not appear to be dismayed at finding such a mixed set of pupils and he was full of energy and determination to make a success of the class.

He produced a book from his pocket and advised each of us to get a copy of it and he agreed to bring a number of copies with him for the next class. Without wasting any more time, he wrote some words on the blackboard, explained their meanings and made us feel it was a night well spent. With hope and his help we looked forward to achieving our objective of learning Irish and he remained our teacher for a number of years doing valiant work.

While we were preparing ourselves learning our language for the wonderful Utopia that we had envisaged, the fate of our country was being debated with a set of slick, practised politicians who had already divided the country. They were now deciding how much of the mutilated body of our country they would return to the guardianship of the rightful owners whose children, over the years, had given their lives to free Ireland from bondage.

Our small group of plenipotentiaries, with Document One given them by de Valera as a basis for discussion, must have been sorrowful indeed when pleading their country's case against such unyielding strength and terrifying injustice which they witnessed in their opponents. Words were twisted; sentences were given different meanings for each side and undreamt obstacles and cajolery were introduced into the talks. At the same time, speed was demanded so that a decision would be reached without delay.

The Irish Plenipotentiaries were divided in their opinion of the final draft. Michael Collins and Arthur Griffith signed it and, after much heartburnings, the others did likewise. There was no lightness in the hearts of the men who returned to Dublin with the document they had signed and who offered it to their organization and recommended its ratification. Each man in his own way defended his opinion for signing.

There were a lot of hot angry words spoken at the meeting called to examine the signed agreement. Almost all of the abuse was hurled at Michael Collins since someone had to be the scapegoat. He was made to take the blame for their bitter disappointment and although he had been reluctant to take part in the talks, he bore the brunt of his comrades' anger and the stigma of accepting an inferior agreement. How he must have suffered when he was called a traitor and when discretion was thrown to the wind in the uproar that ensued.

Michael Collins defended his signing by pointing out to those who chose to listen to him that what he saw in the agreement was not the final settlement of their claims but a means to attain a greater freedom. It was a stepping stone that he was not ashamed to recommend to the Irish people for their acceptance. A vote was taken and a small majority agreed to accept the agreement. There was pandemonium as the minority began to leave the room with the avowed intention, in their madness, of continuing the war against Britain. Whatever the wishes of the general public might be did not concern them.

In the days that followed, it was made abundantly clear that the public was sick and tired of the disturbance and longed for a normal life again. If they had been consulted, they would have accepted the agreement. Remember, we had gone through seven years of continuous strain and we had wholeheartedly supported the movement when it was most needed and without which this bid for freedom could have ended, as had previous attempts, without reaching the stage of negotiation with Britain.

Friends argued with friends on the merits or demerits of the Treaty and out of this predicament two opposing groups emerged - the Treatyites and the Anti-Treatyites also known as the Irregulars. After a great deal of wrangling and some months of peace-making efforts between the major parties, a civil war broke out that was to destroy the country and to breed a terrible bitterness among the people. We Irish were to suffer a greater tribulation than ever before in the history of our country. To know that brother was against brother, that father was against son and that households were simmering with hatred was something not readily understood by any of them. How was it that those who had given up their freedom for so long and who had suffered such untold hardship in the fight were now equally ready to destroy that for which they had been fighting?

It seemed to those who favored the Treaty that the majority vote for its acceptance should have been respected and that all fighting units should have taken their part in forming a government to implement the Treaty. They should have used their united strength and knowledge to make the weak articles strong and the unsuitable articles weaker.

The minority, in their blind fury and bitter helter-skelter haste, decided to resume their fight against Britain. They gave no thought to the fact that the vote taken was a majority one and that their fight now turned not against Britain but majority rule, freely expressed. Anti-Treatyites, who in bygone days longed for leadership, now assumed the most coveted roles and led their followers where they wished. The rank and file, not knowing who was in charge, obeyed orders. They knew Dev was on their side and nothing else mattered to them.

Those who accepted the Treaty formed a government and started to take control of the various departments. Michael Collins, as Army Commander, took over each military barracks as it was evacuated by the British Army. At the same time, he installed a section of the newly-formed Irish Army in them. He was also busy trying to find a peaceful solution to appease his former comrades and to restore unity once more. With so much work to be done and with good jobs ready to be filled, he longed for them to be with him and to take their rightful party in the making of a new Ireland. He appealed to de Valera to do something to restore order amongst the break-away group and he relied on Dev's influence over them. In that he was mistaken, for others better informed knew that Dev had lost his leadership and that 'the tail was wagging the dog'.

We carried on with our daily tasks hoping that soon we would have peace. One Saturday afternoon in 1922, the Misses

Yeats took us to a performance at the Gaiety Theatre and afterwards to tea at Jammet's where our special treat was Jammet's famous pancakes. Our evening's entertainment was saddened by the arrival of a special messenger from the Yeats's house in Churchtown with a cablegram from New York announcing the death of their father John Butler Yeats.[12]

Weeks and months slipped by without any sign of the peace for which we hoped. Unbelievable atrocities became daily occurrences between the Treatyites and the Anti-Treatyites, the legitimate ones endeavouring to form a government and build a worthy state and the lawless one disrupting and hindering every effort made. Tempers were frayed[13] and judgments blinded with the result that lootings, burnings, arrests, executions, revenge and reprisals now took place between former friends. The British Cabinet had mercenaries on both sides, among the men who had joined the Irregulars as well as those in the newly-formed Irish Army. The British openly wished that a state of civil war would show the world that the Irish were not fit to be free.

During this uneasy time, Arthur Griffith, President of the infant Free State, died unexpectedly, to the grief of his friends and to the loss of his party. After a lying-in-state he was accorded a military funeral the likes of which was never before seen in our capital city. As the funeral procession wound its long, mournful way past government buildings and through the streets to Glasnevin Cemetery, onlookers saw, for the first time, the men in charge of the State walking slowly and sorrowfully, in military formation, behind their dead leader, to the haunting drumbeat of the funeral march.

In the days that followed, work resumed in the Dáil Eireann and William T Cosgrave was elected President to replace Arthur Griffith. Michael Collins continued on his journey inspecting the military barracks throughout the country in order, in his thorough way, to become conversant with the conditions and needs of the men for whom he would be responsible. On these journeys he hoped to meet and to make peace with former friends. It was on one such journey that he met his death in his native County Cork only ten days after the death of Arthur Griffith.

Once more Ireland grieved for the loss of a brilliant and beloved son. The streets of Dublin vibrated once again to the sound of marching feet, and the notes of the march for the dead. Many were the bitter tears shed by young and old on the brilliant August day and heavy indeed were the hearts who remembered his age, his accomplishments and his cheerfulness as he repeated his advice, 'Stop talking and get on with the work' to his friends. If it could only be that they would stop fighting and get on with the work. Surely the Anti-Treatyites had time to reflect on their rash actions and realize that the majority of Irish people did not sympathize with their actions.

During this year of tumult and change, Miss Lily and Miss Lolly were faced with the difficulty of finding suitable new premises for the Industry, for the fifteen-year lease on the Churchtown cottage had expired.[14] It was a sad ordeal for them, as well as for us, to contemplate leaving the nice cottage and its surroundings to which we had grown so attached. We had a slight distraction from our worries when Mrs Lane-Poole (Ruth Pollexfen) returned with her two children and their nurse to enjoy a short holiday with her Yeats cousins before sailing to Australia to make her home in the city of Perth. Mr Lane-Poole, having been appointed head of the Australian Forest Commission, was already there. The pleasure of the visit was made sad for Miss Lily who thought of the great distance that would soon divide them. To us workers, after our months of gloom, it was a pleasant distraction to have the frequent visits of the two little girls with their nurses, to listen to their baby chatter packed with mischievous, innocent fun and to answer their many questions.

A strong rumour of romance brought to our attention one of our other village characters. She was an eccentric middle-aged lady who had a great love for cats. She lived alone in a derelict two-storied detached house a short distance from the main street of Dundrum with numerous cats of various breeds and ages reported to number in the hundreds. She was a gentle, nice person who lived here for a number of years without interference, who walked around smilingly and who carried on her clothes the obnoxious odour of cats. Now she left the village as quietly as she came but this time she had as her companion a demobbed Black and Tan. Since nobody had any details of her departure, we speculated about her courtship. Was he unknown to her? Had he heard of her wealth? Had he visited her in her smelly house of cats? At least we hoped he was kind to her after her marriage.

The proprietress of the private asylum I described earlier in my childhood recollections died at an advanced age and the house with contents were billed for auction. Viewing was confined strictly to catalogue holders and each catalogue cost two shillings and sixpence, no doubt to keep out the idle non-buyers. I was fortunate in getting a copy from a friend so I could see the inside of the house. I had known the outside since childhood. What a thrill it was to walk though the numerous odd-shaped rooms and passages that for so long had been a mystery to the local inhabitants.

The front entrance to the house, off Main Street, had a short avenue on a slight incline. The hall door and most of the front of the house was hidden from sight by a mound with evergreens and small flowering trees that acted as a barrier to anyone entering or leaving the house in a hurry. The house was the usual type of two-storied building with rooms on each side of the hallway where the family lived. The patients' quarters were narrow and stretched a long way to the rear where the house widened again to become almost a replica of the front.

In the narrow passages for viewing, the auctioneer arranged a vast collection of old statuettes on shelves, tables and window-recesses. They were long-forgotten objects, left over, beloved property of past inmates. Cupids of varying sizes outnumbered all the other nudes. There were a few Adams, more plentiful Eves, Diana, Aphrodite, Venus, Pan with his pipes and one 'Love Boy with Thorn'. A local wag had covered all the naughty parts with odds and ends of dress material, pins and twine. It was a bizarre spectacle and greatly amused the viewing public who enjoyed the unexpected sight and perhaps forgot about what they had come to inspect.

Jimmy Hyland, Sara's twin, as a young man

CHAPTER EIGHT

(1923-1928)

Death of Jimmy Hyland - Cuala moves to Merrion Square - Commuter trains - Dublin newsboys - 'At the Hawk's Well' - James Stephens - Jack B Yeats - Cottie Yeats - Irish college in Cois Farraige - Pádraic O Conaire - Cuala moves to Lower Baggot Street - W B Yeats at Cuala - Robin Flower - Christmas sale of work - Irish college in Rosmuc - Australian commission for Government House - Gaelic League outings - First flight - Irish college in Carraroe - An American patron.

In the beginning of 1923, my twin Jimmy died of an incurable disease from which he had suffered over a period of years. He had a quiet, retiring nature, so he made no fuss of his illness. He just quietly passed away leaving us to mourn his loss. With the passage of time, in common with our neighbours, our family unit changed. Deaths reduced our numbers and marriages increased our household bringing a new generation. As we grew older, extra responsibilities were thrust upon us.

In this year as well, a friend promised the Misses Yeats the lease of a suitable flat to house the Industry in the Baggot Street area of the city.[1] The Yeatses hoped that we would move from Cuala Cottage at the end of January, but unfortunately, there was a delay in obtaining clear possession and there was a possibility of a further delay.

Mr and Mrs W B Yeats and their young family of a girl and a boy[2] were now living at 82 Merrion Square,[3] a short distance from the location of the new work-rooms. When they heard of the difficulty, they very considerately offered to accommodate the Industry until the promised flat would be available. We were given the use of the large rooms off the hall-door passage for our work with the smaller ones towards the back of the house for cloak rooms and offices. In the end, we remained at Merrion Square for a couple of years before moving to Baggot Street.

I had spent sixteen very happy years with Miss Lily in the embroidery department out in the country where the air was clean and life was unhurried. Each season brought with it its own particular delights as year succeeded year. We were a very happy, contented group of workers enjoying our employment with such wonderful people as the Yeats sisters. There was not time to visualize what the change of work-rooms would mean to us before the move was complete. In the meantime, we were warmly welcomed in Merrion Square during a time of great upheaval in our country.

Since most of our group lived in or near the village of Dundrum, our first change was that we travelled by train to Harcourt Street Station and thence walked to Merrion Square. We tried all the different ways that would take us there in the shortest time. We found that the various routes were equal in length but that the Hatch Street-Fitzwilliam Square route offered more variety and gave good shelter from the north wind and rain. Our way took us by the side of University College, Dublin, Alexandra Girls' College, and the entrance gate of 'An Túr Gloine' (The Tower of Glass)[4] in Upper Pembroke Street. 'An Túr Gloine' was founded by Miss Sarah Purser, RHA, who was well known to us through our visits to see her stained glass exhibits. The flowering shrubs in Fitzwilliam Square with its collection of thrushes, blackbirds and finches was sufficient compensation for our loss of countryside. The fellow travellers we met in our daily journeys were a distraction and supplied us plentifully with gossip. Our interests did not diminish; they expanded.

Trains to meet the needs of suburban dwellers on the Bray

to Harcourt Street line ran frequently from seven o'clock in the morning and continued until midnight. There were period tickets for unlimited family travel offered at a reduced rate. Individuals enjoyed the same reduced fares. The train consisted of a coal-powered steam engine, a driver and a stoker, several carriages divided into first, second and third-class compartments and a large luggage van/guard's van at the rear that was fitted with a lamp that glowed with a red light in the dark. The guard was in complete charge of the train.

The first-class compartments were lavishly upholstered and were fitted with head rests covered with linen or lace antimacassars, moveable armrests, window curtains with elaborate edgings, window blinds, pictures or mirrors under the luggage rack, individual reading lights and good quality carpet. They resembled miniature drawing rooms.

Upholstery in the second-class compartments was less substantial. There were no head or armrests, no extra curtains, less expensive floor covering and general lighting. Third-class furnishing was at a minimum with nicely-shaped, comfortable but plain wooden benches. The majority of train passengers travelled third-class.

Standing on the arrival and departure platforms it was easy to distinguish the first-class passengers - mostly businessmen or lawyers - who walked briskly up and down whilst awaiting the arrival of the train. They wore well-pressed clothes of expensive material, trilby or half-tall hats and highly polished boots often partly covered by garters, and they generally carried a rolled umbrella and a briefcase and sported a flower in their buttonhole. Second-class travellers were considered a snobbish lot who ignored their neighbours, showing off that they could afford the extra expense of the travel ticket. It was third class that carried the largest number of passengers.

In wintertimes junior porters lit coal fires in the first-class waiting room. In summer, flowers bloomed in beds along the platform and stationmasters vied with each other for the variety and quality of the flowering plants and bushes. Prizes were awarded each year by the company for the best-kept station.

The Stationmaster at the Harcourt Street terminus was a most impressive-looking individual when he came out of his office on to the platform dressed in a formal suit of striped trousers, long-tailed coat, smart waistcoat and tall silk hat. He generally carried a pair of folded leather gloves or a roll of paper. He watched the trains enter and leave the station, and trains did not move out until he gave the guard leave to blow his whistle.

One day, soon after we moved from Churchtown to Merrion Square, an amusing incident occurred in our work-room that highlighted the difference between city and country life. A newsboy was running hurriedly along Merrion Square calling, 'Stop Press, Stop Press', and one of our workers quickly raised the large window as he drew near. Leaning out of the window, she shouted, 'What's up? What's up?' A Jewman shook his shirt over the Liffey and "drownded" all the flays [fleas]', he replied. 'You're very smart, aren't you?' said the girl. Had she been home in Churchtown, she would have got all the information free from those she asked. She did not realize that the newsboy wanted to sell his papers for the news they contained.

One morning on my way to work, I was pleased to see a notice-board outside Conradh na Gaeilge in Ely Place that stated the days and hours of the language classes held there. I was disappointed that the Dundrum classes had not re-opened the previous September as expected. I had made good progress and had hoped to continue with my study of Irish. That evening I called to the house hoping to become a pupil. I was fortunate because the very tall young man who interviewed me was the Chief Executive Officer of the newly-formed County Dublin Vocational Education Department.[5] On hearing my story, he immediately arranged to have the Irish classes in Dundrum restored under the Vocational Education Committee with all expenses paid. Our enthusiastic teacher was engaged once more to be our guide and we enjoyed our class meetings, concerts, weekend outings and other activities over a number of years. Later we were awarded scholarships to the Gaeltacht.[6]

Having our Industry workrooms in Merrion Square, in the home of the poet W B Yeats, now a member of the Senate, was a great honour for us workers. That our being there happened to take place in the early stages of our newly-formed Irish government and our freedom from the domination of a hostile foreign one added greatly to our pleasure.

One evening, soon after our arrival in Merrion Square, the poet was entertaining a very important visitor; I believe it was the Indian poet Tagore.[7] As part of the evening's activities the verse play *At the Hawk's Well*[8] was performed by some members of the Abbey Theatre company. The senior work-girls were invited to be present at the performance which took place upstairs in two large rooms that could be opened to one room by folding back the dividing door. The audience was seated on the floor on rugs or cushions in the darkness when we entered, and some of the players were already in their places under a very subdued greenish light, at an imaginary stage in a corner of the room farthest away from the audience.

My recollection is of shadowy figures moving about singing or speaking their various verses. The first player recited: 'I call to the eye of the mind, a well long choked and dry, and boughs long stripped by the wind.' After a very short time, another masked player entered the room from the landing outside, and he moved through the players where he became one of them. It was easy to recognise him from his great height even if Dr Oliver Gogarty[9] had not said in an audible whisper, 'Lennox[10] is in great form tonight'.

The play was directed by Mr Yeats in the manner for which he had written it many years before. It reminded me of the Gospel story of the sick man who had lain for many years by the water's edge waiting for the angel to come from Heaven to stir the water and give it healing power. On our way upstairs to the performance, Mrs Yeats introduced May and me to the playwright Sean O'Casey,[11] a very shy young man without any conversation, who looked tired and ill on that occasion.

The Yeats's little daughter Anne, who had stolen a march on her nurse to see what wonderful things were happening downstairs, came out of the improvised theatre room in her night dress. Mrs Yeats called out to her, 'Come here, Anne, and say how do you do to Mr Simpson'. The child came forward, saying as she did, 'Sim-saun, what a funny name'. She then ran away laughing as the nurse came to fetch her. Our privilege to be present at the play and the sociability of all members of the Yeats family will show how noble and considerate the members of the Yeats family were to each other and to those around them.

Moving to Merrion Square meant many changes in our style of work, our way of living and even our way of thinking. We could not readily understand our feeling of lightness and wonderment. Perhaps they were caused by our newly-won freedom, the loss of which had been responsible for so much suffering and bitterness down through the centuries. Our Merrion Square workrooms were separated and we were completely cut off from our fellow workers in the Cuala Press. No longer did we see the unfinished pages or books or poems that we delighted in reading as they lay about awaiting completion in the printing room. Even our visitors seemed different and when they left the embroidery room we seldom saw them again before they left the premises.

On our way to and from work we met many artists and literary people whom we knew by sight or by reputation. One day while walking along St Stephen's Green, Miss Lily met James Stephens, author of *The Crock of Gold*. He held his right hand tightly closed as though it held something very precious. He explained to Miss Lily that he was taking home to his own pussycat the smell of the cat he had just been fondling through the railings of the park. James Stephens was an extraordinary looking little man with rather short legs and a very square kindly face with a huge forehead.

At that time, Mr and Mrs Jack Yeats were living in Fitzwilliam Square[12] where they each had a work studio. We often met Mr Jack in Merrion Row walking to or from the city centre. He had an unusual style of dress and manner of walking that distinguished him from other men. He was tall and slightly built. His long overcoats of tweed or heavy cloth with velvet collar were fluted at the back from the waist downward, giving a slight fullness to the heels which dipped a little in front from his forward and ever so slightly sidewards manner of walking, as of a person ascending a hill. He was good-looking with beautiful eyes, long-shaped, clean-shaven face, good skin and nice complexion. He acknowledged seeing any of us by smiling and raising his right hand in salute, thumb and forefingers together with little finger extended. He told Miss Lily we were not to pass him without recognition.

Mrs Jack,[13] also an artist, was equally friendly, and she made many beautiful designs for embroideries by Miss Lily or one of us workers. They were a great delight to work on account of their rich, curving lines and minute detail. Such articles were sure to win a prize for the Industry when entered in a competition at an art exhibition. She also made many drawings for Christmas greeting cards and pictures suitable for

Miss Lolly's hand-printing department. Mrs Jack was a frequent visitor to our Merrion Square workrooms. She was very picturesque in her well-designed clothes and exquisite jewellery which suited her face and her figure of small proportions. Her house had hand-painted furniture and other hand-made articles of pleasing design which she herself invented and executed. She was always delighted to show her latest addition to any of us workers who called on an errand to her house.

In 1925, the first Irish language college was established by our government in the Cois Farraige Gaeltacht in Connemara.[14] The local parish priest[15] made arrangements with his parishioners to accept a number of pupils into their houses in August. Classes were held in the National School. The County Dublin Vocational Education Department awarded scholarships to members of the evening language classes who passed a simple test conducted by Department examiners, a test to determine who would benefit by hearing the language in daily use. Most of the children in the Gaeltacht had no knowledge of spoken English and a great many of the older ones had forgotten the little they learned since they had not used it in their homes.

I was fortunate to obtain a scholarship and elated at the thought of attending school, but alas, I was filled with some apprehension. We were to live in strange houses and I worried that there might be fleas in the beds. Fleas were a great torment to people with sensitive skin and although their numbers were slowly decreasing at that time, there were still far too many about to be comfortable. Since I was a sufferer, I prepared myself for action by taking a box of flea deterrent with me. I did not have to use it then or on any of my subsequent visits. All of the people and the houses in Connemara were spotlessly clean in every district where I stayed.

We travelled by train from Broadstone Station to Galway. It was a most boring journey across the midlands. I could scarcely believe my senses that so many miles of my land could be so unlovely. To add further to the monotony, there were too many of us crowded together. Nobody thought of requesting or of providing a corridor coach for our comfort and we had to stand up from our seats in relays in order to avoid cramps. The difficulty in taking the tea we brought with us was sheer pandemonium as the train swayed violently on its uneven tracks which had been laid on soft ground. We were allowed to alight on to the platform for a short while at Athlone where we heard the joyful news that the rest of our journey would be quicker. Of course, the scenery improved after we crossed the Shannon.

Cois Farraige, Irish College

At Galway we transferred to privately-owned motor coaches that took us to our destination in Connemara. The journey had its share of discomfort as we were bundled into small coaches with our luggage, some of which we carried on our knees. Our feet were cramped with suitcases and packages on the floor, because there was no provision for carrying luggage on the tops of the coaches. The engine of one of the coaches required a lot of attention to keep it going and that caused us further discomfort.

Public transportation was only in its infancy in the remote parts of Ireland, so our stop near our destination provided a great diversion for a group of young children who knew of our expected arrival and were waiting for us. As the faulty-engined motor coach came to a forced stand-still, they came leaping and bounding, barefoot, over the stone walls towards us with their loose home-spun grey dresses swirling above their heads as they leaped down from a height on to the road. In these backward places, a number of young boys wore this type of feminine garment long after their contemporaries in other parts had exchanged them for the more masculine trousers. We must have looked very strange to those children in our different style of clothing: stockinged legs, variety of footwear, straw hats, cotton dresses and long and short coats. They gazed in silent wonderment at us and when we tried to speak to them in their language with our faulty pronunciation and our high-pitched voices, they ran away like frightened deer to hide behind the stone walls.

After a short while spent in coaxing the motor engine to further action, we were on our way again and soon arrived at the schoolhouse where the parish priest with some of his parishioners awaited us. A list of accommodations had been prepared and friends were sent together to different houses. I went with four other girls[16] to a two-storied, modern slate-roofed combined shop and dwelling place where the local curate stayed when in residence in the parish. He had gone away that day for a month's holidays. The shop, which was served by the *bean a' tighe*, opened when a customer came in requesting flour, grain or other household necessities; otherwise, it remained closed.

The houses in the parish were scattered over a wide area and some of the pupils, before coming, had been advised to bring their bicycles with them. They were housed in Inverin and Spiddal, several miles from the schoolhouse. Most of us had a long walk each day to the school and we seldom met other pupils after school hours. The sea, Galway Bay, which looked so inviting and tantalising near to us at the house where I stayed, was more than a mile distant without a roadway or a cart track leading to it. We were separated from the sea by numerous walled, stony patches peculiar to Connemara. They looked from a distance like tiny fields of pale-coloured, wild flowers and lichen - the yellow of the more prolific *buachalán buí*[17] dominating the scene - with a few faded thistles or patches of heather here and there. There was not sufficient soil in all those acres to give substance or colour to any plant; yet, it was a pleasant sight to look at - the low stone walls of varying grey shades making a distinct pattern to enclose the weakly growth struggling for existence on the rocks edged by the blue sea.

The ground northward from the seashore inclined upward to the main road and this gave a full view of Galway Bay south to the Cliffs of Moher in County Clare. The land continued its gentle rise but was quite fertile beyond the main road where the houses were built. There were fuschia bushes, veronica and hydrangea to give a little colour to the scene, an occasional field and numerous fresh, spring water wells. After our first trial of finding a pathway to the seashore through the tangled wilderness, we gave up in despair and contented ourselves with viewing its glorious splendour from the distance. The sea seemed to put on a special act daily for our pleasure by clothing itself from shore to shore with what looked like myriads of gigantic bubbles, dancing and sparkling in the sun rays from early morning until late evening, most days showing the entire outline of the Cliffs. Unfortunately, we could not see the outline of the Aran Islands or the Beanna Beola from our holiday home, neither did we ever get to the seashore.

Our lessons at the school were varied and full of life. On certain days a local *seanchaí* came to tell us stories which we were expected to re-tell and to ask the meaning of the idioms. It was all very entertaining and exciting. One day Seán Pádraic O Conaire[18] called the school during our study hours. He was known to most of the pupils through his published books of short stories which we used as textbooks in our Dublin classes.

He pushed his tweed cap on to the back of his head and pursing his lips, he told an amusing experience that he said he had while travelling in a train. He named the story *An Seanchaí ar Iarraidh.*[19] To us it was an oft-told tale, but with his little additions and physical demonstrations of the search, the story became alive and exceedingly funny. He also repeated some poems and rhymes. It was a wonderful meeting for those of us who were familiar with his writing but who had not ever seen him. Now we could visualize him in the future when reading his works.

One Saturday morning, an old man came to the shop on an errand. I was in the kitchen when he opened the door and entered with the usual salutations to which I replied. The *bean a' tighe* was upstairs and I said she would be down shortly. Anxious to try the extra knowledge of Irish I had gained, I said, *'Sílim go mbeidh áthru ann sar i bhfad ar na capaillí bána ar an bfharraige inniú*'.[20] He looked at me very blankly without saying another word, but the baby of the house[21] got up off the floor where she was seated and ran to the window to look out at the sea. At least I had the satisfaction of knowing that she understood what I had said.

She was about three years of age. She never made friends with any of us, and since her elder sisters were living with their grandparents whilst we were occupying their house, she was a lonely child. In our first year we had no share in the family life. We were catered for in an excellent manner. We had good and varied meals, home-made tea cakes and sweetmeats, but we always remained strangers to those people who had their own daily work to do in addition to looking after our wants. We seldom saw the *fear a' tighe*.[22] He was away to the bog harvesting the winter supply of turf before we got down to breakfast; or, if the tides were suitable, he was gathering seaweed for manuring the land. It was a very busy time of the year.

After the old man left the shop that morning, I told the *bean a' tighe* that I had failed to make conversation with him. She said that he was a little deaf and that he would not have understood my reference to the sea waves as having white horses on them. The Irish expression was, '*Tá blath bána in iarraidhe an iascaig inniú*'.[23] Thus, I learned a new expression which gave me good copy for my homework which was part of our training. In church on Sundays, the Epistle, Gospel sermon and prayers were in Irish and we had Irish prayer books to help us in our studies.

After four marvellous weeks we returned home to Dublin bursting with enthusiasm for our Irish language and full of ideas for future visits to the Gaeltacht. Our homeward journey seemed much quicker and we made ourselves more comfortable in the train by occupying more space in the carriages. We made a number of new friends and we were anxious to be with these friends during our last few hours. We planned to exchange letters, to meet for further outings, and to continue with our studies so as to visit Connemara the following year.

We were met by a host of excited friends when we arrived at Broadstone Station. Parents and relatives were reunited with students with much kissing, hugging and happy laughter. After the silence of Connemara, it was a great change to walk out into the lighted streets to hear the clip-clop of horses' hooves, the rumble of cabs and cars, the swish of the electric cables of the tram cars which kept them in motion as they rocked their way downhill through Parnell Square, the loud clanging of the warning approach bell operated by the impatient foot of the driver, the lesser sound of the few motor horns and the gib-gab of the pedestrians.

We soon lost each other in the confusion of the traffic as we walked across the top of Parnell Square to board the trams which would take us home or to a railway station for the short journey convenient to our homes. When I reached Dundrum, I was completely taken aback by the realisation of the narrowness of the space I returned to, by the closeness of our houses to each other and by the small amount of sky that could be glimpsed over the house tops or through the divisions between the detached houses. Everything was so different to that which I had left less than twelve hours ago. We were one island, indeed, but two vastly different worlds. The immensity of my experience suddenly appeared staggering and I wondered whether I would be able to give a coherent account to my friends of the wonders I had seen. However, I soon recovered my appetite for the work and the scenes which I had left behind four weeks previously.

During my absence in Connemara, the Cuala Industries moved from Merrion Square to 133 Lower Baggot Street, a spacious flat over the public offices of a busy building contractor's premises. The wide hall-door leading to the street was always open making it convenient for the customers. The new workrooms were large and airy with a combined sitting room/office for the Misses Yeats. We workers had the use of a large kitchen downstairs, nicely fitted out for meals, and a rest room.

Our previous customers and many new ones came here to visit us, and, in addition, Mr W B Yeats found the large embroidery room an ideal place for the occasional informal meeting with the casual author or playwright who requested an interview. Always early for appointments by fifteen or twenty minutes, he spent the waiting time chatting with Miss Lily about her embroidery in which he took a great interest.

In her absence, he would stand very erect at the end of the

large room, his shapely hands clasped behind his back, looking amusedly through the window down on the stream of traffic passing on the busy street below and listening to the ever present sounds. Presently he would unclasp his hands, leaving the left one where it lay palm outwards, fingers curled awaiting to be reunited with the right one again. Chanting or humming in an undertone he would start tapping out a rhythm on his trousers leg whilst composing or reshaping a new verse.

On one such occasion I was very excited to see Mr Robin Flower[24] enter. I knew him by sight and had knowledge of his great interest in the Irish language. Mr Flower came on behalf of a young author[25] who had just written a novel in Irish and needed help to have the manuscript accepted for publication. Mr Flower was loud in his praise of the work he recommended and he soon obtained Mr Yeats's promise to co-operate in the project. I was agog and thrilled at the conversation I overheard and at the probability that I would be able to read the book when it was published. Unfortunately, at this time Miss Lily's health[26] was causing her some anxiety and often was keeping her from the Industry for short periods, so I did not get the opportunity to tell her what I overheard. As soon as the book was published, I obtained it from our local library.

One day an ardent Gaelic Leaguer, who had adopted the kilt for everyday wear,[27] called to the Industry to enlist my help in fund-raising for the League. He was an entertaining talker and the Misses Yeats made him very welcome. He found a great many things to interest him at the Industry and he came often after his first visit. The Misses Yeats liked to hear him speak Irish and they were glad that I was able to speak to him in the native tongue.

The ease with which our visitors and customers could enter the new workrooms during the day was a great help to business. Foreign visitors came frequently during the tourist season. The embroidery department obtained a great deal of enquiries and commissions from the different government departments and we were also kept busy with Lodge banners for the Orange Lodge in Molesworth Street who were recommending our work to their different branches throughout the country.

The annual Christmas sale of work, hitherto held in a hired hall, now took place in our spacious workrooms in Baggot

Street. An ever increasing number of notable visitors attended. We also continued to have a stall at the Aonach held in the Mansion House on Dawson Street where it had been transferred from the Round Room of the Old Rotunda. From its inception in 1903, the Industry patronized all of the art exhibitions, including the Spring Show and the Horse Show held at the Royal Dublin Society in Ballsbridge.

After a further winter of study in our language classes, the Vocational Educational Department announced there would be additional scholarships to the Gaeltacht, a reward for the progress in Irish made by the former recipients. Second year scholarship pupils were sent to Rosmuc where the college was supervised by Pádraic Og O Conaire,[28] nephew of the scholar and author Sean Pádraic O Conaire whose quaint statue is to be seen in Galway's Eyre Square.

Rosmuc was the birthplace of these two famous men and it had a further distinction in having been the summer residence of Pádraic Pearse, of immortal memory, who went there to study and to perfect his knowledge of the Irish language. It was there that he wrote many short stories of soul-stirring beauty and pathos into which he wove the spirit of the people with their musical-sounding names and the manifold musical-sounding district names.

While I was lucky to win one higher scholarship, I was a little uneasy about asking for four weeks leave during our busy season; however, Miss Lily, always so considerate, solved the problem by suggesting that I should take a simple piece of work with me. I could work whilst having my annual holidays thus my absence would not be felt. She seemed to settle all our difficulties promptly and with great ease and the idea proved very satisfactory.

Now, in later years, I find I do not have many memories to record of my visit to Rosmuc; for the second time, I was not to become a member of a family group. I lived with several other young strangers in an unused house on Pádraic Og's property. His mother, helped by a local girl, looked after our wants. After breakfast, attended by the girl who was instructed not to speak any English to us, we left for school. We returned for our mid-day meal, a most appetising dinner prepared by Bean uí Chonaire in her own home situated a short distance from our house. After dinner I retired to my bedroom or to the out of

134

doors, to get on with the work I had promised to complete before returning.

I did not get to see or know much about the place. My recollection is of a small enclosed village with a good many small fertile patches here and there. There were trees and bushes of succulent texture and depth of colour, very uneven-shaped small dark lakes like deep holes in the road, bumpy roads and very pleasant, friendly people. The mail van went each morning and evening to the Maam Cross railway station to collect and dispatch the letters and parcels that kept us in touch with the outside world, the world from which we seemed cut off in this remote place.

I learned a number of nice, tidy phrases in Rosmuc. When I had the time and opportunity to chat with old Bean uí Chonaire, she explained some idioms to me. At the end of the course we returned by train from Maam Cross to Galway Station and then to Dublin passing through the places made familiar to us in Pearse's story '*Bríd na nAmhrán*'.[29]

Now that the Civil War was finally cleared up, we were much happier people. We could work with greater vigour to restore our native language. There were no surprises for me on my second return to Dublin from Connemara. At the Industry we continued to be busy. We got a sizable order from Australia secured for us by Mrs Lane-Poole, Miss Lily's cousin, who had been commissioned to furnish and to decorate the Government House for the new city of Canberra.[30] The House was to be opened by the Duke and Duchess of York, later King George VI and Queen Elizabeth.

In the embroidery section we embroidered and made up two bedspreads, one of which was of pale blue satin material patterned all over in a design composed of bunches of spring flowers made by Mrs Jack Yeats and embroidered by Miss Lily. The other, the masculine one, was designed by Mr Jack and was of red and blue shot silk. It was of abstract design with a jewelled crown in its composition. I embroidered this one and finished it with a wide hem of variegated stitches. Some hand-printed and coloured goods and some small embroidered pictures made the enjoyable order complete.

Since we opened our workshop in Baggot Street, the number of visitors calling daily never diminished. One day a very happy and excited young couple[31] from the Abbey

Theatre Players called to see Miss Lily to announce their engagement. While she was entering into their happiness, her maternal instinct remembered the meagre salaries paid by the Company and she said, 'Oh, you poor things, how will you live?' Continuing her soliloquy, she said, 'Oh love, I suppose'. The young girl with great spirit and determined courage said, 'Oh, we'll manage', and there was much laughter between them.

They had come together to show their admiration and affection for Miss Lily by making her almost the first recipient of their glad news. Such was the feeling and admiration that people had for a very charming lady and, no doubt of late, they had missed her regular attendance at the Theatre. As months passed, unfortunately her health did not improve; yet, she continued to come to the Industry. Mr W B Yeats was trying to encourage her to embroider some large drawings of an artist he had recently met and of whose work he had a very high opinion.

We now used mercerised cotton thread[32] in our work instead of silk. England had imposed a high tax on all articles that used silk. They collected tax on the full value of the finished article irrespective of the amount of silk used. As we were now a separate country, we had to submit to taxes imposed on our goods. The mercerised cotton, manufactured in Scotland, was a delight to handle and very easy to divide into finer thread when necessary for light work. It was made in every conceivable colour in unlimited shades; it was sun proof and could stand up to endless washings. It gave us new ideas, and we enjoyed the change which, at first sight, appeared to create big problems.

During this year our language class grew in strength and we had numerous outings and concerts. Enthusiastic young Gaelic Leaguers came from the city and the surrounding districts to help at our concerts and exhibitions. They were seeking stage practice, hoping one day to make a name for themselves in public theatre. They were successful in this and today many are famous as dancers, singers and instrumentalists. They were all very young boys and girls then who gave their talents for free and helped fill our coffers with cash so as to enable our branch of the League to spend more money for awarding additional scholarships to those Departmental ones to Connemara.

We extended our picnics and outings to faraway historic

places like Clonmacnoise, Newgrange, Dunsink and the Hill of Tara. Closer to home, we went by train to Carrickmines Station to walk by fields and roadways to seek out and study the ancient monuments located in different places on the way to the Scalp near Enniskerry. We generally walked back to Dundrum as the roadway was all downhill.

My first air flight was an important event. Larry, the brother I had left behind in Liverpool at the beginning of the first World War, was now a Customs and Excise officer and about to be married.[33] On one of my regular visits, he took me on a trip to Southport one Saturday afternoon to see an aeronautical display. On this occasion the young air force were giving the public an exhibition of looping the loop, smoke screen messages, acrobatic tricks and landing and taking off from the very wide seashore.

Presently, they offered the public a short air trip at the cost of £1 per two passengers with the money going to an agreed on charity. At first they did not get many volunteers as one or other of the couples watching the display was too frightened to venture. Larry longed to go on the plane, so I agreed to go with him. We climbed up a short ladder to the open cockpit to sit beside the pilot.

An official closed and fastened the door which appeared to form a collar-like opening that left the tops of our heads free above it. By looking straight ahead we could see the houses and gardens and the sea below us, but we could see nothing beneath us. I remember thinking that the plane was shaped like a bullet, but I have no recollection of its having wings.

During our short flight, we had the horrible experience of feeling that we were dropping down into a bottomless pit. Then, with a slight shudder - as though we had reached a straight path - we were sailing smoothly again. On alighting and thinking the pilot had made an attempt at looping the loop while we were in the air, I questioned him about it. He smiled and said no, that we had been in an air pocket. The flight left a horrible impression on me and as Larry did not discuss it, I gather he did not like his first trip either.

In 1927, the Gaelic college was in Carraroe in Connemara. It was a glorious holiday but once again I was not to become a member of an Irish-speaking family group. This time I was placed with my own school friends and a few strangers in a spacious, isolated bungalow surrounded by small trees and bushes. A woman came each morning to prepare breakfast and stayed to cook our dinner while we were at school. In the evening after tea she left for home. It was a very exciting experience for the younger girls. After the first two weeks, we had a change of pupils because they had been awarded scholarships for only a fortnight and had to leave and make room for a second batch of pupils.

I found myself left without a companion and thought I would be very lonely; instead, I enjoyed walking about myself. I enjoyed the freedom to walk where I wished and not have to go where my companions wished. I brought my bicycle so during the second fortnight, after school hours, I explored the surroundings.

One afternoon when I was cycling on the main road towards Rosmuc,[34] I noticed a side road that was smooth and firm like the main road but almost hidden from view by bushes and small trees. I dismounted from my bicycle and walked along the road to find that it led to an inlet of the sea over which a half bridge was built. Looking down over the bridge wall which terminated in a natural-looking harbour, I saw hundreds or more jellyfish of varying sizes and colours lying - I should say standing - side by side, closely packed from wall to wall like a seamless carpet. They were motionless except for the sea's wave which rocked gently up and down toward the edge that extended out of sight under the bridge.

To me, all alone, it was an amazing and almost terrifying sight to see such a gigantic number of living creatures looking as though they had been hypnotised. I felt a shudder of fear as I looked down on that living mass. Suppose an unseen hand tipped me over the parapet? What would I do? I would not be able to extricate myself and I certainly would have been stung to death. I hurried along from the place and did not meet with anyone to whom I could relate my experience or whom I could take to see the sight.

On another afternoon, I saw a picturesque little bungalow approached by a wide short avenue and lined on both sides with a wonderful variety of hydrangea bushes laden with massive flowers in shades of pink, blue, mauve and pale green. I enjoyed these solitary outings in the stillness of the place where one could recall the poet's words 'seeing a world in a grain of sand and a heaven in a wild flower'.

During the summer we were taken on a trip to the Aran Islands in a locally-owned turfboat. While going over the sea in a sailing vessel on a bright sunny day, it was a wonderful experience to watch the young boys adroitly tighten or unloosen the sails as they were ordered by the captain. On our return journey we had the thrill of being in a race and it was exciting to see the sails being maneuvered to get the most out of the wind. I was not on the winning boat.

That summer I caused a little excitement by reading aloud from my newspaper that came to me by post daily from the *Irish Independent* that Dev and his party had entered the Dáil[35] and had taken their seats in Leinster House, the home of the Free State government. The unexpected news was a bombshell to most of his followers who were present and I took a secret, fiendish delight in watching their facial expressions and hearing their reaction to the news. Some scoffed at the idea; others, incredulous, said, 'Dev would never do that'. Alas, their idol had feet of clay after all.

I returned to my work hoping the next eleven months would pass quickly so that I could return to that haven of bliss once more. At the Industry I was engrossed in embroidering a beautiful Morris-style design by Mrs Jack Yeats. It was roses and carnations on a silk shawl that was destined, when finished, for Australia. There was no hurry about the order so that I could, and did, do other jobs between times. An American widow millionairess,[36] who travelled over to Europe at least twice a year, visited Dublin and found our type of embroidery pleasing to her taste. She gave the Industry many orders for linen ware which often required an elaborate design of her monogram, intermingled with species of flowers in which she was interested. She never failed to call on us when she was in Dublin.

Aonach Tailteann Art Exhibition.

Dear Sir or Madam,

        I have pleasure in informing you that you have been awarded a medal in your class at the above exhibition.

        You are requested to attend the opening of the exhibition on Monday, 6th. inst., at 11-45.   His Excellency the Governor-General will perform the opening ceremony at 12 o'clock sharp.

                        Secretary.

Letter informing Sara that she had won the Tailteann medal

CHAPTER NINE

(1928-1933)

Tailteann Games - The wireless - Calary Point to Point - Sara wins a Tailteann medal - Irish college in Tully - Connemara dress - Colmcille tradition - Basket-making - Household crafts - Spinning - Red petticoats - Movies come to Cois Farraige - Sara wins another Tailteann medal - Lily Yeats's health worsens - Eucharistic Congress - Funeral in Ballynahoun - Matchmaking - Cuala Stations of the Cross - Belfast exhibition, 1931 - Lily retires from Cuala - Lolly Yeats - Death of Annie Hyland - Cuala visitors.

The end of 1927 brought the Christmas sale of work in the Baggot Street workrooms and the annual Aonach in the Mansion House. Those completed, we held our own Christmas tea party for the giving and receiving of presents between the Misses Yeats and their staff. Having arranged the holiday period for the remainder of the festive season, we closed down until the new year of 1928.

The new year was an eventful one. The freedom we now enjoyed enabled us to take part in the revival of the Tailteann Games[1] held, as was customary, every four years. The old traditions were studiously followed to recapture and to perpetuate some of our ancient culture and to encourage those who were proud of their Irish heritage. There were nation-wide competitions and exhibitions in arts and crafts and music and drama, and there were tests of skill and endurance throughout the country in every branch of sport. Prizes were awarded for successful competitors. There was also a week-long tattoo in Croke Park and other events to enjoy with friends and overseas visitors.

With his Christmas money, my brother purchased a crystal wireless set early in 1928. It consisted of a pair of headphones and a small, shallow, oblong box that contained a few fine wires. In the centre of the lid was a slight hollow containing a piece of rough crystal and a tiny piece of flexible wire called a 'cat's whisker'. The whole lot was embedded in an easy-to-manipulate midget cylinder. When the cat's whisker touched a sensitive spot on the crystal, the sound broadcasted by Dublin 2RN[2] came into the set loud and clear - with the help of an aerial and a ground connection. It was a small medium indeed, but one capable of great development.

The great disadvantage to the pastime of listening to the wireless was that the participant became virtually a manacled prisoner during the broadcast and was often frustrated by the live crystal spot weakening and fading out. It was then necessary for the listener to search frantically with the cat's whisker for a new connection while the headphones seemed to increase in weight as they slipped about with every movement of the listener. Sometimes, in order to maintain the programme, the crystal had to be removed and a spot chipped off to expose a live spot of mica. Absolute quiet was essential to the listener and this was difficult in a small, busy household such as ours.

Somehow I did manage to hear a few programmes. One I never forgot was an episode in the Irish language *Gobán Saor* series. It was so distinctive that I understood and remembered it for a long time afterwards. The story is a fascinating one about the old craftsman being gifted with the wisdom of Solomon but it loses much of its magic when it is translated into English. On the occasion when I listened to the story on the wireless, I was fortunate to be alone in the house. Generally, I would say that the crystal set was not worth the trouble except for the wonder that such a small medium was capable of so much. It was not long before the crystal wireless was replaced by a larger, more complicated affair called a battery set which had a loudspeaker so that people in the vicinity could hear the programme whilst continuing with their work.

One spring weekend my friend Kate and I set out by bicycle to the Calary Point to Point races. I stayed at Kate's house in South County Dublin so that we could set off early in the morning with lunches and tea packed in light, waterproof wear which we brought in case of a mountain mist or a light snowfall. We put these in carrier seats in a pilgrim basket. We found a new way to reach the field by cycling through the Glen o' the Downs and turning right at Jamesons' corner. It was much shorter and offered a less crowded hill to climb. Of course we missed the togetherness and fun that takes place on the trek of the long hill, the main approach to the field taken by pleasure seekers from Dublin and the surrounding district.

Calary was a glorious place to be on a bright spring morning with the vastness of natural beauty invaded for one day by happy, excited, carefree people. Old friends were re-united and beribboned horses trotted around for examination and admiration, and there was whispered tipping of winners. There were also fences worth watching for jumping skills and spills, ballad singers, three-card tricksters, hoop-la, Aunt Sally, and coal braziers burning brightly and clearly. Bookmakers called out their prices to the punters. Everybody moved about in search of friends or to try their skills at the amusement marquee. When the last race was called, there was a general bustle among the crowd preparing for the long road home with their pleasant memories to carry them forward to the next year.

At the Industry I completed the silk shawl designed by Mrs Jack Yeats and it was entered in the Art Section of the Dublin Horse Show held in Ballsbridge and for which silver or bronze medals were awarded. The medals were imprinted with a classical drawing of the head and shoulders of the ancient Irish queen Tailte in whose honour the games and competitions took place in olden times. I am the proud owner of one of the bronze medals, second place in the costumed figure section for the first revival of the Tailteann Games of 1924.[3]

The work for the Irish language continued in our evening classes and I continued my interest. We had our ups and downs in the classes, including some losses, as the result of introducing politics into a two-side or divided party. That generally led to much bitterness.

Our summer school that year was held at Tully, Ballinahoun,[4] the continuation westward of the parish where we first had our college. We travelled there from Dublin in a fleet of privately-owned buses that had previously carried us from the Galway railway station to our holiday homes in Connemara. Going all the way by road was an exciting change.

In Tully, on my fourth visit to Connemara, I was delighted to become a member of a family unit at last. Our house was a spacious one beside Loch na Cruimhinne on Cloughmore, Tully, Ballynahoun. Five young girls and I set off late one night from the Tully Schoolhouse. We walked, stumbling and struggling uphill in silence and wonderment, making our way over the uneven ground which seemed endless until we reached a house beside the lake. A large turf fire was burning on the hearth and kettles of boiling water were singing to the chirping accompaniment of the crickets - my first time to hear them. A large table was set with home-made soda bread, butter and jam for our supper. We were shown our rooms where we removed our coats and had a wash up before sitting down to the table. Apart from ourselves, the house seemed deserted.

The bean a'tighe, helped by her daughter, looked after us in silence. We were shy and tired and they seemed bewildered by us. Our hostess's decision to accept 'scholars' was a late and rather sudden one; consequently, family life was disorganized for a couple of days after our arrival. I noticed that the tea was let boil a little before being removed from the heat. I disliked boiled tea, so when the *bean a'tighe* poured a little tea in my cup, I raised my hand saying, *'Is leor sin'*.[5] She continued to fill my cup with tea. I wondered what was wrong with my Irish that I had not been understood.

From sheer exhaustion and good air I slept soundly that night to awaken early next morning to see and hear the lake water lapping on the large stones that were between the gable end of the house and the lake. What could have been more romantic or more of a change from my home in Dundrum. Since it was Sunday, we set out after breakfast to walk to Mass accompanied by the youngest member of the family as our guide.

When we reached the larger boreen, we were on a height that gave us a view of the distant main road as well as the road from the north which formed the crossroads near the schoolhouse. Looking down on those roads, I saw a pattern of groups walking to church that was familiar to me from reading *Iosagán*[6] by Pádraic Pearse.

We saw barefoot little girls in their Sunday dresses talking and running excitedly around each other and older girls linked arm-in-arm whispering so not as to be overheard. Women in brilliant petticoats and patterned shawls, with smaller head shawls, walked slowly in small groups gossiping stopping now and again to explain a point in their conversation.

Little boys in bawneens and long grey trousers silently tried to keep in step with the older boys who used their arms like propellers to swing themselves along quickly so that the younger ones had to break into a trot in order to keep up. The old men, who left home early, sat on the stone walls outside the church smoking their pipes and waiting for the priest to arrive.

When we reached the church we went inside immediately. The first couple of rows had been left, in politeness, for the 'scholars'. The older and more feeble parishioners took their places in the back rows. The door faced the sea and that day it was wide open during the Mass. Other days it was closed if the wind was blowing in from that direction and the opposite door was opened. That was the same arrangement that applied to all the houses in Connemara.

After our dinner our little guide brought us to the sea shore and there the Atlantic in all its majesty lay before us. She called the place Trá an Tobair[7] and told us that it took its name from St Colmcille's Well which she pointed out to us. The huge stone, shaped like a boat, was also of interest. The local people believed firmly in the legend of those two stories.

According to folklore, St Colmcille stood in the boat-shaped stone when he was being harassed by his enemies on the Aran Islands. The stone moved miraculously out to sea with him and brought him safely to the mainland at Tully. Legend tells us that Colmcille laid his hands on the well-stone when he stepped out of the miraculous boat. Ever since, there is always fresh water in the hollow of the stone.[8]

Our house was a spacious, low building with a loft at one end that could be used as a bedroom which was reached from the kitchen by a moveable ladder. There were numerous outhouses and a barn opposite the house in a cobble-stone, oblong yard which was enclosed by a wide iron gate with stone piers and a stile beside the gateway.

There were four boys and two girls under the age of twenty in the family. Along with their parents, they left the house to us and made a temporary home for themselves in the barn and outhouses. It was a few days before we became acquainted with the family. Then they started to come into the kitchen each night to recite the family rosary and they stayed afterwards to talk with us.

Tully was an ideal place to hold a scholarship course. The schoolhouse was situated near the crossroads, close to the main road that led east to Galway city, west to Casla Bay, south to Ballynahoun and the seaside and northwest to Clifden. There was ample accommodation for students and their friends.

Our principal teacher was the local National School teacher[9] who knew all the local people and therefore made us feel like one large family. Before our arrival the people resolved that they would make a success of the summer school by helping us in every way toward our gaining proficiency in the language and in understanding local traditions. We were encouraged to take part in their daily lives.

We went to the bog after school hours to watch the cutting and stacking of turf, to learn the names of the various implements and the reason that turf was stacked in a particular way. We learned that turf cut in the present year would not be used until the following year or even later.

We learned, too, about basket-making. The panniers carried by the donkeys were made of sally rods that grew in profusion beside the lake. They drew a circle on a smooth patch of ground, usually beside the lake, and the strongest staves were inserted upright to a particular depth evenly around the circle. The *fear a' tighe* sitting on a low stool which he moved as he worked wove the strong staves together with a lighter one made flexible by steeping it in water. When the required depth was reached, the upright staves were folded over a strong rim woven close towards the centre to make a firm indestructible base. The basket was then removed from the ground to plait the uprights into a smooth firm opening. If the basketmaker wanted a white basket or a potato strainer, the sally rods were boiled and peeled before working them into shape. These industrious people made full use of all that nature provided.

The *fear a' tighe* fished in the sea from the rocks at dawn using hooks and lines. The fresh mackerel grilled on tongs over the hot coals made a tasty breakfast. Rockfish and haddock were also plentiful and any fish not used the day it was taken from the sea was dried for later use.

Seaweed for fertilising the fields was gathered at low tide as was carrigeen growing as nature intended it - close to the shore in a small pool. One bright and sunny afternoon, when the tide was suitable, I was directed to the enchanted spot. The tide had gone out leaving its edge quietly rocking the plants in the pool. Removing my shoes and stockings and folding my skirts into my waistband, I was able to step into the water which reached my knees.

Mosses of different growth, texture and colour grew on the rocks and the warm sand between them, sparkling in the sunlight, was covered with minute particles of various coloured sea shells which presented a picture of a magic garden in a confined space. Carrigeen is dark red while growing. After harvesting when it is spread on the headland to dry, it bleaches and becomes brittle. Before cooking, it is steeped in water. When boiled in milk, it makes a firm jelly.

Sunsets in this wide open space, with neither tall buildings nor trees to interrupt the view, were another joy. While they were always beautiful, the difference between them was not great. Occasionally, nature showed its versatility and produced something of staggering beauty. One evening, as I sat in my usual place beside the gate pier watching the sunset, the horizon appeared to explode sending shafts of the rainbow's seven colours all over the sky. The white clouds over my head became floating masses of rose pink that reflected brilliantly on the lake water where the colour intensified rising to flood the whitewashed cottages and bushes with a rosy light. Meanwhile the sun became a deep orange ball emitting shades of yellow and blue that stretched far and wide across the evening sky. The yellow became paler and paler till it turned a soft green and finally silver. Surely, I had seen 'heaven's embroidered cloths'[10] that W B Yeats immortalized in his poetry. It was the most spectacular sunset I had ever seen and it brought to mind the words 'Thy glory fills all Heaven and Earth'.

Another evening, sitting in the same place at dusk, I was startled to see a huge column of moths rising into the night air from the loose stone wall that bordered the boreen. They rose silently as if answering a command and they kept their formation, which stretched a considerable distance, until they vanished from my sight into the darkness above. I wondered whether they were part of the army that would later invade the houses to flutter about the lighted lamps. Did they visit the same house and what was their purpose? The moths were a perfect weather guide for us, for if they were so numerous as to black out the lamp light, the next day would be wet. No one ever thought of 'shuffing' them off as the firelight was sufficient to illuminate the whole house.

Another mystery to unravel was the noise of the crickets around the fireplace without actually seeing one. I was told one night to wait until after the light was extinguished and the house was quiet. I stole into the kitchen and shone my electric torch on the chimney breast. What a sight! There were hundreds of long-bodied insects who, seeing the light, rushed madly to escape back into their hiding place through tiny holes that looked no bigger than pinpoints in the plaster of the chimney breast. The family of the house would not have dreamed of interfering with any of these creatures.

Every member of the household was busy from morning to night with household chores. The *bean a' tighe* was ever cooking, churning, knitting, or spinning sheep's wool into yarn. It looked so simple that I longed to try to do it. Alas, I did not manage it as the spinning wheel was very old and it wobbled a bit at each rotation. The spinner was so familiar with the wheel that her hand yielded to each wobble as she held the wool and thus was able to produce an even thread. When a certain amount was spun, the thread was measured by winding it around a large wooden square frame that held pegs or hooks in each of its four corners. The required length was then sent to the local weaver who made the yarn into cloth on his hand loom.

Before the thread for the red petticoats[11] worn by the women went to the weaver, it was dyed from a household recipe that was handed down from one generation to another. When the petticoat was made, it was finished with a row of black braid above the hem line. I remember being told on my first visit to Connemara that the wealth of a family could be told according to the number of rows of braid worn by the *bean a' tighe*, but I never inquired whether there was any truth in it.

One day a travelling entertainment company moving from Galway city to Clifden stopped at our school and left some of their party to put on a show that evening after school. They erected a small marquee with stage and seating accommodation on long, low forms. When opening time arrived, the place filled quickly with students and local youths. Those who were refused admission because of overcrowding found their way in by lifting out some of the tie down pegs and crawling in under the canvas.

The programme opened with a cinematic picture and when the signature MGM lion flashed on the screen giving its 'Yap, Yap,' a local youth shouted, '*Oh, feicigí ar an madra mór*'.[12] Some of the audience thinking a big dog had entered the tent stood up to see it thereby blotting out the screen. As they rose higher and higher, only a small part of the screen top was visible and it showed the silhouetted heads of the gapers.

There was lots of laughter by those who realized that the boy thought the MGM lion was alive and just a big dog. With so much confusion, the canvas seemed about to burst, so most of us got out quickly so as not to be entangled in the canvas when the crash came. Afterwards, those who stayed were treated to an entertainment of conjuring tricks, songs and dances.

Toward the end of our summer term, we students organized a Sunday afternoon of games and sports for the local people in appreciation of all the help they had given us. There was a great deal of talent among the students and the local people and it was a beautiful day. The pleasure of the old people was a joy to behold. They were wild with excitement watching bouts of tug-of-war, potato and spoon races, three-legged and sack races and other spontaneous activities.

The postman called to the National School each day with letters and parcels. During the last week of my stay he brought me an unexpected surprise - a registered packet from Miss Lily that contained a first prize, silver Tailteann medal engraved with my name and that of the Industry. The silk shawl designed by Mrs Jack Yeats and embroidered by me had won first prize in its section. I am sure Miss Lily wanted my Irish language friends to know of my success and to see the beauty of the medal awarded for work well done.

We very reluctantly left Tully at the end of the term, for it was such an ideal place; however, we were assured by our teachers that the course would be held there again. Returning to Dublin to take up our work again was no longer a problem. We viewed it as a necessary evil to be endured in the interval between our yearly visits to Connemara. I had many stories to retell of that summer but, alas, we were sad and upset by Miss Lily's frequent absences for health reasons.[13] Miss Lolly took over the management of our embroidery department[14] and we were kept busy executing familiar orders, but our parties and outings were reduced to a humdrum minimum.

Sara's first prize silver Tailteann medal

The following year Dublin city was the center of activity when the Catholic Church celebrated the centenary of its emancipation.[15] Services were held in every church throughout the country and these culminated in a Sunday afternoon ceremony on O'Connell Bridge that was attended by thousands. General Eoin O'Duffy[16] won acclaim for his organizing skills and the press played its part by publishing details of assembly points for parishes and instructions for people planning to attend. Details were also given regarding the hymn singing, prayers and manner of departure. Everything went like clockwork, with suitable decorum, and those taking part felt that they had been re-baptised and that a bright future lay before them.

The following months were filled with the usual rounds of work and pleasure until it came time for the annual scholarship trip to Connemara. I was beginning to feel ashamed of my eagerness to compete with my fellow Irish language workers who, by this time, were much younger, but I wanted so much to return to Ballynahoun to visit the delightful family where I stayed the previous year and where I felt there was still so much to learn.

I received a hearty welcome from the family when I returned and I took up the threads where I had left off. I was only with them that year for two weeks as I already had an extended Easter holiday to attend my brother Larry's wedding in England. During my first summer in Ballynahoun the problem of no fresh vegetables other than potatoes and onions had been a vexation, but the second summer there was a small garden plot near the house with a variety of vegetables. The carrots were the juciest I ever tasted, and the green peas which grew in profusion were perfectly succulent.

One afternoon on my way back from school the *bean a' tighe* met me on the main boreen to take me with her to a wake and funeral. The house of the deceased neighbour was a short distance from us on *Bóthar na Trá*. When we reached the house, the men were seated in groups on the low stone walls surrounding the house and the women were gathered in the large kitchen where the corpse was 'waked' in her coffin in a very spectacular way.

The coffin rested on a heavily-draped table under a niche or window recess that was also heavily curtained with white material to form a pelmet which looped in the centre with full side pieces falling to the ground. The whole effect was that of a crib or a shrine. The corpse, very small and dainty, was clothed in white with a frilled mob-cap that showed up her waxen face and grey hair. A few small white posies and some lighted candles had been placed on the table.

The neighbouring women were seated closely against the walls while the younger ones squatted on the floor in front of them. A neighbour woman helping the bereaved family handed around some snuff on tea plates and each woman took a pinch of snuff which she liberally applied to each nostril. Later the women were each served a drink of poteen from a large, narrow jug. It was poured into a cup or glass which was passed from person to person to drink as much or as little as they liked. When the glass was nearly empty, the dregs were tossed back into the jug and the glass was refilled to serve the next person until all the mourners had taken some of the poteen.

When the parish priest was seen approaching, a great silence fell on the house. We all stood when he entered with his usual blessing to all present. After speaking some words of condolence with the family, he recited some prayers and left the house accompanied by one of the members who had arranged a table and some chairs in the yard.

Now I learned the meaning of 'making a wake' in these remote parts of Ireland. The priest stood at the table with the son of the house and thanked each individual as he came forward to place his money offering on the table, each giving as much as he could afford. The money, so given, was for the benefit of the priest as there was not a collection at Sunday Masses. I don't know what other collections were made for the support of the clergy.[17]

The wake in the house having concluded, the funeral procession got under way to the burial ground. On leaving the house, each member of the family, in order of seniority, contributed a loud wailing lamentation, a 'keen for the dead',[18] giving a list of the successes and valiant deeds of the departed one now sadly missed. The dirge continued, without any repetition of deeds accomplished by the deceased, all the way in the slow-moving procession until we reached the graveyard, a stony spot almost on the seashore, enclosed by cement-built walls and an iron gateway. The coffin was laid in a grave which consisted of stones, stones and still more stones.

On this visit to Ballynahoun I was allowed a little insight into matchmaking which was a serious undertaking and very desirable and commendable in those remote places where contact between boys and girls ends with school leaving. A lot of loving care was exercised in the practice and persuasion without force was strongly used. The intending couple were always consulted and satisfactory and happy marriages were the outcome.

When I returned to Dublin we had big changes in the moving pictures when sound was introduced so that performers spoke or sang their parts. It added greatly to the entertainment value. A further amenity was a daily motor bus from Dundrum to the city and back.

Miss Lily's health improved and she resumed her regular attendance at the Industry. She was embroidering large pictures of Saint Colmcille writing in his book of prophecies[19] and of Saint Francis surrounded by birds. Both were drawings done by Mr Jack for the collection previously used as sodality banners. The banners were embroidered by Miss Lily and her staff at Dun Emer for presentation to the Loughrea Cathedral by Edward Martyn, a wealthy patron of the arts and a constant visitor to Dun Emer in its early days of 1903.

Miss Lily was happy doing this type of work and she discussed the possibility of building up a collection of embroidery pictures with Mrs W B Yeats who lived nearby at Fitzwilliam Square. Yeats had recently met an artist whose work he admired[20] and he thought he could obtain designs from her. Our wealthy American patroness[21] on her yearly visit to Rome saw the pictures and on her return journey through Dublin she asked to have a set of the familiar fourteen Stations of the Cross embroidered on Irish poplin of old gold colour. They were to be similar in size to the banner drawings and they were to be ready for her to take back to America the following year where they would be mounted and framed.

Mr W B Yeats commissioned a young Dublin artist, the daughter of an artist father, to make the drawings which he presented to Miss Lily. The pictures were beautifully drawn and although of such a sombre theme, the young artist managed to get a great deal of feeling into such a painful journey. There were even a few tiny flowerheads peeping occasionally through the rough stones on the way, as though offering their sympathy.

We workers never failed to be impressed by the manner in which Miss Lily, as she worked them, placed each picture on the floor or on the table at a distance to make sure that she was getting her stitches in the direction most suitable for the effect she wished to obtain. The embroidery cotton which we used was ideal for working on poplin and with its many colours, blending to fulfill the artist's expressions was much simplified.

With the difficulty of Customs and Excise regulations operating between Ireland and England and with her health problems, Miss Lily had not visited her English friends and

Industry patrons for some time. Boxes of our products were sent by parcel post to some of her friends who took a lot of trouble to conduct sales in her absence. One of those friends who had connections in Northern Ireland arranged to have a week-long exhibition and sale in Belfast during the autumn of 1931 and with a senior worker from the printing department I was selected to take charge of the embroideries.

It was an experience and an awkward adventure to have our handiwork examined at Goraghwood[22] and at the Free State's Customs Department on the return journey and at Dundalk, a short distance away, similar formalities were imposed. It was a horrible, frustrating barrier in a small island that should have been left as one unit if complete justice had been done to the memory of those Irishmen who had sacrificed their lives for its independence.

Our visit to Northern Ireland was a profitable one for the Industry and a pleasant working holiday for us as we were able to see some of the beautiful scenery and to enjoy the everyday lives of our compatriots during our two long week-ends. The family with whom we lodged was happy and care free and did not bother about politics or religion or any goings-on outside their own house. To some of us in the South, the partition of our country was a crime, but to England, by keeping a grip on part of Ireland meant that her national flag, the Union Jack, could still fly as her emblem in other parts of the world.

During 1931, Miss Lily worked on the American order for the fourteen pictures comprising the Stations of the Cross. When questioned by one of her staff as to which picture had the most appeal for her, she replied, without hesitation, 'Number Six'.[23] It was typical of her own gracious character to admire a woman who so compassionately gave all she could, as she herself would have done, in giving a towel to the Saviour of mankind to wipe his bespattered face on that terrible journey.

While she worked on the Stations, it became obvious that Miss Lily would not be able to continue with her work. It had been necessary for her to take rest periods before completing the set. She finished the Stations, and this unique set, somewhere in America, is a tribute to the young artist who designed them and the older artist who embroidered them. It was Miss Lily's last work in the Industry, for at the end of the year, complying with her doctor's instructions, she very reluctantly decided to close her embroidery department.

When the decision was made to close, each worker as she finished her last item left the Industry to take up other employment thus avoiding an abrupt end to a very pleasant living. May and I as the senior workers stayed on to finish the orders that were there and to fill those orders likely to come in until it was known that Miss Lily had retired owing to ill health.

Miss Lolly moved some of her hand-pressed finished items into the spacious room where her workers continued with the hand colouring of wall prints and Christmas greeting cards which were mostly exported to America. Miss Lolly also undertook the correspondence dealing with the embroidery orders. Her letter writing had always been a wonderment to us workers and the vast amount she got through in her large script must have covered reams and reams of paper.

In this aspect and in her slim figure she resembled Mr Jack but her stiff, unyielding attitude and quick temper[24] was similar to that of Mr W B Miss Lily had the soft placid character of Mr Jack and resembled the poet, whom she admired very much, in appearance. There was a great bond of friendship between Miss Lily and Mr W B Yeats.

I worked some months into 1932 when my mother became ill and it was necessary for me to stay home and attend her. After a brief illness, she passed away meeting death in the valiant way she had instilled in her children.[25] She was happy that she had known the joy of experiencing the Eucharistic Congress in Dublin - a truly fitting end to a well-spent life.

Shortly after my mother's death I returned to work at the Industry and was kept busily employed for a number of years. Except for the depletion in the number of workers and the absence of Miss Lily, it was like old times to be surrounded by printed sheets straight from the handpress in the next room as they awaited completion. Once again we could read and memorise verses and poems which kept our minds occupied as we silently worked the embroidery stitches.

Unlike Mimi in *La Bohème*, I did not regret that the flowers had no perfume, because when drawn by Mrs Jack or with the master touch of William Morris, they had all the beauty necessary to satisfy. Miss Lily paid occasional visits to the Industry when her health improved and she seldom missed the opening of the Royal Academy or any other big art display.

Eileen Colum, the poet's sister, spent a lot of her working hours in this room with us. She had a fund of knowledge of all the literary giants in Dublin past and present and was a good talker. She told us of their houses, entertaining eccentricities, successes and mistakes in an amusing and an unspiteful way.

American visitors continued to call when on a travelling holiday. Some were customers of long standing who had stacks of Miss Lolly's lengthy letters written over the years which had described Dublin and some of its citizens. They spent many leisure hours browsing over our exhibits possibly hoping to meet an Irish notable. Often their patience was rewarded for we had a number of unexpected callers each day.

One visitor, idly chatting, suddenly said, 'How would you spend the Irish Hospitals Sweep money if you were lucky to win it?' The question was so unexpected that none of us was inclined to answer it. Fortunately, at that moment, one of our weekly street musicians with his moth-eaten barrel organ struck up its out-of-season tune, the Christmas hymn, 'Adeste Fideles' which he played at a galloping speed. It was followed by 'Come Back to Erin' at an even greater gallop. One of the workers, on hearing it, said, 'I would go out and buy that appalling organ and make a bonfire of it'. I feel sure the questioner often told that story back in the States as a quick-witted Irish reply. She certainly enjoyed the answer as a huge joke.

CHAPTER TEN

(1933 - 1938)

Sad changes at Cuala - Lily's retirement - Change of government - Working at the Dundrum polling station - James Dillon - Patrick McGilligan - W B Yeats's health - Rose Hodgins - Irish Army flags.

When I returned to the Industry after the death of my mother the atmosphere was very different and I felt life was unreal and desolate. I had so recently lost my mother; Miss Lily was absent, and May, my lifelong workmate and dear friend, had to stay home to nurse her mother through a very tedious illness. On the advice of the doctor, May left the Industry, for she was not able to give any time even to the smallest item.

The large embroidery room was partly taken over by Miss Lolly for the colouring of wall prints and for Christmas cards. I was finishing off the orders that had kept May and me busy since Miss Lily's retirement. Miss Lily in her loneliness kept herself busy by reading, knitting small garments for the poor and doing pieces of embroidery. She looked forward eagerly to visitors and luckily they were many and varied. Some of her friends with motor cars took her for drives through the country lanes which she loved. Other times she visited Mr W B at his house in Rathfarnham.

May and I visited her frequently to keep her informed of our work and recreation. My absorption into politics amused her. Because of her lifelong interest in our education, her real interest was finding out how much I knew of the system of proportional representation under which our government was elected. She wanted to instruct me and to explain points of interest if necessary.

Fortunately, I was fascinated by the system and had satisfied myself of its intricacy by reading the many articles that always appeared in the newspapers when an election was in the offing. There were those who were vehemently against proportional representation saying that it had been imposed on us by Britain. Others, who were in the majority, favored the system. I was in favour of PR.

After the general election of 1932, we had a change of government which I disliked and feared. The new leader,[1] in my opinion, was like a fussy old hen who having got possession of a well-built nest looked at it with a jaundiced eye and decided that it would have to be torn apart and rebuilt to her taste leaving as little of the foundation as possible. That could be dealt with at a later date.

First, her chicks had to get a golden claw-shake, so that when she would 'cluck, cluck', they would come running to her bringing their relations and friends. The bigger the following, the better. Quantity not quality was what mattered most. I had my own opinion about how the quantity was obtained. It would be good for the work that had to be done to blot out all traces of the heroic deeds and acts executed under very difficult circumstances by the country's former builders and architects. The mythical stepping stones suggested by Michael Collins and followed by warm-hearted Irishmen were first on the destruction list. The written words known as the Constitution had to be altered to open doors that were tightly closed against non-nationals securing high positions in the government of the country.

As I was always deeply interested in politics, I kept my mind busy with daily events and speculated about the future. I thoroughly enjoyed the excitement of my first working election day, the outcome of which was so wrapped up in mystery. There was a great deal for me to learn. I had lately been encouraged to take an active part working for a political party during the election. I put all my mind and strength in this. Being a local person, I was well acquainted with all the workers and most of the voting public and this was necessary to make a success of my usefulness.

I enjoyed the frayed tempers and petty squabbles on polling day. They provided good material for recalling later. Having read all the official instructions to make sure of points appertaining to the different function of the day, I found it very uplifting to be in a position to point out to my opposite number or to a bumptious official that their actions were not in accordance with the written instructions provided for their guidance. Obviously, they had not read them and were prepared to brush aside complaints as minor trivialities unless there was an efficient party agent present.

Election day began with the poker-like stiffness of officialdom, the regular established ones working silently putting paper and seals in order for the day's work and the newcomers opening wrong packets and trying to do too many things at the same time while feverishly hoping that their clumsiness was not noticeable.

The presiding officer for each polling booth was obliged to obtain signed secrecy and appointment forms from each party agent wishing to sit at his table during the day to protect the candidates' interests. There were a very intricate network of rules to protect equally the observers, the public and the officiating officers.

The voting place assumed a prison-like austerity for the day. Large notices of warnings, penalties and byelaws were posted outside the building and the place was policed by guards. Mirth was restrained, voices hushed and friendship dropped to zero. Suspicious glances were cast on every action of the opposition party by their counterpart. Advances were quietly accepted or completely refused according to the character of the person approached; each regarding the other as an enemy to be avoided, at least for that day.

The work became monotonous as the morning wore on and we gladly welcomed the first meal break. The party helpers outside the building rivalled each other in the timing and quality of the meals served during the day. Tea, coffee and biscuits were brought in before eleven o'clock and cigarettes, sweets and soft drinks were given to us by well wishers.

At the polling station where I usually helped, there were three large rooms to accommodate five booths that catered for an electorate of approximately two thousand voters. Later the number of booths and stations increased as the district population increased. Each party contesting the election was entitled to have a member at each booth to safeguard their interest during the casting of votes. They were also permitted an agent who moved about from place to place and was responsible for all of his party workers.

The day had its moments of secret fun not covered by the secrecy act which we had to sign. One memorable day a well-intentioned food committee member of a particular party thought their helpers should have a hot meal during the day. At mid-day large dinner plates extravagantly filled with meat and two vegetables were brought in to their workers. The second vegetable was of the dried pea variety. Either the cook was careless or had no knowledge of how to deal with them.

The worker at my table received his plate with obvious pride and satisfaction thinking to himself how considerate and proper his chosen party were to workers. Space being limited at the table, it was necessary for him to place the dinner plate on his knees. A very silent and dour young man, he tackled the peas, chasing them relentlessly with his fork round the plate while they skidded about in all directions, some hitting the floor with a distinct plop, plip, plop. After partaking of some meat and potato, he made a further onslaught on the peas. Gathering some on the broad of his knife, he lifted them to his mouth only to find that some of them had rolled off into hiding down his sleeve. Undaunted, he tackled them again and again while I watched, unashamed, the game of the rebellious peas.

Presumably he was unaware that his actions were being noted and I, in turn, was also the object of several pairs of eyes. No doubt it was rude of me to act in such a manner but I really got lost in watching the game of the peas and the conquering hero. Probably my facial expression was registering points awarded for capture and disapproval for failure so that my interest was an amusement to those who could see me but not the performance.

I often wonder if I had acted like 'The Hurler on the Ditch', offering some advice or applauding a neat capture, what would have been the outcome of my rudeness. I got a great deal of fun out of that episode and can do so to the present day by giving a real live description of those rebellious, uncooked peas and their determined captor.

The day after the votes were cast I was present at the counting of the votes. Officials were in charge of different constituencies. First, the containers were examined to make sure that the seals were intact. Next, signed documents were noted. Then the votes were counted with their numbers compared with the relevant papers. Any discrepancies were recorded. Finally each number one vote cast for a candidate was placed in a receptacle bearing his or her name, rechecked by another official and tied in bundles of fifty.

Each worker was followed by another with an official who checked again to make sure of accuracy. All the work was done under the scrutiny of the public party helpers working in a candidate's interest. Spoiled papers were put aside for further examination by a higher official who decided whether to accept or to reject the paper. The number of valid casts were divided by the number of seats to be filled plus one to find the quota; thus, in a three-seat constituency, the number would be divided by four.

Occasionally, a very popular candidate received a great number of votes in excess of the quota. They were called a surplus and they were the first extra votes to be dealt with. It was a complicated business, because the whole number of votes had to be gone through to find the second preferences for other candidates. Then the second preference votes in excess of the quota were distributed in proportion to the named candidate which could result in the election of another member of the same party.

The next stage and more general one was the elimination of the name of the candidate with the lowest number of votes. Those candidates having been declared unsuccessful and perhaps having had to forfeit their deposit, the count continued through all the stages in a similar way until all the seats were filled. It was a very fair way of electing a government if the electors gave the system as much consideration as it deserved and required and if the successful candidates followed its principle through to the end.

I loved the election work and the excitement it inspired and

I collected many little bits of gossip to amuse my friends. Miss Lily showed a lot of interest in hearing my account of the wonderful orators that my chosen party had in abundance. I told her that I was particularly struck with the appearance and the hand actions of James Dillon,[2] his easy flow of words when making a point, the silence and attention of his listeners, his whole demeanor giving great expression to his delivery.

The clipped sentences of the gaunt-figured Patrick McGilligan[3] in his delightful Northern accent as his message came across to his audience in a trim and jocular manner. The sombre quiet flow of explosive passages from J A Costello[4] in his effortless legal way. I also told her about many other speakers. Miss Lily would then talk of her father's boyhood friend Isaac Butt[5] and other friends whom my talk would recall to her memory.

During the Easter holidays of 1934, May's mother died leaving yet another gap in a world that had become for both of us a place of sorrows.[6] She continued with her housekeeping and her part-time work in the local Carnegie Library. Being wellversed in literature from her early youth and later from her contact with the Yeats family while she was employed in Cuala Industry, she was an ideal librarian.

We both paid our weekly visit to Miss Lily where we were always welcomed and comforted. The health of Mr W B Yeats at this time was causing him some trouble and much anxiety to his friends.[7] He was living in a flat at Fitzwilliam Square in the home of Dr Solomons. Both his children were in boarding schools. After a short period he became hale and hearty again with renewed vigour and zest for his work.

His return to good health was always reflected in Miss Lily who idolized him. She talked endlessly of their young days together, particularly at their grandparents' house in Sligo with their many elderly relations and young cousins some of whom we knew personally from their visits to Dundrum and others of whom we knew from her detailed descriptions. We felt we knew the great man from babyhood to manhood, his triumphs and failures. He in turn showed much admiration for her and for her embroidery work.[8]

The health of Mr W B Yeats having deteriorated during the past few years, his doctor recommended that he take a house in the country away from the turmoil of the city, rest from his work and spend the winter months in a warm climate. He found a nice convenient house in the Rathfarnham[9] area where he could walk about and enjoy the fresh air in complete solitude with the happy companionship of a nice dog, a murmuring brook, whispering trees and sighing rushes - a complete haven for a poet such as he.

In the winter of 1936, he went to Rapallo to visit his friend Ezra Pound staying there until it was summer time again in Ireland.[10] From Rapallo he returned with ideas of the work he must and could do. He was full of praise for his wife's nursing ability. During that year he accomplished a great deal of his programme to the delight of Miss Lily and his many friends. The following winter he went to Spain and once again repeated the magic of a return to health and energy.

In 1937, the Misses Yeats suffered a great loss in the death, at an advanced age, of their much beloved cook Rose Hodgins,[11] a Sligo girl. She had been with the family all through the years, coming to the household after the marriage of John Yeats and Susan Pollexfen in 1864. Many were the nice little stories that Miss Lily recounted of her faithfulness and untiring devotion to each member of the Yeats family. Rose herself liked to talk about her happiness and the pleasure she had in being attached to such a lovable family.

One of the many stories Rose told of 'her girls', as she termed the Misses Yeats, happened in London when their mother was very ill and unable to look after the housekeeping. It fell to Rose's lot to take charge since Miss Lily and Miss Lolly were both working. One day Miss Lolly came to her in the kitchen with her two hands cupped together holding a quantity of gold coins which she left down on the table saying as she did so that there was enough money to pay all the bills and have some left over.[12] One can understand their grief at Rose's passing. Her remains were interred[13] in the local churchyard close to the roadway so that her many friends would remember her when passing by.

Feeling very lonely and unable to make a change because of my unwillingness to sever a connection with a life that had become an enchantment, an event occurred to bond me to my work. While out shopping in the city one afternoon, Miss Lolly met a young friend[14] who was exhausted in her search for a studio to try out a new project. Miss Lolly suggested to her friend that she might consider using part of the large embroidery room which was ideally suited to her requirements.

She accepted the offer. When she moved in to work it was as if a new limb had grown on a well established tree bringing with it a new growth of variety and activity. There was ample room for me to work and to retain my cupboards and when she settled in, the visits of her friends brought in a breezy and mirthful atmosphere with them of fun, frivolities and wishful thinking, but alas the printed sheets that I enjoyed so much were moved back to the printing department.

For me a totally different life began. Some of the daily routine was packed with amusement and explosive situations only to be found amongst the young and carefree. I was kept busy but not tied to time so that I found I could pay an occasional afternoon visit to Miss Lily and also to May who lived a short distance away on the same road.

Back at the Industry, Miss Lolly's young friend, after a short time, lost interest in her project. Her companion had joined another circle that offered more fun and free hours while at the same time they could earn good pocket money doing pleasant easy work. She soon packed up so as to be with her friends and once more the printed pages of poems and cards were distributed about the embroidery room for drying and for finishing by one of the workers from that department. Life for me became as near as it could to the old familiar pattern. I was kept busy with the work I loved and the companions I enjoyed.

As I continued with embroidery orders, an enquiry came from the Irish Army Headquarters requesting an estimate for the embroidering of fifteen banners required for military divisions. They sent details of the materials that could be supplied, and design of the pattern to be followed. In addition, they invited me to meet the designer to hear an explanation of the work she required to be carried out in the additional centre-piece.

There was an embroidered copy of the main design. It had been used for some time without a centre-piece. The centre inset piece depicting an historical incident from an ancient Irish battle was to be distinctive to each banner. Competitors were given identical small portions of the new design to embroider and to submit with a completed tender form by a specified date.

Miss Lily advised and encouraged me to apply for the work

knowing I was capable of doing it and, if successful, that I would be usefully employed at the Industry for a considerable length of time. After a good deal of thought I decided to submit two styles of treatment of the tiny soldier-like figures drawn to illustrate the historical incidents.

After several months when once again I was about to pack up my work and seek other employment,[15] Army Headquarters accepted my tender and gave me the contract for the making of three banners.[16] My second style of embroidery was selected for the centre-piece with interlacing adjustments here and there. I was pleased and felt it a compliment to receive the contract and lost no time in getting it started.

After completing the centre-piece to my own satisfaction, I was fortunate in getting the help of an experienced embroideress to work with me on the main design, a Celtic pattern in the shape of a flame carried out in shades of green silk threads with interlacings of gold threads. This replica of the Army badge was embroidered solidly in metal thread which rested on the point of the flame that was incorporated in the main design. A wide enclosed border of Celtic bosses across the top finished it off.

The whole effort was a most delightful combination of colour giving the effect of gold silver and enamel tracery on a rich silk poplin. It was very pleasing to the eye. When taken off the work frame, the banner was finished on three sides with an untarnishable metal gold fringe and mounted as a flag to be carried with the tri-colour in important Army parades. Alas, it was too heavy with the amount of silk and metal thread together with the lining necessary to help the silk poplin support the weight of the embroidery.

I was bitterly disappointed when I saw the banner in use. Mounted as a flag and hanging in such heavy folds along the staff, a hurricane wind could not have shaken it into a flutter. Its great weight must have been a burden to the bearer. With such an unsatisfactory ending to so much labour, I did not undertake to make the remaining twelve banners.

Times were changing so rapidly that the small embroidery orders had ceased to come in. I had not noticed this while I was so busy working on the banners, but now it was imperative that I should seek other employment.

Detail of a cushion embriodered by Sara and designed by Jack B Yeats

CHAPTER ELEVEN

(1938-1943)

Sara becomes a teacher - Death of W B Yeats - World War II - Death of Lolly Yeats - Classes and pupils - Irish and embroidery - Last glimpse of Lily.

I enrolled at the Municipal Art School in Kildare Street to obtain the necessary certificates required by the Department of Education to which I hoped to apply for a position as an embroidery teacher in one of their many art classes held throughout County Dublin.[1] I continued to work at the Industry at the small jobs sent in by regular customers and I continued to visit Miss Lily at her home in Churchtown to give her accounts of my lessons under the different teachers most of whom were known to her for many years.

Miss Lily liked to talk to me about new ideas and hopes for the future, planning what I should do and describing the things to avoid. Having a lot of young nieces and nephews, I occasionally took them to visit her[2] because she was lonely and she loved seeing and talking to children. My hope was that they would remember a gracious lady in her home surrounded by beautiful portraits painted by her father and the other art treasures from friends which provided her with great pleasure in her declining years. Miss Lily's bed had been moved downstairs and fitted up in a corner of their large sitting room because at times during the day she needed a good deal of attention. At night she had the attention of a nurse during her critical periods.

In 1938, Mr W B Yeats went for the winter months to the south of France.[3] His health had been precarious and troublesome during the year. On this visit it was hoped that he might recover some of his past strength, but as the weeks went by, hope of recovery was abandoned and feeling that the end was near he asked his wife not to call him back this time but to 'let him go on his last long journey'. These words were told to me by Miss Lily.

Mr W B Yeats died in France on the 28th of January and there he was temporarily interred[4] awaiting arrangements to be made for the removal of his remains by one of his ancestor's trading vessels for reburial in the churchyard of Drumcliffe, County Sligo where his grandfather had ministered in the early nineteenth century. The epitaph of the headstone composed by himself reads, 'Cast a cold eye on Life, on Death. Horseman, pass by'.

Toward the end of 1939, World War II started and with it came problems of many kinds hitherto unknown to us. As a nation we had gained freedom from Britain for the greater part of our country and had a government to make laws to guide us in our own decisions. This country declared its neutrality which raised many awkward questions in the British Parliament.

As heretofore, our boys joined the British Army in numbers to fight against Hitler and his wicked plan to become dictator of Europe. The rationing of foodstuffs became essential but unlike our previous experience in World War I, it was not so strict. Having a small merchant fleet of our own and protected by neutrality laws, we were fortunate enough to obtain the necessities needed to keep our industries working and transport extra foodstuffs as well. We were able to live a normal existence except for travel to Britain to visit relatives and friends.

The British ports were closed to us unless we could establish a legitimate reason for entering the country, then a passport would be issued. England suffered a great deal during the war. We, who rarely suffered even the common cold, did not escape some disaster although we appeared to be living as usual.

In the autumn of 1939, Miss Lolly's very robust health suddenly failed.[5] Following a period in the hospital and in a nursing home, she passed away at the age of seventy-two on the 16th of January, 1940, only twelve months after her famous brother. A funeral service was held in St Nahi's, her favourite small church, and she was laid to rest in the graveyard that surrounded the church. It was but a short distance from the Yeats's home in Churchtown.

Mrs W B Yeats, now living in Fitzwilliam Square, took charge of the Industry ably assisted by its trustees and former subscribers. All the equipment and a small staff of the old employees were given a place in her home where the work continued on its established lines for many more years.[6]

I now was employed in the local Girls' Technical School as a part-time embroidery teacher.[7] It gave me great happiness and it gave much pleasure to Miss Lily who immediately gave me permission to use all of her embroidery designs with only one exception - the fourteen Stations of the Cross that she had worked for an American customer. These I was to burn at her death. I piously hoped it would be a long time before I had to fulfill her instructions.

My first class consisted of sixteen juniors. We began by making pretty printed cotton bags to hold their materials and this gave me time to formulate an idea as to how I should instruct them so that each pupil would have something completed at the end of the session.

From then onwards, I got classes of senior pupils at the night schools in South County Dublin.[8] Very soon I realised that some of those attending had difficulty threading a needle. To start their lessons, I decided that they would make samplers of strong linen so that each would have a finished hem-stitched article before an embroidery motif was marked on it. All the patterns would be alike except for the colouring which I considered the most important part of their work. Thus a new life began for me, and with it, a good monthly pay packet. I was able to add to my small savings for 'the rainy day'.

I visited Miss Lily more frequently at this time because she was lonely and I knew that my work awakened in her memories of her own working days with May Morris at the Morris School of Embroidery. The family at Gurteen Dheas was reduced to one and Maria, the maid. A young schoolgirl was engaged to come in every day after school hours to help Maria with her housework and to remain overnight to keep her company. At this time, Miss Lily did not require any special attention; however, when help was needed, a night nurse was again employed and she stayed until Miss Lily recovered.

After a time, with the responsibilities left in Maria's hands, she adopted a jealous, animal-like protective attitude toward the house and person of Miss Lily.[9] It was almost impossible to pay a visit or to have a chat with her unless Maria wished it. This difficulty was mentioned to a friend by Miss Lily and she conveyed the message to Mr Jack. With his assistance and advice from the local doctor, Maria was sent for treatment to a mental hospital in the city. She escaped after a few weeks treatment and came back to Gurteen Dheas where she made a dreadful scene on finding a stranger in her place.

As soon as she had been missed from the hospital, the authorities notified Mr Jack by telephone and he came by taxi to Churchtown arriving almost at the same time as Maria. He reasoned with her about the state of her health and with the help of her local clergyman, the doctor and the Gardaí, she was taken to a different hospital where she died after some months, detention.

Following such an upheaval, Mr Jack and Mrs W B undertook Miss Lily's welfare.[10] This they did in a most generous manner giving her peace of mind and body for the remainder of her life. Unfortunately, this was interrupted by her usual short or long periods of distressing illness to which she never referred only speaking of the kindness she had received from her nurses. She was so placid. Her attitude to life was of one who 'counted her blessings every day'.

It was such a pleasure to be able to speak to Miss Lily freely once again and to know she was being cared for in such a special way. I visited her a great deal at this time bringing her samples of my young pupils' work and telling her of the unusual remarks which I overheard them making among themselves about their friends, their homes and the world in general. The odd and often private questions put to me by the more courageous ones never failed to amuse me.

I modelled my instructions on the same pattern as I had

been taught and I answered all their enquiries as I had been answered and instructed by Miss Lily who never lectured or rebuffed anyone. I succeeded in keeping their attention and interest in their work by talking of current events and childhood days that were so different to theirs.

Since I was very keen on the Irish language, I told short stories to the younger pupils in their native language.[11] Afterwards, I expected to hear them repeated in Irish or in English which afforded me the opportunity to explain the great expressive beauty of their own language so that they might develop an interest in it.

One thing I noticed that was common to girls of all areas was their fear of speaking Irish because of their mispronouncing the words. Why are they not taught to imitate the sounds? Also, teachers should be obliged to take a refresher course in pronunciation every year in order to make them word perfect or nearly so. Fear of being misunderstood is a great stumbling block to learning any language.

I enjoyed my working days as a teacher in those classes meeting children of a new age. This was of immense interest to Miss Lily who talked endlessly of her recollections of the wonderful people of her young days, our patriots and our beautiful country. One could listen to her reminiscences for hours on end. She approved of my method of teaching for it was a repetition of my own training under her careful management.

On one occasion as I was paying my usual visit, Miss Lily startled me by saying, 'I will come and visit you'.[12] She was referring to a period after her death when her remains would be laid to rest in the churchyard close to my own and May's families' burial spots. Previously she had announced her great consolation in the fact that her final resting place would be among friends.

Sara at work, in later life

EPILOGUE

(1943-1972)

Although she was the more delicate of the two sisters and she was incapacitated by emphysema, Lily Yeats survived Lolly by nine years. Like W B and Lolly, she died in the month of January - 5 January, 1949. She is buried with Lolly under a single stone in St Nahi's graveyard. The words on the tombstone are hers:

> Elizabeth Corbet Yeats,
> Gurteen Dheas, Churchtown,
> daughter of John Butler Yeats
> and her sister Susan Mary Yeats

Sara continued to teach until 1962. While she followed Lily in the matter of her methods and designs, she also experimented with innovations of her own. She invented a new darning stitch that she incorporated into a piece of embroidery, unfinished, that her grand-niece Diane Dixon owns. Her pupils remember her for her enthusiasm for the Irish language and Irish folklore, for her very neat appearance: black cardigan and skirt, a blue-flowery blouse, black boots or laced-up shoes, a straw hat in summer, and for her own sense of style. Always eager to learn, Sara enrolled in French classes when she retired; however, very much in character, she gave up the lessons because she said she knew more French than her teacher. In the same spirit, when James Plunkett published *Strumpet City* in 1969, she announced that Plunkett did not know about Dublin and that she was writing her own account of the city in the first decades of the twentieth century. She was seventy-three.

Sara sought advice from Monk Gibbon whose own reminiscence of W B Yeats, *The Masterpiece and the Man: Yeats as I Knew Him*, was published in 1959. The Gibbons and the Yeatses were related and Gibbon's father was Canon of St Nahi's and a Cuala patron. Lily's embroidered pictures decorate the Church; Gibbon's sister attended Lolly's Saturday morning brushwork classes, and both sisters were generous and encouraging to young Monk Gibbon. Lily took him to the Abbey and Lolly printed some of his early poems as Cuala wall cards.

A man with the sensibilities of his time, Gibbon allowed that Sara's picture of her life and times was interesting; however, 'the publishers will want celebrities',[1] so he encouraged her to include ' a little not-unfriendly gossip'. While he himself called the Yeats sisters 'heroic', he advised Sara to marginalize those remarkable women and 'to concentrate on Jack and Willie'. He especially wanted Sara to include a story that she had about Lolly believing that Gibbon tried to get W B to church,[2] a story he no doubt wished he had had for his own book - critical of Yeats the man - that included gossip unfriendly as well as friendly. His descriptions of the sisters - Lily's laboured breathing and Lolly's high-strung fidgeting and the carefully constructed co-existence of their later lives - would have struck Sara as disloyal. She followed Gibbon's counsel to concentrate on the Yeatses but she maintained in her Memoir the manner of her Cuala work life: loyalty, discretion and a certain awe of her employer and her family.

Sara also had support for her Memoir from Thomas Mac Greevy, poet and Director of the National Gallery of Ireland from 1950-1964. Sara would have known Mac Greevy from the late fifties when he purchased[3] from her the transfer designs for the Loughrea Saint Colmcille and Saint Asicus banners (1903) that Lily had given Sara when the embroidery section of Cuala closed. Mac Greevy also encouraged Sara to write her account of working for the Yeats sisters. It was probably Mac Greevy or Gibbon who helped her to arrange to send her unfinished manuscript to the London publisher Routledge and Kegan Paul who expressed an interest but who wanted more about the Yeats family.

The manuscript was never finished. In 1969, Sara suffered a stroke though she insisted that she was disabled from falling over a dog at church. She never fully recovered her speech or the use of her arm. Her brother Larry returned from England in 1971 to share Sara's care with Cissie. When cataracts made work on the manuscript difficult, Sara's neighbour Mrs Smith copied Sara's Memoir and her nephew Ken Dixon arranged to have the copy typed.

1.   James Hyland - Annie Kiernan
                      I

Joseph (1889-1973), Bartholomew (1891-1942), Sara (1893-1972), James (1893-1923), Lawrence (1896-1966), William (1899-1966), Patrick (1901-1939)

2. Larry Hyland recalled that in addition to the Hylands, their seven children and their niece Bridget Gaffney who was reared in the house, the family had a lodger from time to time.

3. The Hylands lived at number 10 Pembroke Cottages, one of the twenty-six brick and granite cottages located just off Main Street in the village of Dundrum. Built by the Earl of Pembroke for his workers in the late 1870s, the project may have been included under the Cross Act: *Artisans' and Labourers' Dwellings Improvement Act of 1875*, which authorised loans to local authorities and to private individuals to put up cottages for artisans and labourers (O'Brien, p.25).
Batty Hyland purchased the cottage from the Pembroke Estates in the 1930s. The cottage is currently owned by Hyland's grand-nieces, Diane and Hilary Dixon.

4. When Sara started school, Mr Sheehan was the Master. He lived with his wife, also a teacher, opposite the barracks in Dundrum.

5. The Dundrum National Schools were located at the back of Holy Cross Church on the site of the present church hall (Nolan, p.65). Holy Cross was consecrated in 1878; its three altars are by Patrick Pearse's father, James Pearse.

6. Dundrum was on the Harcourt Street line which was opened in 1854 and closed in 1959. Some traces of old roadbed remain.

7. The Church of St Nahi was built in 1760, but the site is associated with the monk Nahi who lived in the seventh century and was associated with the monastery in Tallaght (Carleton p.36).

8. Big houses in the Dundrum area included Taney House, Friarsland Hall, Mount Anville, Roebuck Manor, Woodlawn and Glenville, now the site of the Dundrum Shopping Centre.

9. Diana, the Roman goddess of the hunt, is sometimes represented as driving a chariot drawn by four stags.

10. Father Brady was killed about ten years earlier than Sara reports. 'In 1866, Reverend T Brady, who had been previous chaplain, was annexed to the parish, but two years later, he got a fall from his horse from the effects of which he died' (Donnelly, p.123).

11. Edward Fitzgerald (1809-1883) translated the work of the eleventh century Persian poet, Omar Khayyam. Sara quotes the last lines of the *Rubaiyat of Omar Khayyam*:

        And when, like her, O Saki, you shall pass
        Among the Guests star-scattered on the grass,
        And in your joyous errand reach the spot
        Where I made One - turn down an empty glass!

12. The official name of the Union located in Loughlinstown was the Rathdrum Union workhouse.

13. British coinage was used in the Irish Free State until 1928. Senator

W B Yeats chaired the committee charged with selecting the design for the first Irish coins.

14. Pluck is the name for the heart, liver and lung of an animal used for food.

15. The child was Lawrence who was born in 1896 when Sara was three.

16. The lines appear in the refrains of Irish, Scottish and English traditional ballads. One of the ballads, 'The Butcher Boy', has a Dublin setting.

17. The line is from Samuel Lover's 'The Fairy Boy'.

18. 'The Fairy Boy' and Mrs Hyland's changeling story describe the belief popular in the Irish countryside in the last century that fairies abducted young children, particularly little boys, and substituted a 'changeling' or fairy brat. Infants and small children who failed to thrive were often thought to be changelings.

19. Mrs Hyland's body-snatching story appears to be located somewhere in north County Dublin; however, there is also a body-snatching tradition associated with Kilgobbin Church (Carleton, p.9).

20. Electuaries were mixes of powdered medicine and honey, jam or syrup. Senna was used as a cathartic.

21. The custom of families reciting the Rosary each night was widespread and demonstrates its central role in Irish spiritual life at the time.

22. A traditional belief was that mirrors attracted lightning.

23. The Manor Mill Laundry was located on Sandyford Road, later the site of the PYE Agency. The Laundry closed in 1942. Some of Sara's neighbours in Pembroke Cottages worked at the Manor Mill. One of them, Mrs Sarah Kennedy of 20 Pembroke Cottages, was the Laundry representative to the Irish Women Workers' Union (Nolan, p.59).

24. Queen Victoria visited Mount Anville in 1900 (Donnelly, p.124).

25. Eoin MacNeill circulated a letter in June, 1893, inviting those interested to meet together to discuss establishing an organisation for the purpose of promoting Gaelic as a spoken language. The meeting held on 31 July, 1893, concluded with the founding of the Gaelic League.

26. 'Give me a penny for the Irish [language].'

27. In 1902, Augustine Henry invited the Yeats sisters to join in a venture that involved employing Irish girls to make Irish crafts of a high standard (Murphy, *Secrets*, p.89). The enterprise lasted until 1908 when the Yeats sisters started their own Cuala Industries.

NOTES TO CHAPTER TWO

1. Grush is an old Dublin custom. Sara's neighbour and past pupil Marie Mason remembers that grush was thrown when one of the Guinnesses was married at St Patrick's. Sara's grand-niece Diane Dixon recalls seeing grush thrown by a wedding party in Ballyfermot in 1988.

2. Palles (1831-1920) was the only Catholic to hold the position of Lord Chief Baron of the Exchequer in Ireland (1874-1916). He was also a Commissioner for National Schools and Intermediate Education. The Palleses lived at Mount Anville House from 1850-1920.

3. Reverend Edward Matthews was made Canon in 1898.

4. The asylum was probably Ashgrove. Located behind the Eagle, it is the present site of Ashgrove Court. The property appears on the 1912 Rathfarnham map.

5. The accident happened on 14 February, 1900. The engineer was a William Hyland, age twenty-two (Mulligan, pp.34-36). There is no indication that he was related to the Dundrum Hylands.

6. The stationmaster was Mr McElheron ('DSER'); his foreman was Mr Reilly (Nolan, p.35).

7. William Hyland was born in 1899.

8. Kruger was President of the Transvaal, one of the two Boer farmer republics that challenged British colonial expansion. The Boers had some early success in the War that lasted from 1899-1902. Lady Gregory recorded a number of examples of Irish popular support for the Boers in her *Kiltartan History Book* and in *Poets and Dreamers*.

9. Sara might have delighted in the reports of the little larks, but her mother probably was attracted to the story for its moral: self help is the best help.

10. William Balfe's *Bohemian Girl* was a Dublin favourite, sometimes to the despair of critics (O'Brien, p.45). James Joyce used a song from *The Bohemian Girl*, 'I Dreamt I Dwelled in Marble Halls', in his story 'Clay'. Joseph O'Brien's discussion of operas in *Dear Dirty Dublin* suggests something of its importance in the Dublin of Sara's youth. In Joyce's *The Dead*, the conversation at the Morkans' Christmas party turns to the tenors who visited Dublin with travelling opera companies.

11. Referred to as the 'bun lady'. There is no record of the identity of Sara's benefactress.

12. Sean O'Casey describes a similar street cry in *Inisfallen, Fare Thee Well*: 'Fresh Dublin Bay herrin's thruppence a dozen; thruppence the dozen. The Dublin Bay herrin's fresh from the say' (O'Casey, p.199).

13. John Butler Yeats (1839-1922) took his degree from Trinity College, Dublin, then trained for the Bar. After he married Susan Pollexfen of Sligo, he became a portrait painter in Dublin and later in London. In 1901, Sarah Purser organised a Hone-Yeats Exhibition in Dublin. Encouraged by its success, Yeats decided to return to Ireland and to settle with his daughters in a house called Gurteen Dheas (the lovely little field) in Churchtown.

John Butler Yeats went to America in 1908. he stayed in New York until his death in 1922; he never returned to Ireland.

14. Susan Mary 'Lily' Yeats (1866-1949) and Elizabeth Corbet 'Lolly' Yeats (1868-1940) returned from London to Dublin in 1902 to take up their partnership with Evelyn Gleeson.

15. Evelyn Gleeson (1855-1944), trained as a painter, took up carpet design. Nicola Gordon Bowe discusses the history of the Dun Emer Industries in *The Irish Arts and Crafts Movement* and William Murphy examines the Yeats sisters' role in the Dun Emer Industries in *Family Secrets* (pp.86-144).

16. Runnymede (also Runnimede) was a villa on the Sandyford Road that was built in 1816. Evelyn Gleeson rented the house from Commissioner Hogan and changed the name to Dun Emer (Carleton, p.25).
17. Lily Yeats studied embroidery with William Morris's daughter May. Lolly Yeats prepared for her work as a book designer and hand printer by taking a short course at the Women's Printing Society in London (Bowe, p.177).
18. The Yeatses lived at 6 Sydenham Villas until Gurteen Dheas, their house in Churchtown, was available. They moved to Gurteen Dheas in October, 1902. Both houses still stand.
19. Norma Borthwick's *Ceachta Beaga Gaedhilge* (Little Irish Lessons), a series of reading lessons in the simplified spelling of Irish that she advocated, appeared in 1902 with illustrations by Jack B Yeats. Gifford Lewis's *The Yeats Sisters and the Cuala* includes reproductions of the title page and a sample page of text and drawings (Lewis, pp.58-59).
20. Sara probably collected the milk from the Lamberts who lived on Kilmacud Road.

NOTES TO CHAPTER THREE

1. The shop, now the site of Mulvey's, was called Sandler's.
2. Sara refers to Baron Karl von Munchausen, a soldier and hunter best known for his tall tales.
3. Marie Mason remembers her father telling her about the headless coachman or the *cóiste bodhar*. 'Ghost of Dundrum', a story collected by Damien Byrne and John Forrest, may be a version of the legend:

> Long ago (in the penal days) there was an open four-
> wheeled coach which was conveying some parishioners
> to a mass rock above Kilmashonge near midnight on
> Christmas Eve. They were met by an ambush of British
> soldiers who beheaded the driver but the coach
> continued on its way with the headless coachman still
> in his seat. The legend is that he still appears
> shortly before midnight every seventh Christmas. (Byrne

Mss. p.92, Dundrum Library).
4. Sara is probably referring to the 1910 election when William Cotton, the Nationalist candidate, received 5,223 votes to Captain Bryan Cooper's 5,090. According to *Thom's* (1915), Cotton's address was Hollywood, Roebuck, Dundrum. In 1900, John Joseph Mooney (N) defeated two Conservative candidates: the Right Honourable Horace Plunkett and Francis Ball, but Mooney is listed in *Thom's* as a resident of Killiney.
5. The Barn Elms Dairy was on Churchtown Road. The house still stands and is owned by the Cosgrave family.
6. Larry Hyland remembers walking past Mount Anville to Booterstown Avenue to the sea. He said they carried lardy bread or

bread with drippings for the day's outing.

7. The image is very similar to the one at the beginning of *An Craoibhín Aoibhinn's* 'The Return of the Fenians', the celebration of the Gaelic League that Lady Gregory translated for *Ideals in Ireland*. The 'Englishing' of Ireland is described as a cloud '... like the great black wings of a crow stretched out between us and the blessed light of the sun' (p.65).

8. Richard 'Boss' Croker, born in Clonakilty, County Cork, in 1843, emigrated with his family to the United States in 1846. He rose to be the political boss of New York's Tammany Hall, the Democratic political machine. After the Ice Trust Scandal, Croker returned to Ireland and purchased Glencairn on the Murphystown Road. The Glencairn Stud produced 'Orby' which won the Epsom and the Irish Derbies.

9. In Charles Dickens's novel, Dora Spenlow was David Copperfield's child-wife.

10. The telephone exchange was located in one of the cottages near the site of the present jewellry shop in Dundrum.

11. In Sara's time, the Dundrum Post Office was located at 8 Main Street (Nolan, p.119).

12. Purcell's would have been one of a number of small acting companies that toured Ireland. William Fay describes such companies in the eighties in his autobiographical *The Fays of the Abbey Theatre*. In Dundrum, the field they used, Bob Doyle's or Mellon's field, is opposite the barracks.

13. The Carl Rossa Company was a British touring company that was visiting Dublin regularly by the mid 1870s where they played at the Gaiety (O'Brien, p.46).

14. A serial by this name did not appear in the *Saturday Evening Herald* between January and March of 1907. It may have appeared in a different paper or in the *Herald* in a different year.

NOTES TO CHAPTER FOUR

1. By the time Sara joined the Yeats sisters at the Dun Emer Guild, their joint venture with Miss Gleeson was proving difficult. On 1 October, 1904, two co-operative societies were established. Miss Gleeson's was the Dun Emer Guild; the Yeats's embroidery and printing business became the Dun Emer Industries. All were located in Dun Emer House in 1907.

The name Dun Emer, the Fort of Emer, refers to an episode in the *Táin Bó Cuailgne* when Cuchulain goes to see Emer and finds her teaching embroidery to her foster sisters (Kinsella, p.26). Emer was the motif of Lolly's Dun Emer pressmark. It was designed by Elinor Monsell.

2. A photograph of Lily and her assistants taken in 1903 identifies the girls as: Eileen McCabe, Sarah Mooney, Jane Gill, Máire Walker and Eileen Colum; a companion photograph features Lolly and her

printers: Esther Ryan and Beatrice Cassidy (Murphy, pp.258-259). Jane Gill married a man called MacClusky and she was replaced by her sister Molly Gill who worked for Dun Emer/Cuala for sixty years (Nolan, p.24).

3. Lily planned to go to the Irish Exhibition in Madison Square Garden in January, 1908. At the last minute her father decided to join her. They sailed in December on the *Campania*. The Exhibition turned a profit for the Industries and Lily was a great success in New York (Murphy, *Prodigal Father*, pp.328-233). When it was time to return to Ireland, JBY elected to stay on in New York and Lily sailed alone.

4. Ruth and her sister Hilda joined the Yeats sisters when their parents' marriage dissolved. Ruth and Lily were devoted to each other and that caused problems with Lolly who felt an outsider. Ruth was in charge of the embroidery when Lily went to New York. She married Charles Lane-Poole in 1922 and moved with him to Australia.

5. The cottage, called Peach Cottage, was located on the Lower Churchtown Road. The Yeats sisters leased the cottage from 1908-1923. It was later called Laeken Cottage. Gibbon called it Rose Cottage in *The Masterpiece and the Man: Yeats as I Knew Him* (p.26).

6. The Cuala Press succeeded the Dun Emer Press. Its first title was W B Yeats's *In the Seven Woods* (1903).

7. By 1908, the 1904 arrangement with Miss Gleeson proved impossible, so the Yeats sisters set up their own Cuala Industries (Miller, pp.49-50).

8. When the Cuala Press started in 1908 the staff included: Beatrice Cassidy, Máire (Molly) Gill, Esther Ryan and Eileen Colum who had been transferred from the embroidery section in 1906 to look after the administration of the Press and to do hand colouring (Miller, p.55). Two of the three girls in embroidery would have been Sara and Máire Walker (Máire nic Shiubhlaigh).

9. On St Agnes' Eve (21 January), girls try to imagine their future husbands. Tennyson treats the theme in religious terms. The nun is the bride of Christ.

10. John 14:1. Lily reassured Sara with an ecumenical reading of the lines from St John.

11. William Morris (1834-1896) became interested in embroidery in 1855. After his marraige in 1859, Morris experimented, with the help of his wife Jane, with medieval embroidery. He later created his own patterns for his firm of Morris, Marshall and Faulkner. Lily worked for Morris's daughter May as an embroidery assistant from 1888-1894.

12. William Morris's people were evangelical Christians. As a young man he became interested in Anglo-Catholicism and went to Exeter College, Oxford, with the intention of becoming an Anglo-Catholic clergyman.

13. Christina Rossetti (1830-1894) was a Victorian poet and sister to the Pre-Raphaelite poet and painter Dante Gabriel Rossetti.

14. Edward Burne-Jones (1833-1898) was an artist and close friend of Morris's. Burne-Jones did the figure in Morris's fabric designs.

15. In 1881, Morris moved his Kelmscott Press to an old printing works near Merton Abbey in Surrey. The site included a glass studio, a weaving shop and a dye house (Poulson, p.84).

16. Lily worked at Kelmscott House, Morris's house in Hammersmith where he lived from 1878 until his death in 1896 (Poulson, p.78). Lolly learned typesetting with Emery Walker, Morris's friend and partner in the Kelmscott Press. She also took a short course at the Women's Printing Society; however, she knew nothing about practical press work before she started the Dun Emer Press (Sheehy, p.160).

17. Sara probably refers to the International Exhibition of Industrial Arts (the Great Exhibition) housed in the Crystal Palace.

18. A letter from Lily to her father (11 October, 1908) describes a garden work party on a Saturday afternoon:

> *Yesterday we had a gardening party at Cuala, not a*
> *garden party. Four of the girls stayed on all*
> *afternoon and we planted and cut the grass and did*
> *wonders and had our tea out under the trees. The*
> *landlord is so pleased with what we have done to the*
> *garden that of his own free will he has offered to*
> *plant creepers up the cottage and some silver beeches* (Yeats

Mss, 31.112. National Library of Ireland).

19. GK Chesterton (1874-1936) was an essayist, novelist and critic. Chesterton knew the Yeats family during their years at Blenheim Road.

20. Katherine Tynan (1861-1931) was a prolific writer. A close friend of the young W B Yeats, they corresponded regularly until she married Henry Hinkson in 1893.

21. Susan Langstaff Mitchell (1866-1926) was the Sub-Editor of the *Irish Homestead*, later the *Irish Statesman*. She was known for her wit and satirical verse. She lived with the Yeatses in London from 1897 - 1899 when she was a paying guest and companion to Lily.

22. Sir Horace Plunkett (1854-1932) founded the Irish Agricultural Organisation Society in 1894. He was later a Senator of the Irish Free State.

23. George Russell 'AE' (1867-1935) joined Plunkett's Irish Agricultural Organisation Society as an organiser in 1897. Painter, poet and mystic he also edited the *Irish Homestead*.

24. Susan Mitchell's song 'Cuala Abu' is reprinted in Liam Miller's *The Dun Emer Press, Later the Cuala Press* (pp.78-90).

25. Lily described the 1909 Halloween party in her letter of 2 November, 1909, to her father:

> *... on Friday we had a party for the girls at Cuala*
> *and Dun Emer. Hallow Eve in the proper manner, dancing*
> *burning nuts and melting lead till 11 o'clock. We got*
> *home about 11.30 then heated soup over the fire and*
> *talked.*
> *We retired to our rooms to rest while the girls were*
> *melting the lead but could hear their remarks which*
> *were shouted. The lead is melted in an iron spoon then*
> *poured through a key into a pail of water picked out*
> *and read by an expert, such readings as 'You'll be an old*
> *maid surely', and then 'Holy St Joseph, you won't. Here*
> *are two heads on one pillow, and what in the living earth*
> *is this we have for Miss Lolly? A man in an armchair'.*

> *Ruth made a great hit by seeing a sick calf for one girl*
> *and sure enough a calf of theirs died on Sunday.* (Yeats Mss,

31.112.). National Library of Ireland.

26. Among the artists represented in the run of 123 Cuala Christmas cards are: Jack B Yeats, Mary Cottingham Yeats, Lolly Yeats, Nano Reid, Elizabeth Rivers and Hilda Roberts. Jack Yeats regretted that his designs were on Cuala cards. He wrote to W B Yeats, 'If I had the ready money, I would buy the copyrights of all the prints of mine which Cuala publishes' (Pyle, pp.123-124).

27. Sara either did not know or loyally chose not to mention that Máire Walker had been the centre of controversy twice during the early Dun Emer/Cuala years. In 1906 while Lily was in Germany, Lolly was critical of W B's treatment of Máire. He had wanted Máire to sign a contract with the Abbey for fifteen shillings a week. Not only was Máire offended by this small salary, she was infuriated with Yeats's plan that she play second fiddle to Sarah Allgood (Murphy, *Prodigal Father* p.296). Lolly's January, 1906, letter to Lady Gregory defending Máire's position reveals something of the maternal sense of responsibility that the sisters felt for the girls who worked for them:

> *I do think she needs more care and much more rest and*
> *a more regular life - early to bed when possible. I*
> *don't think her mother knows the importance of this and*
> *unless she is actually ill, she sits up to all hours.*
> *I wish we could have her out with us for some weeks and see*
> *what early hours and quiet would do for her.* (E C Yeats to J

B Yeats, 8 January 1906, NYPL).

Máire later left Cuala to work for Miss Gleeson and the Abbey for the rival Theatre Company of Ireland. In 1910, at Lady Gregory's invitation, she returned to the Abbey.

NOTES TO CHAPTER FIVE

1. Lily probably stayed with the Chestertons or with the Cadburys.

2. The popular novel by Sir James Matthew Barry (1860-1937) had a second success when it was adapted for the stage.

3. This may be Margaret McCabe. Lily's diary for 1903, which was donated to the Sligo Library's Yeats Collection by Sara, indicates that a Margaret McCabe joined the embroidery staff on 11 May, 1903.

4. John Yeats, Rector of Drumcliffe, lived from 1774-1846. Lily was the family historian.

5. Yeats's biographer Joseph Hone identified Yeats's birthplace as 'Georgeville', a semi-detatched house on Sandymount Avenue about one half mile from Sandymount Castle (Hone, p.9; Murphy, *Prodigal Father* p.45).

6. The folklorist Kevin Danaher writes that the belief that the sun dances at Easter was common all over Ireland (p.74). The belief even travelled to the United States. Francis Phelan's autobiographical *Four Ways of Computing Midnight* (1985) describes the custom observed in

his Pittsburg household in the late 1920s.

7. Pat Liddy included a drawing and a description of the Bottle Towers in *Dublin Be Proud* (p.71). The Towers, house and outhouse were built by Major Hall in 1742.

8. The Central Criminal Lunatic Asylum was established by an Act of Parliament in 1845. The facility, still in use, was renamed the Central Mental Hospital of Dundrum in 1961.

9. Sara's friend was May Courtney. After she left the Cuala Industries, she served as a librarian at the Carnegie Library in Dundrum.

10. 'The Lady of Shallott' and 'The Lotus Eaters' are poems by Alfred Lord Tennyson. Both treat mythological themes: the Arthurian tradition and the Greek.

11. The original site of the Municipal Art Gallery was 17 Harcourt Street; it moved in 1930 to the top of Parnell Square. The Gallery opened in 1908.

12. Sir Hugh Lane (1875-1915) was Lady Gregory's nephew. A London art critic and picture dealer, Lane became involved in art in Dublin after he saw the Nathaniel Hone and John Butler Yeats Exhibition in 1901. He was appointed Director of the National Gallery of Ireland in 1915. and served only three months before he was lost on the *Lusitania* in May, 1915.

13. Guides in Christ Church Cathedral point out the old stocks of the Liberties which date to 1670. The Dean of the Cathedral had the power to put parish offenders into the stocks.

14. The Abbey Theatre opened in 1904 at 27 Lower Abbet Street, the site of the old Mechanics Institute. The theatre burned on 18 July, 1951; it reopened in 1966.

15. According to William Murphy, Ruth Pollexfen married Charles Poole on 20 July, 1911 not 1912 (*Secrets* p.382).

16. Eileen had two younger sisters: Maisie and Susan. Sara doesn't indicate which of the girls worked at Cuala.

17. Richter's Manchester-based Halle Orchestra appeared nearly every year in Dublin until 1907 (O'Brien, p.49).

18. Lady Ishbel Aberdeen founded Beaumont during her second tour (1906-1915) in the Viceregal Lodge. She also organised the Irish Industries Association which encouraged Irish designs and Irish manufacture (Sheehy, p.147).

NOTES TO CHAPTER SIX

1. Lily took a great interest in the supernatural and was said to have had 'second sight'. Her vision of a funeral coming from Dun Emer was followed by the death of Miss Gleeson's nephew (Murphy, *Prodigal Father* p.308). It is not clear whether Sara realised how serious Lily was about Sara's dreams.

2. The significance of fish for the Yeats family does not appear to be documented; however, there was a tradition that a white seabird was a harbinger of death for a member of the family (Murphy, *Prodigal*

Father p.217). Yeats's poem 'In Memory of Alfred Pollexfen' alludes to that tradition and draws on Lily's report of Pollexfen's death.

3. Lily did tell Yeats about her girls' dreams. He refers to one in *Memoirs* (12 March, 1909), but he does not identify the informant (Yeats, p.183). In his letter dedicating volumes one and two of *Plays for an Irish Theatre* (1911) to Lady Gregory, Yeats wrote that his play *Cathleen ni Houlihan* was based on a dream (Yeats, *Plays and Controversies*, p.164; *Varoirum*, p.232). The play was written by Lady Gregory.

4. Yeats gave a lecture at the Abbey in March 1913, on 'The Poetry of Rabindranath Tagore'. The lecture that sounds more like the one Sara describes was 'Ghosts and Dreams', a talk given on All-Hallows Eve, 1913, before the Dublin Branch of the Physical Research Society (Frayne, Vol.2 p.407).

5. A passage in *John Sherman* (1891) describes that moment. 'Delayed by a crush in the Strand, he heard a faint trickling of water near by and it came from a shop window where a little water-jet balanced a wooden ball upon its point' (Yeats, p.92). See also Yeats's *Autobiographies*, 153.

6. Jack B Yeats married Mary Cottenham White on 24 August, 1894 (Pyle, p.110). They moved to Greystones in 1910 (Caldwell, p.107).

7. Yeats describes Miss Lucy Middleton as 'the only witch in the family' (Kelly, Vol.1 p.321n).

8. The cinema became a feature of Dublin life by about 1910. There were thirty-seven cinemas by 1914 (O'Brien, p.47). James Joyce was involved in one of Dublin's first cinema ventures, the Volta (1900) at 45 Mary Street. It was not a success.

9. Lily stayed at Beaconsfield with GK Chesterton and his family.

10. The Carnegie donation provided buildings not grants for books (O'Brien, p.59). The Dundrum Library was designed by Rudolph Maximillian Butler, Professor of Architecture at University College, Dublin.

11. According to her family, Sara rode a bicycle for nearly thirty years. She was still cycling in 1942. She would take her bicycle on the train and cycle from the depot to the schools where she taught needlework.

12. Larry stayed in England until 1971 when he returned to Ireland, to Dundrum, to look after Sara.

13. Joseph Hyland married May Margaret James.

14. The notice sent by the Industries at the end of 1914 describes the War's impact on Cuala:

> *Owing to the War, the usual exhibitions have not been held, and the promoters of this Industry find it very difficult to keep their girls employed.*
> *On patriotic as well as artistic grounds it would be a great pity if the movement were allowed to suffer for want of the necessary encouragement, and it is hoped that all interested in Home Industries will take this opportunity of seeing and acquiring some of this beautiful work.* (Miller, p.68).

15. The final lines of Yeats's poem 'To Ireland in the Coming Times'.

16. The Grand Lodge of the Masonic Order, 17 Molesworth Street, has

banners made by the Cuala Industries.
17. Irish poplin was used used for dresses till Queen Victoria's time; then it was used for neckties (O'Dwyer, p.33).
18. Alice Furlong was an ardent nationalist and poet popular in periodicals and in the press.

NOTES TO CHAPTER SEVEN

1. The Easter Rising began on 24 April, 1916. While Sara notes that the Yeats sisters liked to work on bank holidays, Lolly was off in Scotland and only Lily was at the Industries that day (Murphy, *Prodigal Father* p.450). Lily's letters to her father and to John Quinn describe how the Rising affected the girls and the always fragile finances of the Industries. It appears that she did not know the extent of the girls' or their families' involvement in the nationalist movement. Two girls, one of whom was Mollie Gill, were lifted by the authorities for their Cumann na mBan activities (Carleton, p.50).
2. Sara quotes the refrain line from Yeats's poem 'Easter 1916' to describe the change in public opinion after the executions of the 1916 leaders.
3. Yeats married Bertha Georgie (George) Hyde-Lees in London on 20 October, 1917.
4. The lines are from the essay 'Earth, Fire and Water' (*The Celtic Twilight*):

> *We can make our minds so like still water that beings*
> *gather about us so that they may see, it may be,*
> *their own images, and so live for a moment*
> *with a clearer, perhaps even with a fiercer life*
> *because of our quiet.* (Yeats, *Celtic Twilight*, p.136). The
Cuala print is Number 57.
5. The Irish suffragette movement was founded as the Irish Women's Suffrage and Local Government Association in 1876 by a Quaker couple, Thomas and Anna Haslam (C Murphy, p.182). Sara may have been referring to the Irish Women's Franchise League started in 1908 by Francis and Hanna Sheehy Skeffington who were friends of the Yeatses.
6. O'Reilly was Michael Collins's devoted aide. He was with Collins in London, during the Rising and in British prisons after the Rising. He later became Collins's Aide-de-camp. James Matthews, Frank O'Connor's biographer, said that when O'Connor was preparing to write his biography of Collins, his friend Richard Hayes, Director of the National Library, told him if he wanted to know about Collins, that O'Reilly would be his best source. Later when O'Connor interviewed O'Reilly, he had the eerie experience of seeing him take on Collins's persona (Matthews, pp.120-121). O'Connor himself described the session with O'Reilly in *My Father's Son* (O'Connor, p.141).
7. Joseph's adventures as Collins's driver are described in *Taxi-Driver to Michael Collins*. A pass was issued to Joseph on 30 April, 1916. He

had a number of narrow escapes driving Collins and doing his errands. Canon Maurice O'Shea, the late Canon of Sandyford, recalled that Michael Collins and a companion (perhaps O'Reilly) took refuge in the area near Mount Anville (Centenary, p.21).

8. Lily's devoted friend Helen was Helen Laird who appeared in the Abbey under the name Honour Lavelle. She was the first Maurya in *Riders to the Sea*. By 1917, when Lily was ill with boils and anthrax, Helen Laird was married to Constantine Curran, a barrister who later wrote the definitive work on Dublin decorative plasterwork, a reminiscence of James Joyce and a memoir of literary Dublin.

9. In anticipation of the birth of his first child, Yeats asked Sturge Moore to design a cover for a child's cot that Lily and her girls would work. Lily couldn't promise the particular colour that Moore stipulated because of the difficulty in getting the colours she needed. Moore was firm. 'My design is not suitable for working on any ground chosen by an idiot' (Bridge, p.32). Moore made peace with Lily and the project went ahead.

10. Joseph was Collins's regular driver but Sara's other brother Batty, also a taxi driver, held a permit to drive for the authorities.

11. In his memoir *Army Without Banners* (also titled *On Another Man's Wounds*), Ernie O'Malley describes how members of Collins's Headquarters staff were referred to only by the initials of their rank. They also used code names for arms, ammunitions and operations (O'Malley, p.224). Tom C may be Tom Cullen and Bill T might be Liam Tobin. Tobin was Collins's lieutenant for intelligence-gathering; Cullen was one of Tobin's close associates. Devoted as she was to Lily Yeats, there is no indication that Lily ever knew from Sara that the Hylands were working for Collins.

12. John Butler Yeats died in New York on 3 February, 1922. He was eighty-two. His body was not returned to Ireland; he is buried in Chestertown Cemetery in upstate New York. The Yeats sisters had taken the girls to Jammet's, Dublin's best restaurant, which was located at the corner of Andrew's Street and Church Lane until 1926 when it moved to Nassau Street. A Dublin institution, it closed in 1967.

13. Dundrum was cut off for a week in the autumn of 1922. In a letter to Mrs Julia Ford, one of the Cuala Industries American patrons, Lolly wrote regarding her father's *Early Memories*, 'It won't be ready till spring because of the fighting. There wasn't any mail at all from September 10 - September 30, 1922' (E C Yeats to Julia Ford, 3 October 1922, Yale University Library).

14. The lease expired in the spring of 1922.

NOTES TO CHAPTER EIGHT

1. The Yeats sisters leased the second floor of 133 Lower Baggot Street for the Industries.

2. Michael Butler Yeats was born on 22 August, 1921 in Thames, England (Murphy, *Secrets*, p.212).

3. While the move to 82 Merrion Square was a temporary one, the Industry was housed there from August 1923 till at least February 1925. Sara reports that the move to Lower Baggot Street was completed while she was in Connemara during the summer of 1925. It was during this time that Lily became seriously ill again and that George Yeats took over the embroidery room. From then on, until her death in 1968, she was the person who bore the burden of the Cuala Industries.

4. An Túr Gloine (The Glass Tower) was the co-operative stained glass works founded by Sarah Purser (1848-1943).

5. The officer was probably Sean Beaumont.

6. The County Dublin Vocational Educational Department awarded scholarships to members of the evening language classes.

7. W B Yeats produced Rabindranath Tagore's play *The Post Office* at the Abbey Theatre in 1913, the same year that he contributed the introduction to the Indian poet's *Gitanjali* (1912).

8. W B Yeats's play *At the Hawk's Well*, was written in the style of the Japanese Noh theatre. The lines:

> *I call to the eye of the mind*
> *A well long choked up and dry*
> *And boughs long stripped by the wind*

are the opening lines of the play which are recited while the musicians unfold a black cloth (Yeats, *Variorum Plays*, p.399, 11 1-3).

9. Oliver St John Gogarty (1878-1957), Dublin surgeon, sportsman, writer and wit, served with W B Yeats in the first Seanad Eireann.

10. Lennox Robinson (1886-1958) was an Abbey director and playwright. The night of the production of *At the Hawk's Well* at 82 Merrion Square, Robinson played the part of one of the musicians (O'Casey, p.280).

11. Irish dramatist Sean O'Casey (1880-1964) left his own account of the evening in *Innisfallen, Fare Thee Well*, an account that reflects the shyness and discomfort that Sara reported:

> *No one spoke to him, and, right or wrong, he felt that*
> *they were uncomfortable with a tenement dweller in their*
> *midst.* (O'Casey, p.290).

O'Casey claimed only the portrait painter Estella Solomons spoke to him that evening.

12. The Jack Yeatses moved to 18 Fitzwilliam Square in 1929 (Caldwell, p.108).

13. Cottie Yeats's designs included many of the female saint figures in the set of twenty four sodality banners commisioned for St Brendan's Cathedral, Loughrea.

14. Leon O Broin reported that the first Irish college in Cois Farraige was in Spiddal in 1917 (*Just Like Yesterday*, p.13). The first college further west was held at Cnoc in 1925. It was not established by the government; Philip de Bhaldraithe of Ballyhaunis founded the college. I am grateful to Máirtín O Flathartaigh for information about the Irish colleges in Cois Farraige during the 1920s.

15. An tAthair Séamus O Ceallaigh was the parish priest during the first summer of Irish college at Cnoc.

16. Sara and the girls went to the house of Meait Diolún and his wife

Bríd which was located in Teach Mór, a townland east of the village of Indrebháin (Inverin).

17. Ragwort or ragweed was a plant associated with fairy belief.

18. Seán Padraic O Conaire (1883-1928) provided much of the literature in Modern Irish in the first two decades of the twentieth century. His short stories are on the syllabi of secondary school and university Irish courses.

19. O Conaire did not publish his version of the story or he did not publish it under that title. The story does not appear in An tSr Eibhlín ní Chionnaith's list of his works.

20. I think there will be a change on the white horses of the sea (white caps on the waves) today.

21. The young child in the Diolún household was Bairbre. I am grateful to her sister Jude Diolún Uí Fhatharta for her recollections of the time and her memories of Sara Hyland and of the other Irish students.

22. The *fear a' tighe* or man of the house was Meait Diolún.

23. The sea is dappled with foam.

24. Flower (1881-1946) was Deputy Keeper of Manuscripts in the British Museum. He is also associated with the literature of the Blasket Islands. He visited the Islands first in 1910 and encouraged Blasket writer Tomás O Criomhtháin (1856-1937) whose *An t-Oileánach* (The Islandman) was translated into English by Flower. His own *Love's Bitter Sweet* was published by Cuala in 1925.

25. The young author may have been another Blasket writer Muiris O Súilleabháin (1904-1950) whose autobiography *Fiche Blian ag Fás* (*Twenty Years A-Growing*) was published in 1933.

26. Lily's poor health was acute from 1923 until 1929 when her condition was properly diagnosed as an abnormal thyroid (Murphy, *Secrets*, p.240). She was in England from the summer of 1923 until the early spring of 1925 and then was able to go into Cuala for only a few hours each week (Murphy, *Secrets*, p.230).

27. Lord Ashbourne as President of the Gaelic League wore kilts (O Broin, p.54). Sara may have been referring to another kilt-wearing Gaeilgeoir named Claude Chavasse who had also stayed at Tighe Dhiolún.

28. Pádraic Og O Conaire (1893-1971) was not related to Seán Phádraic who was born in Galway in 1882 and went to an uncle in Rosmuc when he was about eleven (de Bhaldraithe, p.5).

29. Pádraic Pearse's story is of an old traditional singer from Connemara who loses a singing competition to a younger woman but who nevertheless walks to Dublin to sing in the Oireachtas. She wins first prize, but she dies from the hardship of her journey.

30. Ruth Pollexfen Lane-Poole, who promoted Cuala in Australia for Lily, got the commision for the bedspreads made for the visit of the Duke and Duchess of York in 1927. The Duke's bedspread was exhibited in the window of Freke's store in Dublin and there was a story about the bedspreads and Cuala in the *Manchester Guardian* on 7 February, 1927 (Murphy, *Secrets*, p.236).

31. It is hard to identify the pair. FJ McCormick who married Eileen Crowe was forty-two in 1926 and Arthur Sinclair and Máire O'Neill

married in 1926 after Máire O'Neill was widowed. Sheelagh Richards married Denis Johnston in 1929 but they do not fit Sara's description.
32. In 1844, John Mercer invented a way to process cotton for dyeing by the use of chemicals.
33. Lawrence Hyland was married in July 1928.
34. Sara may have been referring to Sruthán, a small harbour on the right of the main road out of the village of Carraroe. There is a stone bridge and a harbour for turf boats going to Aran.
35. De Valera's 'empty political formula' description of the oath of allegiance enabled him to devise a ceremony whereby he could enter his name in the Dáil book but not take the oath. In that way de Valera and his Fianna Fáil party could enter the Dáil in 1927.
36. Elisabeth Curran Solterer has suggested that this is probably the Papal Duchess Genevieve Garvan Brady, though she was not widowed until 1930.

NOTES TO CHAPTER NINE

1. The ancient gathering at Tailteann (Tara) in the honour of the god Lugh featured competitions, especially horse-racing. A nice connection to Sara's prize is the mention in the medieval *Acallamh na Senórach* of three noted embroideresses who provided dazzling garments for the Tara festival (Mac Neill, p.328).
2. Dublin 2RN, the Irish broadcasting service, began on 1 January, 1926. Leon O Broin describes the early broadcasts in *Just Like Yesterday* (pp.167-168).
3. Diane Dixon has Sara's silver medal; Hilary Dixon has the bronze medal from the Tailteann competitions. The bronze medal was for second place in the Costumed Figures; the silver was for a first prize award (1928), a silk shawl designed by Cottie Yeats and worked by Sara.
4. Ballinahoun is in the parish of Cnoc. Like Loch na Cruimhinne and Cloughmore, the townlands are located in west Galway where Casla Bay empties into Galway Bay.
5. That's enough.
6. In Pearse's story, Old Matthias watches his neighbours go to Mass, but he does not go himself. He is reconcilled with the Church when a boy messenger, Iosagán, comes to him with a message of peace. Sara was reminded of Pearse's description of Sunday morning Mass-goers:
> All the people were gathered into Mass. Old Matthias
> saw them going past, in ones and twos, or in little
> groups. The boys were running and leaping. The girls
> were chattering merrily. The women were conversing in low
tones (Pearse, pp.229-230).
7. There are two holy wells in An Bhánrainn Bhán Theas, Banraghbawn South (Robinson, p.132).
8. The annual pattern in honour of St Colmcille that Sara mentions continues today every ninth of June. The stone is known locally as

Mullán Cholm Cille, Colmcille's Boulder (Robinson, p.132).

9. The local National School teacher was Seán O Coisdealbha. While O Coisdealbha is Costigan, he was called Seán Costello. He went to the Meath Gealtacht in 1932 where he taught in Rath Cairn. I am grateful to Máirtín O Flathartiagh for this information.

10. 'Had I the heavens' embroidered cloths' is the first line of W B Yeats's poem 'He wishes for the Cloths of Heaven'. In another poem 'A Coat', '... a coat/Covered with embroideries/Out of old mythologies' is a metaphor for the poet's song.

11. The red dye was made from lichen and plants such as heather and briar root (Dunleavy, p.166). There is no indication that the numbers of rows a braid was a measure of wealth.

12. Oh, look at the big dog!

13. Lily was never able to work full-time after her 1923 collapse. She came into Cuala on a part-time basis until the end of 1931.

14. While Sara does not mention it in her Memoir, she confided in Lily who reported to Ruth Pollexfen in a 1933 letter that 'things were very different and she (Sara) could not get on with Miss Lolly' (Murphy, *Secrets*, p.247).

15. Dublin celebrated the Centenary of Catholic Emancipation during the week of 16-23 June, 1929. The Cuala Industries took an ad in the *Catholic Emancipation Centenary Record.*

16. General Eoin O'Duffy (1892-1944) organised the mass gatherings as part of his responsibility as the Commisioner of the Garda Síochana.

17. The general practice was that the family organised the collection for the priest not that the priest collected the money for a funeral himself. The practice existed in other parts of Ireland as well. For example, priests' collections were part of Tipperary life until the 1960s.

18. Sara's report of men as well as women keening is also unusual.

19. The picture was based on one of the Sodality banners designed by Jack Yeats and embroidered by Lily and her staff for the Loughrea Cathedral in 1902. In 1932, the parish priest asked Lily to rework the faces on the banners (Murphy, *Secrets*, p.413, n.45). In 1930, Mrs Oliver St John Gogarty commissioned four banners including the one of St Colmcille (Pyle, *National Gallery*, p.10).

20. The young artist who had designed the Stations of the Cross was Bridget O'Brien, daughter of the painter Dermot O'Brien. Yeats also commissioned designs from Diana Murphy but that was later. On 30 June, 1932, Yeats wrote to Olivia Shakespeare:

> *I have that rarest of things - a success in my own family. You remember those Stations of the Cross. I got three examples designed and worked in preparation for Eucharistic Week. The whole set has been sold and my sister has profitable work till next May.* (Yeats, *Letters*, pp.797-798).

21. The Duchess Brady bought a set of the Stations of the Cross. They are at the Jesuit Novitiate in Wernersville, PA where the Bradys are buried. The Stations, or three of them, won the First Prize for Embroidery in the Arts and Crafts Exhibition of 1932. They were

praised for their 'exceptional high standards and beauty' (Murphy, *Secrets*, p.246).

22. Trains stopped for Northern Ireland Customs at Goraghwood.

23. The Sixth Station of the Cross depicts Veronica giving Christ her veil to wipe his face as He walked the road to Calvary. According to tradition, when He returned the veil, His face was imprinted in the cloth.

24. This is the only time that Sara criticises Lolly directly and she describes Lolly's faults not as individual but as family failings. Lily's letters to Ruth relate Sara's difficulties working with Lolly at the Industries. Sara's complaints supported her own trials with Lolly.

25. Annie Kiernan Hyland died 20 July, 1932.

NOTES TO CHAPTER TEN

1. In the General Election of 1932 de Valera's Fianna Fáil party won the largest number of seats in the Dáil though not a majority. Sara, a firm Cumann na nGaedhealer, was not a Dev admirer.

2. James Dillon (1902-1986), a flamboyant orator, became Vice-President of Fine Gael in 1933 when the party was created from a coalition of Cumann na nGaedheal, the Centre Party and the National Guard. He broke with Fine Gael in 1941 but rejoined ten years later. He was the leader of the party from 1959-1965.

3. Patrick McGilligan (1889-1979), was Minister for External Affairs in the Cumann na nGaedheal government from 1927-1932. He held ministerial posts in the two coalition governments: Finance (1948-1951) and Attorney General (1954-1957).

4. John Aloysius Costello (1891-1976) headed the two coalition governments: 1948-1951, 1954-1957. He declared Ireland a Republic in Canada on 7 September, 1948.

5. Isaac Butt (1813-1879), a barrister and MP for Youghal and later Limerick, founded the Home Rule movement in 1870. He was a friend of John Butler Yeats.

6. When May left Cuala, Sara worked on alone. It apparently was a difficult time for her. While she does not mention problems getting on with Lolly in her Memoir, she confided to Lily that things were not the same and that she was having a hard time getting on with Lolly (Murphy, *Secrets*, pp.247-248).

7. Yeats's biographer Joseph Hone reported that Yeats's poor health began in October, 1927, with lung congestion (Hone, p.393).

8. While Yeats was devoted to Lily and admired her work, he felt new designs were necessary. In 1937, he gave her Diana Murphy's design for 'The Land of Youth'. She wrote to Ruth that she thought it 'queer and modern' but she said she would work it for Yeats (Murphy, *Secrets*, p.250).

9. The Yeatses gave up 82 Merrion Square in 1928 and moved to a flat at 42 Fitzwilliam Square. In the spring of 1932, George Yeats found Riversdale, a house a mile from the village of Rathfarnham.

10. Yeats went to Rapallo first in 1928 where he met Ezra Pound; he wintered there in 1929-1930 and kept a flat there until June, 1934 (Hone, p.393, p.441).

11. Rose Hodgins was a long-time member of the Yeats household. She was with them at 3 Blenheim Road, London. Murphy reports Rose's death as 15 March, 1930 (*Secrets*, p.241). Monk Gibbon said of Rose:

> *Their one surviving maid - now grown distinctly*
> *elderly herself - ministered to them both, but at*
> *different times and in different rooms. She adored Lily*
> *but if Lolly's name was mentioned by me, she would*
> *cast her eyes to heaven and implied that it needed a*
> *saint out of heaven to survive the caprice of that*
> *volatile personality.* (Gibbon, p.172).

12. Lolly was a salaried teacher in London in the late 1890s who earned £300 a year, a sum she never earned again when she returned to Dublin (Lewis, p.38).

13. Like the Yeats sisters and the Hyland family, Rose is buried in St Nahi's Churchyard.

14. William Murphy mentions a Maureen Franks, the eighteen year old daughter of the Yeats's neighbour, who worked with Sara at the Industry in 1934. While Sara and Maureen got along, Lily reported that Lolly interfered with the girls (Murphy, *Secrets*, p.247).

15. While Sara gives no details about her decision to leave the Industries on 1 January, 1935, she told Lolly that she had to keep house for her brothers. She planned to continue work at home for Lily on a commission basis. On 27 November, 1934, a letter from Lily to Ruth suggests that Sara found it too difficult to continue to work with Lolly (Murphy, *Secrets*, p.247).

16. The Free State Army ordered three military flags at fifty pounds each. Sara gave Lolly a ten-percent commission. Her winning design was a flame in a stylized Celtic pattern. An article in the *Sunday Independent*, 'Commemorating Ireland's Military Glory' includes photographs of Sara working on a flag and the 1st Brigade flag that Sara describes. She was working on the flags in August, 1935.

NOTES TO CHAPTER ELEVEN

1. Sara qualified as an embroidery teacher in 1938; she taught until 1962. She was teaching in the Shankill Library in the 1940s.

2. Sara's niece Josie Dixon recalls that a visit to Miss Yeats was a regular feature of her Irish holiday. She remembers Lily as an old lady in a high bed.

3. The Yeatses had rooms at the Hotel Séjour, Cap Martin. Yeats died in France on 28 January, 1939.

4. Yeats was buried at Roquebrune until his body was returned to Ireland in 1948 for burial in the shadow of Ben Bulben in Drumcliffe Churchyard.

5. Lolly died from heart complications on 16 January, 1940.

6. The Cuala Press left Baggot Street in 1940 relocating in George Yeats's home till her death in 1968.

7. Sara's niece Josie Dixon said that Sara taught in the Dundrum Tech until 1962.

8. Sara taught at the Carnegie Library in Dundrum and at the Stillorgan Library.

9. Maria Brien was hired by the Yeats sisters in 1889. While she worked for them for nearly fifty years Lily never trusted her.

10. While Jack had been giving Lily money, George Yeats provided most of Lily's financial support (Murphy, *Secrets*, p.262). Lily had a stroke in August, 1943, which left her unable to embroider.

11. Marie Mason, who started studying with Sara when she was thirteen, remembers Sara speaking Irish and trying to get her pupils to speak Irish. She told them stories about the legendary craftsman, the Gobán Saor.

12. Sara thought Lily was referring to the proximity of the Yeats and Hyland grave sites. Lily, who was known to have second sight, was probably speaking about returning in a vision or in a dream.

NOTES TO THE EPILOGUE

1. Gibbon wrote this advice to Sara in a letter dated 31 January, 1969. The letter is in the possession of the Dixon family.

2. Gibbon mentioned the incident in two letters to Sara: on 11 February 1969 and on 22 May, 1969.

3. Photographs of the transfer designs appear in Hilary Pyle, *Jack B Yeats in the National Gallery*, Plates 10 and 12.

Notes

WORKS CITED:

Birmingham, Stephen. *Real Lace. America's Irish Rich*. New York: Harper and Row, 1973.

Bowe, Nicola Gordon. 'The Irish Arts and Crafts Movement, 1886-1925', *Irish Arts Review Yearbook*, 1990-1991, 172-185.

Bridge, Ursula, ed. *W B Yeats and T Sturge Moore. Their Correspondence 1901-1939*. London: Routledge and Kegan, Paul, 1953.

Caldwell, Martha B. 'Jack B Yeats. A Chronology of Major Personal events, Publications and Exhibitions' in *Jack B Yeats. A Centenary Gathering*, ed. Roger McHugh. Dublin: Dolmen, 1971.

Carleton, Karen et al., *Beneath the Granite Throne. Sandyford-Dundrum-Ballawley and Surrounding Areas*, from *Times Past*. Dublin: Blueprint Ltd., n.d.

'Comemorating Ireland's Military Glory', *Irish Independent*, 22 August, 1935.

Coote, Michael H. *A Short History of Taney Parish*. Dublin: Beacon, 1968.

Crookshank, Anne O. *Irish Women Artists from the Eighteenth Century to the Present Day*. Dublin: The National Gallery, 1987.

Danaher, Kevin. *The Year in Ireland*. Dublin: Mercier Press, 1972.

de Bhaldraithe, Tomás, ed. 'Réamhra', *Scothscéalta*. Baile Atha Cliath: Sáirséal agus Dill, 1962.

Donnelly, Most Rev N. *A Short History of Some Dublin Parishes*, 111. Dublin: Catholic Truth Society, n.d.

Dunleavey, Mairéad. *Dress in Ireland*. London: BT Batsford, 1989.

Fay, WG and Catherine Carswell. *The Fays of the Abbey Theatre. An Autobiographical Record*. London: Rich and Cowan, 1935.

Gibbon, Monk. *The Masterpiece and the Man: Yeats as I Knew Him*. New York: Macmillan, 1959.

Gregory, Augusta. 'Return of the Fenians', in *Ideals in Ireland*, ed. Lady Gregory. New York: Lemma Publishing, 1975 (1901), pp. 65-73.

Heilbrun, Carolyn G. *Writing a Woman's Life*. New York: Norton, 1988.

Hone, Joseph. *W B Yeats. 1865-1939*. London: Pelican, 1971.

Joyce, Weston St John. *The Neighbourhood of Dublin*. Dublin: Gill, 1913.

Kinsella, Thomas. trans. *The Táin*. New York: Oxford, 1970.

Lewis, Gifford. *The Yeats Sisters and the Cuala*. Dublin: Irish Academic Press, 1994.

Liddy, Pat. *Dublin Be Proud*. Dublin: Chadworth, 1987.

Mac Neill, Máire. *The Festival of Lughnasa*. London: Oxford, 1962.

Matthews, James. *Voices. A Life of Frank O'Connor*. Dublin: Gill and Macmillan, 1983.

Miller, Liam. *The Dun Emer Press, Later the Cuala Press*. Dublin: Dolmen Press, 1973.

Mulligan, Fergus. *One Hundred and Fifty Years of Irish Railways*. Belfast: The Appletree Press, 1983.

195

Murphy, Clíona. '"The Time of Stars and Stripes" - the American Influence of the Irish Suffrage Movement', in *Woman Surviving*, eds. Maria Liddy and Clíona Murphy. Dublin: Poolbeg, 1989, pp. 180-205.

Murphy, William. *Family Secrets*. Syracuse: Syracuse University Press, 1985. *Prodigal Father*. Ithaca: Cornell Universtiy Press, 1978.

Nolan, J. *The Changing Face of Dundrum*. 4th ed. Dublin: Elo Press, 1987.

O'Brien, Joseph. *Dear Dirty Dublin: a City in Distress, 1889-1916*. Berkeley: University of California Press, 1982.

OBroin, Leon. *In Great Haste. The Letters of Michael Collins and Kitty Kiernan*. Dublin: Gill and Macmillan, 1983. *Just Like Yesterday*. An Autobiography. Dublin: Gill and Macmillan, 1985.

O'Casey, Sean. *Innisfallen, Fare Thee Well*. New York: Macmillan, 1949.

O'Connor, Frank. *My Father's Son*. New York: Alfred Knopf, 1969.

O'Malley, Ernie. *Army Without Banners*. Boston: Houghton Mifflin, 1937.

Centenary History of Holy Cross. Dublin: Elo Press, 1978.

Pearse, Pádraic. *Scríbhinní*. Dublin: The Phoenix Publishing Company n.d.

Poulson, Christine. *William Morris*. Secaucus: Quintet, 1989.

Pyle, Hilary. *Jack B Yeats in the National Gallery of Ireland*. Dublin: National Gallery of Ireland, 1986.

Robinson, Tim. *Connemara*. Roundstone: Folding Landscapes, 1990.

Seidel, Linda. 'Celtic Revivals and Women's Work' in *Imagining an Irish Past. The Celtic Revival 1840-1940*. Chicago: University of Chicago Press, 1992, pp. 23-43.

Sheehy, Jeanne. *The Rediscovery of Ireland's Past: The Celtic Revival 1830-1930*. London: Thames and Hudson, 1980.

'Taxi-Driver to Michael Collins', *Michael Collins Memorial Foundation Supplement* (20 April, 1966), p.16.

Yeats, William Butler. *The Celtic Twilight*. London: AH Bullen, 1902. *The Letters of W B Yeats*. ed. Allan Wade. New York: Octagon Books, 1980. *Memoirs*. ed. Dennis Donoghue. New York: Macmillan, 1972. *The Poems of W B Yeats. A New Edition*. ed. Richard J Finneran. New York: Macmillan, 1983. *Uncollected Prose*. Volume 2. ed. John P Frayne and Colton Johnson. New York: Columbia University Press, 1976. *The Variorum Edition of the Plays of W B Yeats*. ed. Russell K Allspach. New York: Macmillan, 1969.

MANUSCRIPT SOURCES:

Byrne, Damien and John Forrest. 'Ghost in Dundrum', *Haunted Ireland*. Typescript. Dundrum Library.

Yeats, Elizabeth Corbet. Letter to Miss Julia Ford. 3 October, 1922. Yale Bieneke Library. Letter to Augusta, Lady Gregory. January, 1908. New York Public Library. Berg Collection.

Yeats, Susan Mary. Letter to John Butler Yeats. 11 October, 1908. National Library of Ireland. 31.112.

INDEX

Abbey Theatre, 15, 17, 77-8,
81, 82, 86, 105, 125, 135-6
Aberdeen, Lord and Lady, 83
Allgood, Sarah, 81, 183n
Anglo-Irish Treaty, 115, 116
talks to negotiate, 112-13,
114-15
Aran Islands, 139
Auxiliaries, 109, 110, 111

Balbriggan, County Dublin, 40,
57
basket-making, 146
beggars, 25
Belfast, 83, 154
Black and Tans, 106, 108, 109,
110, 111, 118
blacksmiths see Dundrum
Boer War, 38
bonfires for celebrations, 49,
112
Book of Leinster
'Táin', 13-14
Borthwick, Norma, 43
Brady, Father, 24
Bray, County Wicklow, 87
Brien, Maria, 170
British Army, 94, 105, 168
conscription to, 96, 104
evacuated from Republic, 116
Browning, Robert, 66
'Bun Lady', 38-9, 53
died, 65
Burne-Jones, Edward, 65
Butt, Isaac, 162

carpet-making, 30, 63
Carraroe, County Galway, 137
Catholic Church, 111
Centenary of Catholic
Emancipation, 150
Eucharistic Congress, 155
Jubilee Year celebration, 42
censorship by British and IRA,
112
Chesterton, G K, 68, 185n
Christmas
celebrations, 13, 34, 69
post, 55
see also Cuala Industries
Churchtown, 68, 100, 102, 118
Barn Elms, 49
Bottle Tower, 73
Churchtown Road, 63, 64, 68
Classons Bridge Road, 66
Gurteen Dheas,16, 20, 42, 63,
117, 167, 169, 170
Sydenham Villas, 42, 43
see also Cuala Industries
cinema and moving pictures
(cinematographs), 34, 89-90,
149
Civil War, 14, 115-16,117
clothes, 20, 33, 35, 78, 97, 123,
148
children's, 33-4, 35, 53, 128-
9, 145
of Cuala girls at wedding, 15,
78, 81
in England, 92
at funerals, 93

fabrics, 33,97
  in Connemara, 148
footwear, 33
kilt, 133
at weddings, 33, 81
of Yeats sisters, 59
coinage, 26
Cois Farraige Gaeltacht
  (Connemara), 127
  see also Sara Hyland: Irish
  language summer school
Collins, Michael, 11, 14, 103,
  104, 108, 109, 110, 158
  Commander of Irish Army,
  116
  death of, 117-8
  in Treaty negotiations, 113,
  115
  smashes British spy system,
  103-4
  see also Joseph Hyland
Colum, Eileen, 69, 82, 156
Colum, Padraic,69
Constitution, 158
co-operative movement in
  Ireland, 68
Cosgrave, William T, 117
Costello, J A, 162
County Dublin Vocational
  Education Department
  scholarships, 124, 127, 134
Courtney, May, 15, 74, 75, 76-
  8, 79-80, 82, 86, 108, 125,
  155, 157, 158, 162, 164
Craig, James Herbert, 17
Croker, Richard 'Boss', 50, 62
Crowe, Susan, 25
Cuala Industries, 11, 14, 15, 16,
  150, 162, 169
  Baggot Street premises, 121,
  132-4
  Christmas sales, 133, 141
    Aonach, 69, 134, 141
  Churchtown Road (Cuala
    Cottage) premises, 14, 63-4,
    66-7

embroidery department, 13,
  59, 63, 64, 67, 71, 74, 82,
  126, 132, 135, 154, 155,
  157, 164, 165
  baby clothes made by, 97
  banners made by, 97, 133,
    153, 164-5, 174
  sewing 'bees', 80
  see also, Lily Yeats
  garden allotments at, 94, 96,
    97, 105
  Halloween parties at, 68, 87
  Merrion Square premises,
    122, 124, 125-7
  patrons of, 90, 97, 133, 135,
    139, 153, 154, 174
  press room, 15, 64, 82, 101,
    126, 155, 157
  see also Lolly Yeats
  visitors to, 15, 64-5, 71, 83-4,
    88, 101, 126, 133, 135, 156
    literary readings of, 65, 71,
      74
    music of, 83
  see also Dun Emer Press;
    Sara Hyland: employment;
    Lily Yeats; Lolly Yeats
Customs and Excise
  between Ireland and
    England, 153
  between Republic and
    Northern Ireland, 154
  see also Larry Hyland

dances, 82
Daylight Saving Bill, 105
death, funerals and wakes, 54
  in Connemara, 151-2
  in England, 92-3
de Valera, Eamon, 104, 109,
  110, 111, 113, 116, 158
  in America, 104, 108
  Document One, 114
  entered the Dáil, 139
Dickens
  David Copperfield, 51

Dillon, James, 162
Doyle, Bob, 56
Dublin, 12, 82
  Alexandra Girls' College, 122
  Baggot Street, 121, 122
  Ballinteer, 102
  Ballsbridge
    Royal Dublin Society, 134, 143
  Beaumont hospital, 83
  Booterstown Strand, 49
  Centenary of Catholic Emancipation celebrations, 150
  Christ Church Cathedral, 77
  Croke Park, 142
  Dawson Street
    Mansion House, 80, 134, 141
  Dorset Street, 39
  Dublin Castle, 103
  Dún Laoghaire
    Purty Kitchen, 39
  Ely Place
    Conradh na Gaeige, 124
  Engineer's Hall, 80
  Eucharistic Congress, 155
  Findlater's Church, 39
  Fitzwilliam Square, 122, 126, 153, 162, 169
  General Post Office, 39, 100
  Glasnevin, 14, 99, 100
    Cemetery, 117
  Grafton Street
    Mitchell's, 38
  Harcourt Street
    Municipal Art Gallery, 77
  Hatch Street, 79, 122
  Jammet's, 117
  Kildare Street
    Municipal Art School, 167
  Lower Camden Street, 89
  Merrion Square, 82, 122, 124
  Molesworth Street
    Orange Lodge, 133
  Mount Jerome Cemetery, 65
  National Gallery, 15, 174
  O'Connell Bridge, 39, 150
  O'Connell Street, 76, 100
    Clery's, 77
  Parnell Square, 114, 132
  Pearse Street (Great Brunswick Street)
    Antient Concert Rooms, 103
  Phoenix Park, 100
    RIC depot, 75
  Rathfarnham, 158, 163
    St Enda's College, 82
  Rotunda, 39
    Round Room, 69
    Royal Academy, 156
  St Columba's College, 22, 78, 81
  St Stephen's Green, 126
  Sandyford, 50
  Sandymount Avenue, 72
  South King Street
    O'Neill's, 75
  Terenure, 100
  University College, 122
  Upper Pembroke Street
    An Túr Gloine, 122
  Zoological Gardens, 34-5, 75
  see also Abbey Theatre; Churchtown; Dundrum; Gaiety Theatre; Theatre Royal
Dundrum, 17, 23, 132, 153
  asylum (private), 35-6, 119
  Ballinteer Road, 43, 55, 56, 62
  big houses of, 23-4, 43, 63
    Woodlawn, 23
  Birches Lane, 48
  blacksmith, 22, 23
  Browne's shop, 12, 17, 55-6, 58-9
    fire at, 45
    see also Sara Hyland
  Carnegie Library, 93, 162
  Central Criminal Lunatic

Asylum, 74
characters of, 24-6, 41-2, 118
in Civil War, 14
countryside surrounding, 23, 63-4
Daw's Bridge, 28
Deveney's, 12
drainage scheme, 68
election meetings in, 48-9
Exaltation of the Holy Cross Church, 22, 40
first council houses, 40
gas mains in, 102
Kilmacud Road, 37, 48, 49, 56
Main Street, 22, 32, 47, 54, 56, 73, 102, 121, 119
Manor Mill Laundry, 29, 62, 91
Meadow Brook, 32
Mount Anville
  Convent, 30
  House, 34
Pembroke Cottages, 11, 12
Portobello Barracks, 32
Post Office 54-5
Roebuck Park, 24
Royal Irish Constabulary barracks, 37
St Nahi's Church, 16, 23, 169, 173, 174
Sandyford Road, 35, 55, 56, 62
Runnymede, 13, 42
  see also Dun Emer
schools, 21-2, 23, 62
  present National School, 56
shops of, 23, 47, 63, 73
Slang, river, 22, 62
Station, 11, 22, 24, 36-7, 54, 56, 63
Sweet Briar Lane, 48
Taney Church, 36, 93
Telephone Office, 45, 51
Upper Churchtown Road, 23
Upper Kilmacud Road, 35, 36

see also Dun Emer
Dun Emer, 13, 30, 43, 58, 61, 62, 64, 68, 69, 153
  Dun Emer Press, 14

Eason's, 22
Easter Rising (1916), 14, 99-101, 102, 103, 109
Edward VII, King of England, 62
embroidery see Cuala Industries; Lily Yeats
employment, working hours, 48
Enniskerry, County Wicklow, 12, 31, 137
European Community, 11
excursion parties, 31-2

famine, 72
fire engines, 45
fleas, 29-30, 89, 90, 112, 127
  remedies for, 89
Flower, Robin,133
folklore and the supernatural, 28, 67, 72-3, 86
food, 26, 41, 50
  cooking, 26-7
  ice-cream, 78-9
  shortages
    in Easter Rising, 100
    in World War I, 93-4, 96, 168
    in World War II, 168
  sweets, 22-3
franchise see voting
Free State Army *see* Irish Army
funerals *see* death
Furlong, Alice, 97

Gaelic League, 11, 13, 30, 43, 49, 114, 133, 136
Gaffney, Brigid (Cissie), 57, 99, 175
Gaiety Theatre, 12, 57-8, 79,

117

Galway, 127
  Bay, 129, 130
  Eyre Square, 134
  see also railway
garden 'bees', 80
George VI and Elizabeth, King
  and Queen of England, 135
Gurteen Dheas *see* Churchtown
Gibbon, Monk, 174, 175
  *The Masterpiece and the
  Man: Yeats as I Knew Him*,
  16, 174
Gladstone, W E, 11
Gleeson, Evelyn, 13, 14, 42,
  61, 63
Goff, Dr, 53, 74
Gogarty, Dr Oliver, 125
Gordon, Dr (Medical Advisor
  to the RIC), 75
gramophones, 73, 75
Greystones, County Wicklow,
  87
Griffith, Arthur, 13, 49, 115
  death of, 117

Halle Orchestra, 83
Health Act, 83
Heilbrun, Carolyn *Writing a
  Woman's Life*, 16
Hitler, Adolf, 168
Hodgins, Rose, 163
Home Rule, 13, 96, 107-8, 110
  Second Bill, 11
horse racing, 50
  Calary Point to Point races,
  143
  Curragh, County Kildare, 101
  Leopardstown Racecourse, 76
houses, 19-20
  beds, 20-1
  big houses, life in, 43-4, 63,
  89
    see also Dundrum
  in Connemara, 145-6
  lighting, 29

gas, 102
Howe, Elias, 92
Howth, County Dublin, 51, 108
hunt, a, 32
Hyde, Douglas
  'The Return of the Fenians',
  13
Hyland, Annie Kiernan (Sara's
  mother), 11, 16, 26, 28, 39,
  40, 41, 49, 52, 53-4, 80, 84,
  110
  death of, 17, 155
  death of sister, 57
  employment of, 16, 21
  fables and folklore of, 38
  in Glasnevin for Easter
    Rising, 14, 99-100
  love of music and opera, 12,
  28, 38, 76
  love of paintings, 12, 20
Hyland, Batty (Bartholomew),
  19, 41, 43, 52, 53, 57, 102,
  103
  buys gramophone, 75-6
  chauffeur, 53, 74, 82
Hyland, James (Sara's father),
  20, 49, 53-4, 65, 76
  death of, 84
  as jarvey, 22, 37, 38, 50, 51
Hyland, Jimmy, 19, 21, 41, 54,
  55, 80, 89
  death of, 121
  driver for Dr Goff, 74
  work for Post Office, 61
Hyland, Joseph, 19, 29, 49, 57,
  97, 100, 110, 113
  apprentice to painter and
    decorator, 47, 52, 83
  birth of daughter May, 99-
  100
  delivered newspapers, 41
  driver for Michael Collins,
  11, 14, 104, 109
  taxi driver, 97, 101
Hyland, Larry, 19, 27-8, 175
  wedding of, 151

work for Customs and Excise, 95, 137
Hyland, Patrick, 19, 40
Hyland, Sara
aeroplane flight (1927), 76, 137
attended auctions, 106-7, 119
birth of, 11, 19
'Bun Lady', outings with, 12, 39, 50-1, 63
character and appearance of, 16-17, 173-4
childhood of, 12, 19-59
confirmation of, 53
first Holy Communion, 40
fruit picking, 49
household chores, 52
part-time work, 12
in Browne's shop, 58, 59
milk collection, 43-5
dreams of, 85-6
employment, 16
at Cuala Industries, 13, 14-15, 61-99, 101-2, 105-7, 116-117, 118, 122, 124-7, 132-3, 135-6, 139, 141, 143, 149, 153-7, 164-5, 167
teacher at evening classes, 169, 170-1, 173
teacher at Technical School, 15, 169
see also childhood *above*
friendship with May, 15, 74-5
outings with May, 75, 76-8, 79-80, 82, 86, 108
and Irish language, 16, 133, 171, 173
evening classes, 113-14, 124, 136-7, 143
lessons at Cuala, 97
summer school, 12, 15, 17, 127-31, 134-5, 137-9, 144-50, 151-2
opera, 56, 57-8
political interests of, 13, 16, 158-62
religious convictions of, 65, 77
stars and planets, interest in, 56-7
supernatural beliefs and folklore of, 44-5, 47-8, 101
visits England, 90, 95
cotton factory, 91-2
uncle's funeral, 92-3
visits Lily Yeats, 15, 162, 164, 167-8, 169-71
visits Northern Ireland, 154
Hyland, Willie, 19, 37

Industry, The *see* Cuala Industries
Ireland's Eye, 108
Irish Army, 14, 116, 117, 164, 165
Irish Independent, 39, 139
Irish language revival, 113, 133
see also Gaelic League; Sara Hyland
Irish Literary Revival, 11
Irish Republican Army (IRA), 104, 108, 109, 110, 111
Irish Republican Brotherhood, 96
Irregulars, 115, 117

Joyce, James, 185n
The Dead, 13

Khayyám, Omar, 24
Kiernan, grandfather (of Sara), 12, 40, 57
Kilruddery Estate, County Wicklow, 87

Laird, Helen, 105
Lane, Sir Hugh, 77
Lane-Poole, Charles, 78, 118
Lane-Poole, Captain Dick, 81
Liberal Party, 13
lighting, public, 47, 56

see also houses
Lloyd George, David, 111
London Exhibition, 66
Loughrea Cathedral, County
  Galway, 153, 174
Lusk, County Dublin, 12, 39,
  57, 91

McGilligan, Patrick, 162
MacGreevy, Thomas, 174
MacNeill, Eoin, 177n
magic lanterns, 34
Martyn, Edward, 153
Masonic lodges, 97
matchmaking, 152
Matthews, Canon, 34
medicine
  folk cures, 28
  see also fleas: remedies for
mercerised cotton, 136
Merton Abbey Works, Surrey,
  43, 66
Middleton, Lucy, 87-8
Mitchell, Susan Langstaff, 68,
  87
moneylending, 26
Moore's melodies, 82
Morris, May, 169, 179n, 181n
Morris, Jane, 65-6
Morris, William, 65-6, 155,
  169
  see also Merton Abbey
    Works
  sound introduced in, 152-3
Murphy, Diana, 191n, 192n
Murphy, William, 16
  Prodigal Father, 15
music see opera; street
  musicians

nationalism, 13, 50, 96, 154
  Yeats sisters sympathetic to,
    14
New York Exhibition, 63

O'Brien, Bridget, 191n

O'Casey, Seán, 125, 178n
O Conaire, Pádraic Og, 134
O Conaire, Seán Pádraic, 130,
  134
O Direáin, Máirtín, 17
O'Duffy, General Eoin, 150
O'Gorman, Mrs, 51-2
Old Age Pensions, 83
Old Moore's Almanac, 56
opera, 57-8
  companies, 12, 58
  see also Annie Hyland; Sara
    Hyland
Orby, 62-3
O'Reilly, Joseph, 102, 103, 104
Orr, Monica, 83

Palles, Chief Baron Sir
  Christopher, 13, 34
partition, 154
Pear's Annual, 12, 20
Pearse, Padraic, 134, 176n
  Bríd na nAmhran, 135
  Iosagán, 145
Pembroke, Earl of, 34
phonographs *see* gramophones
plantations, 94
Plunkett, Sir Horace, 68
Plunkett, James
  Strumpet City, 174
Pollexfen, Ruth (Mrs Lane-
  Poole), 63, 64, 67, 71, 78, 79,
    85, 118, 135
  wedding of, 15, 78, 80-2
Pollexfen, Susan, 163
poorhouse *see* workhouse
Pound, Ezra, 163
Proclamation, reading of the,
  100
Purcell's touring theatre
  company, 56
Purser, Sarah, 122, 178n

Queen's Theatre, 17, 79-80

railway, 90, 123, 127-8

Broadstone Station, 127, 131
Carrickmines Station, 137
Dartry Station, 66, 80
Galway Station, 144
Harcourt Street line, 11, 22,
   41, 54, 57, 122-4, 176n
Maam Cross Station, 135
Milltown Station, 41
see also Dundrum: Station
religious practices, 29, 145
   Lent, 42, 59
see also Catholic Church
Robinson, Lennox, 125
Rosmuc, County Galway, 134-
   5, 138
Rossetti, Christina, 65
Royal Irish Constabulary
   (RIC), 75, 102-3, 109
see also Dundrum
Russell, George ('AE'), 68

St Colmcille legend, 145, 153
St Patrick's Day celebrations,
   30
   Industrial Exhibition parade,
   30
Saturday Evening Herald, 59
schools, 21-2
   Protestant, 35
sewing machines, 92
silk, tax on, 136
Sinn Fein, 11, 13, 49
   courts, 104-5
Skeffington, Hanna Sheehy, 14
Sligo, 68, 81
   Yeats family in, 72, 162
   Yeats Museum, 69
Stephens, James
   The Crock of Gold, 126
street musicians, 24-5
   barrel organ grinder, 25, 156
suffragette movement, 102
see also voting
Swords, County Dublin, 40

Tagore, Rabindranath, 124

Tailteann Games, revival of,
   141-2, 143, 149
Tarot cards, 88
theatre-going
   touring companies, 56, 149
   see Abbey Theatre; Gaiety
      Theatre; Purcell's; Queen's
      Theatre
Theatre Royal, 79
time difference between
   England and Ireland, 95
Titanic, sinking of, 83
transport, 22, 76, 81, 87, 128-9,
   132
   aeroplanes, 76
   bicycles, 93
   boat, 139
      Dún Laoghaire to
         Holyhead, 90
      North Wall to Liverpool, 95
   buses, 153
   carriages, 24, 31, 32
   motor cars, 53, 95
   trams, 108
      Terenure tram, 68
   see also Batty Hyland; Jimmy
      Hyland; Joseph Hyland;
      railway
travelling salesmen, 25
truce of 1921, 111-12
Troubles, 14
Tully, Ballinahoun, County
   Galway, 144-50, 151-2
turfcutting, 146
Tynan, Katharine, 68

Union Jack, symbolism of, 13,
   34, 35, 154

Victoria, Queen of England, 11,
   30
Vocational Education
   Committee (VEC), 124
voting, 49
   general elections, 13, 49
      1932, 158-62

see also Dundrum
proportional representation,
  158, 161
for women, 11, 102
  see also suffragette
  movement

wages, 26
Walker, Máire (Máire Nic
  Shiubhlaigh), 69
wedding customs, 32-3
  see also clothes; Ruth
  Pollexfen
Wicklow hills, 23, 64
wireless, 142-3
  Dublin 2RN, 142
women, votes for, 11
  suffragettes, 14
workhouse (Union), 25
World War I, 14, 26, 93-7, 106,
  107
World War II, 168
  Irish neutrality, 168

Yeats, Anne, 106, 125
Yeats, Cottie, 126-7
  embroidery designs of, 126,
    135, 139, 143, 149, 155
  greetings card designs of, 126
Yeats, George (Bertha Hyde-
  Lees), 101, 106, 122, 125,
  153
  manager of Cuala Industries,
    169
Yeats, Jack B, 42, 43, 87, 88-9,
  126, 155, 170, 174
  embroidery designs of, 153
  greetings card designs of, 69
Yeats, John B, 15, 42, 63, 72,
  117, 163
Yeats, Lily (Susan Mary), 11,
  13, 15, 16, 42, 58-9, 62, 63,
  66, 68, 69, 75, 82, 83, 86-7,
  88, 90, 94, 116, 118, 126,
  132, 135-6, 149, 158, 162,
  164

at-homes in Gurteen Dheas,
  67-8
character and appearance of,
  59, 64, 67, 69, 77, 78, 102,
  107, 155, 174
death of, 173
health of, 16, 105-6, 133,
  136, 150, 153, 154, 155,
  170, 173
interest in dreams, 85-6
letters of, 14
manager of embroidery
  department, 14, 61, 67, 122,
  135, 153, 154
  embroidery and designs of,
    15, 65, 169, 174
retirement of, 14, 17, 154-5,
  157, 169-71
taught in England (1908), 71
teaching methods, 66, 72, 171
  see also Cuala Industries;
  Sara Hyland
Yeats, Lolly (Elizabeth
  Corbet), 13, 16, 42, 58-9, 66,
  68, 94, 116, 118, 132, 150,
  163, 174
at-homes in Gurteen Dheas,
  67-8
character and appearance of,
  16, 59, 69, 155, 174
death of, 16, 169, 173
letters of, 14, 155, 156
manager of printing press, 14,
  15, 61, 63, 82, 101, 127,
  157
  see also Cuala Industries
Yeats, W B, 42, 72, 81-2, 86,
  87, 97, 101, 122, 124, 132-3,
  136, 153, 155, 157, 168, 174,
  177n
'At the Hawk's Well', 16, 125
death of, 168 health of, 162-
  3, 168
'Lake Isle of Innisfree', 87
married to George, 101

Annals of the Famine in Ireland
Asenath Nicholson
Edited by Maureen Murphy

Annals of the Famine in Ireland is an eye-witness account of an American woman's experience in Ireland from 1847 to 1949. Nicholson, familiar with Ireland from her earlier walking tour in 1844/5, returned to Ireland during the Famine to do what she could to help the poor. She ran her own soup kitchen in Dublin in the spring of 1847 and later travelled to the West of Ireland to distribute food and clothing, to visit the distressed and to bring the story of the suffering to the world. With an enlightening introduction by Maureen Murphy, *Annals of the Famine in Ireland* is the story of a remarkable woman.

"I've read a great deal about the Famine but I haven't read anything that captures the horrors in so vivid a style, and with such understanding and sympathy. She also writes eloquently about the landscape and the people. Her descriptions make you feel as if you are there ... I could go on. It's so evocative, so moving."

Margaret Ward

£15.99
ISBN: 1 85594 193 7

Women, Power and Consciousness
in 19th Century Ireland
Mary Cullen and Maria Luddy

Presented in a comprehensive and accessible manner, this original and scholarly work charts the lives of eight women whose agitation for educational and social reform and the nationalist cause, changed the course of Irish history. These studies of the work of Anna Wheeler, Margaret Aylward, Frances Power Cobbe, Anne Jellicoe, Anna Haslam, Isabella Tod, Charlotte Grace O'Brien and Anna Parnell are essential reading for students, historians and anyone interested in Irish history and the role of women in nineteenth century Ireland.

£15.99
ISBN: 1 85594 078 7

In Their Own Voice
Women and Irish Nationalism
Margaret Ward

Women such as Constance Markievicz, Maud Gonne, Hanna Sheehy Skeffington, Louie Bennett and countless more fought for Irish independence. Collected and introduced by historian Margaret Ward, this ground-breaking collection gives us the voices of these women themselves, as they wrote in the newspapers of the day and as they explained themselves in autobiographies, letters and speeches. *In Their Own Voice* is a unique and invaluable collection for teachers, students and anyone interested in reclaiming women's contribution to history.

£8.99
ISBN: 1 85594 101 5

Smashing Times
A History of the Irish Women's Suffrage Movement, 1889-1922
Rosemary Cullen Owens

While the Irish nationalists were battling for Home Rule and the affairs of the Land League, Irish women were also battling for the basic right to vote. *Smashing Times* brings to life the Irish women of the 1900s who were active and militant suffragists. It is a unique and enthralling account of how they fought for women's rights, particularly the right to vote, how they set about obtaining their objectives, how they were viewed by the Irish public, priests and politicians. It also examines their historic achievement and their effect on Irish society.

£8.99
ISBN: 1 85594 101 5

From Dublin to New Orleans
The Journey of Nora nad Alice
Suellen Hoy and Margaret MacCurtain

In the autumn of 1889, Nora and Alice, two twenty-year-old women, left the relative security of their Dominican convent boarding school at Cabra in north Dublin. They set off on a journey so far removed from their daily lives that the resulting diaries recording their adventures make engrossing reading. The purpose of their journey was not to make their fortunes but to begin a life in religion as Dominican sisters in New Orleans.

£8.99
ISBN: 1 85594 101 5